ACKNOWLEDGEMENTS

My wife Ann Patricia, for her endurance and wisdom throughout the ordeal.

Edi (Edith) and Ken Butcher, for their encouragement and friendship over many years.

James Crann for his wonderful book-cover design, and for his support, encouragement and friendship over many years.

Paula Jacobs for her brilliant proof-reading, editing, and friendship.

Inprint Copy and Print Services, Colchester.

HSBC Bank High Street Colchester. For their invaluable support and guidance, with special thanks to David, Abby and Stephen.

David 'Dave' Humphreys for his support, encouragement and friendship over many years.

Paul Foot, British Investigative Journalist. 1937 - 2004

Mr P J Simpson, Deputy Chief Constable, Essex Police.

The only thing necessary for the triumph
of evil is for good men to do nothing.
Edmund Burke (1729 – 1797)

THE GREAT SOUTHEND FRAUD
-The Twist in a Tale

CHAPTER 1

Weak sunlight filtered through the courtroom windows illuminating myriad dust particles in shards that disappeared dramatically in the gloom.

Ancient benches and floorboards creaked with every movement as the occupants of Court Number 11 fidgeted, whispering among themselves.

The past 5 days had weighed heavily during this libel action at London's Royal Courts of Justice. Ron Levy had striven desperately to prove his claim that Fred Laws, the plaintiff, had acted maliciously and vindictively towards him.

Fred Laws, Southend Council's Chief Executive Officer and Town Clerk, had done well to employ Patric Milmo QC to represent him in this legal contest. Ron, representing himself, had no illusions: He knew he was no match for the experience and legal dexterity so amply displayed by this ruthless barrister throughout the trial, and his cunning in preparing for it.

The Jury had been out for little more than an hour. Now Ron sat nervously awaiting the verdict.

Looking around at the bored faces gave him no encouragement, doubt creeping in. 'Had I been wise to take on the Establishment?'

At the beginning he had been confident. 'Surely it hadn't been wrong to seek justice and quell the misdemeanours that had been so evident to me and to those that worked with me.' And yet, knowing that written evidence that would make his case more plausible had been suppressed had weakened his resolve. 'Did I do enough to convince the Jury?' He wondered.

The whispering died down, the sudden silence cutting off Ron's thoughts.

The clerk of the court rose resolutely, adopting the posture that he had assumed during his performances in the well of the court over many years. A thumb under each armpit, out-spread fingers stretched across his chest, elbows tucked in to his sides.

Peering over the top of his half-moon spectacles he turned to face the jury, his crisp, officious voice slicing through the silence of the court like a power saw ripping its course with ease through hardest timber. 'Would the Foreman of the jury please rise.'

Ron leaned expectantly forward as the foreman slowly eased himself onto his feet.

The Clerk continued, his tone and manner unchanging. 'Do you find for the plaintiff or the defendant?'

Unaware of how tightly he was gripping the edge of the bench, Ron's knuckles had turned white.

He was suddenly alarmed by the enormity of the blow that the Foreman's declaration was about strike him. A verdict in Fred Laws' favour would send Ron spiralling into the depths of despair:

> 'All my efforts over the past few years to expose corruption and misconduct within Southend Council would amount to nothing. All my friends and supporters would be let down. The guilty ones would get away with their offences.'

The foreman hesitated. He appeared to throw a quick glance towards Fred Laws.

Ron's heart skipped a beat. His head was swimming:

'Did this mean that the Jury had decided in Fred's favour, despite all my hard work? How could they do that? All of them had sat throughout the trial looking thoroughly bored. Few of them, it seemed, had a clue what was going on. I hadn't seen any of them making notes. How could they possibly remember all the important things that had been said; all the salient points that had been extracted from the questioned witnesses; all the evidence that had been before the Court? Although, in fairness to them, they had not actually seen all the documents that I had wanted them to see: Had Patrick Milmo's cleverly prepared ambush succeeded?' Ron wondered.

'To make matters worse, hadn't Fred Laws lied to the Court when he insisted that he *had* immediately reported the fraud complaint to the police? I felt certain that it was a lie... and yet... suppose I had got it all wrong? What if Fred Laws was telling the truth and had reported it to the police.'

'Oh, my God,' thought Ron. 'What on earth have I done? I may have brought the man's professional reputation to the brink of destruction. Whatever possessed me to let it go this far?'

'Is it now my own reputation that is under threat?'
'On the other hand, if the verdict goes in my favour I would be exonerated and my years of struggle to establish the truth, about the way those council officials had behaved, would end in victory. I would be able to return to my family relieved of the burden of suspicion. I might even consider standing again for election to the council.'

As with a drowning man whose past life flashes before

him, Ron found his future life flashing before him, in opposite directions, as he seemed to be drowning in a sea of fear and anxiety. He surfaced rapidly, his whole body trembling, as the foreman, in a disinterested monotone, announced the Jury's verdict...

CHAPTER 2

Anne Archer shifted in her seat, adjusting her dress and posture to ease the numbness. She was weary. For hours she had been sifting through housing applications in her stuffy office at Southend Council's Housing Department and she desperately needed a shower.

She turned round, looked at the door, listening for sounds that may indicate someone was approaching along the passageway leading to her office. Satisfied that her privacy was temporarily secure, she took a handkerchief from her bag and dabbed the base of her neck before unfastening 2 buttons of her blouse and carefully wiping her chest. Then, somewhere along the passage, a door opened. Quickly she reached for her Chanel and sprayed over her bra and neck. She was refastening her buttons when Muckley appeared.

He came in just as he always did: brash, overbearing, sly eyes taking in everything. Without preamble he said: 'Have you finished those applications, Mrs Archer? I have an appointment in an hour and I would like to run through them before I go.'

He studied her face intently. She looked flushed. He knew that she was first class at whatever she did concerning Council procedures and grudgingly admired her.

She was 52 but looked younger. He ran his eyes over her contemplatively as she answered.

'Yes, I've almost finished - just a few more.'

He snatched up the unfinished ones without a word, quickly flicked through them, extracted one, and almost threw the rest back on her desk.

'I'll see to this one. Just complete the rest and let me have them as soon as possible,'

'Oh, which one is that?' Anne asked, her suspicions roused.

'Err... the Wellings'. 'Damn her, he thought. Wasn't she satisfied that he, her superior, was capable of professional adjudication? Who was she to question him?

He was by nature shifty. It was through his deviousness that he had bamboozled his way into the position of deputy chief housing officer. Oh yes, he had done well since the days of being a milk roundsman, and now had the department in fear of him. He was well aware that Anne, having reached her position through hard work and dedication, outranked him professionally, and he strongly resented her being welfare/lettings officer, having earmarked Helen Clarke, one of the young office girls, for the job. Why he preferred her was a matter of conjecture among the department.

'Mr Muckley,' Anne said, 'The Wellings are owner-occupiers with a council mortgage, I'm sure that is so, and under the rules they are not qualified to receive a council house, or even to go on the waiting list, as you well know.' She reached out to recover the file from him. 'Shall I stamp it as non-applicable and save you the trouble?'

Muckley sharply drew the file close to his chest. 'No no. Leave it with me.' He glared at her menacingly, and she knew, infuriatingly, that he would get his own way. He always did. 'Carry on,' he said, and strode impatiently from her office.

Once again, he was going to break the rules. How did he get away with it? Although it was well known that Muckley interpreted the council rules according to his personal benefit, no one complained officially; his bullying, authoritative manner dispelling any hope that matters would proceed to a point where he would be reprimanded.

Anne's anger rose in her throat, bitterness coating her tongue. She was continually frustrated by the goings-on of Muckley. His tall, hawk-like figure seemed to be in the background whatever she thought or did in relation to her work, and her exaggerated politeness towards him, despite his bad-mannered approach towards her, masked her true feelings of wanting to smack his face.

She reached for another application form, but going through the motions made her feel that once again she was going to accept the situation lying down. She paused. No. Why should I? Not this time, she decided. There must be some way in which I could resolve the situation. During her twenty-four years with the department she had known some oddballs, but none as unscrupulous as William Muckley.

Suddenly she felt ashamed of the sick feeling in her stomach. Although not afraid of him physically, she was nonetheless morally at a disadvantage.

It was time to go. 'What is the use of complaining to Muckley's superior?'

Cyril Purrott, as chief housing officer, was in a position to reprimand Muckley, yet he never did and was unlikely to do so, being a quiet, timid man wholly absorbed in his work that precluded personal likes and dislikes. And confrontation was not among his characteristics. He was well aware of what had happened throughout his department but dismissed unpleasantness, subconsciously preferring a quiet life.

He was an officer under the manipulation of a sergeant major, hating Muckley's arrogance yet meekly accepting, through his gentle upbringing, discipline from one whom he should be directing.

Cyril Purrott was a likable man who appreciated his staff. He was content that those around him were professional and none more so than Anne, who through him had been promoted to her present position four years previously, this time despite Muckley.

Anne stopped working. She looked round her office, at the familiar things that she had altered, put in place and reorganised until the whole procedure was compatible with smooth-running efficiency. Sadness crept in and anger dissolved as tears came.

She swallowed and lowered her head in despair as choking sobs closed her throat. 'I must go,' she said aloud. 'I have to.'

Voices echoed along the passageway and she quickly composed herself, drying her eyes with the back of her hand and studying the next application form; but no one came and she completed the pile before tidying up. She took the forms to Muckley's office, but he wasn't there. She deposited them on his desk and went back to her office. Then she noticed the time. The working day was over, but as far as she was concerned there wouldn't be many more of them. She would hand in her notice tomorrow.

The following morning Anne woke early and, before showering, sat down immediately at her home typewriter, carefully wording her resignation. She knew her worth, and vanity over what would cause a shocked reaction from her colleagues overrode despair.

She felt good: resolute. Having had an early night and deep sleep she was ready for whatever the day would bring.

Striding into Purrott's office she placed the neatly typed resignation on his blotter. Then, suddenly, the full impact of what she was doing shocked her, and she was surprised to find herself shaking, but made a quick retreat before changing her mind. She took a deep breath, mixed emotions destroying her confidence as she went to her desk. 'I've done it!' she said to herself. 'That's twenty-four years' service ended - just like that!'

This was it! She nervously busied herself at her desk, squaring or aligning equipment unnecessarily, poking the edge of an A4 sheet of paper into the deepest corners of her desk and removing dust particles, wiping away all traces of what to her was anathema.

She couldn't wait for the others to arrive, and felt the need to get up and move around. She crossed to the window, looking out on the scene below. Victoria Avenue had certainly changed from the time when she, at twenty-eight, had first entered what to her was hallowed ground. How quickly the eight years had passed since all the council departments, which for years had been spread throughout the town, had been brought together in the new civic centre! At that time she had had fourteen years experience in the department behind her and was a dedicated but only moderately ambitious officer. She had returned to work as a young mother, ostensibly to augment her husband's modest earnings - but domesticity had not been easy for her. Being married to Fred, a quiet man, and having two small children to cope with, had domesticated her entirely but had not in any way dulled her quick and lively intellect.

Anne, too, had changed over the past few years. Her once trim five-foot-two frame had gained a little weight, and a few silver threads lightened her dark hair, but she had remained resolute. Her reputation for honesty and integrity was well deserved; she was unflappable, innocent of emotional outbursts.

Studying had been difficult, but by the time the new Civic Centre was commissioned she had worked her way up several grades.

Over those years she had earned her promotion, and as welfare/lettings officer had proved her worth.

But Muckley had invaded her world, and he, among all the friendly colleagues, had arrogantly, and it seemed permanently, changed the atmosphere; and where once it had been a joy to come to work it was from then on soured. She still enjoyed her work, nothing could destroy that, but his presence pervaded throughout, and he was hated by those with whom he came in contact.

Well, this time it would be different. She was determined to put the record straight. She would say exactly how she felt, nothing held back through embarrassment... an all-out effort to end the years of misery caused by a misfit.

Suddenly she heard her name being called, and was brought back to the present.

'Anne.' It was Purrott standing beside her. She warmed to his dismayed expression as he said: 'Would you please come to my office?' He stood back to let her pass, looking at the floor as he did so. He was obviously distressed, but somehow this soothed her anxiety.

He politely guided her to a chair, concern apparent in every gesture. 'Before you give any reasons for wanting to leave us, you must know that I am devastated. You are one of our most respected employees, and none of us would want you to go.' Resting on his forearms he looked deeply into her face for a few seconds, at one with her, but dreading the follow-up that he knew was inevitable.

'Is there really any point in discussing this, Mr Purrott? We both know why I'm leaving, don't we? It's for the same reason that others have left before reaching retirement: one of them a nervous wreck. At least I'm getting out before my health is ruined. Look, Mr Purrott, you and I know, as do most of the staff in the department, what Muckley gets up to. If anyone gets in his way, he destroys them. Well, he has finally succeeded with me: because of him I can no longer carry on. I hate him.'

There was silence for a few seconds. Purrott seemed lost for words. As Anne waited for him to reply she could hear faint voices in the next office.

He wanted to hold her to him, wanted to comfort her, to confess his weakness and despair at his lack of courage when faced with situations that were better left alone as far as he was concerned.

'I have to agree with you. Previously, when others resigned, their reasons for doing so were not always made clear. Those who to all intent and purposes were happy here became disconsolate or had anxiety complexes. It wasn't because of the workload, I'm sure of that. It may be supposition, and I can't speak for them, but I can tell you in confidence, because you are, after all, a friend as well as a colleague that I believe Muckley to have been the root of the trouble caused by loss of competent staff. In your case, especially, I intend to do all I can to keep you, to make you change your mind.'

Anne sighed. This kindly man in front of her was genuine, she knew that. Despite his weak will, part of his idiosyncrasy was his charm, natural and easy-flowing, his willingness to help those in difficulties. His neat small face and clear brown eyes belied his age. At fifty-four he seemed to be in a private world where once chivalry was respected and honour among schoolboys known.

'I *am* happy here, Mr Purrott, 24 years here is surely proof of that! But I am sick of make-believe, of deception. I don't want to leave but I can no longer pretend that all is in order. Please understand that. Something must be done regarding Muckley. There is plenty of evidence against him. Why, oh why, has he been allowed to flout authority? We are all too complacent, of course, unwilling to place another's career in jeopardy; but he deserves all that is coming to him. I appreciate your predicament but surely it is time for action, time to rid the council of him rather than continually destroy others' chances of happiness.'

'Anne, I have an idea. Suppose you rewrite your resignation, put down as many details as you can of Muckley's conduct. I'll take it to the housing chairman. I know it's not normally the done thing, to approach the chairman directly, but I think in this instance it may be worth a try.'

Anne was doubtful. 'Well, Mr Purrott, I'm not sure what it will achieve, but I suppose it's better than doing nothing.'

'I'm sorry that it should end like this, Anne. I don't know what else I can say. Of course, I shall have to report the matter to the town clerk. What his reaction will be I just can't imagine.'

Anne stood up and replied sardonically 'Neither can I, Mr Purrott. Neither can I.'

He extended his hand. 'Thank you for all you've done. Anne I really do wish you every happiness, whatever the outcome.'

'Thank you, Mr Purrott. I shall be here until the end of the month. Hopefully, you will have spoken to the Chairman by then.'

She paused at the door, turned back and said, 'You shall have that detailed resignation by tomorrow, Mr Purrott.'

Closing the door behind her, she felt depressed at the thought of leaving the job that she loved and was angry that Muckley could claim another victory. Too distraught to return to her desk, she went home to complete a dossier listing those details of Muckley's behaviour which had compelled her to resign. She knew how important it was to get the wording right and held nothing back. Muckley would harm her no more.

17

She hadn't noticed that three hours had slipped by. Sighing with a mixture of relief and satisfaction, she read through her five closely written pages 'I think that says it all,' she murmured. 'Perhaps, at last, something will be done about Muckley.'

The following morning Anne typed and photocopied her new resignation and took it straight to Cyril Purrott's office.

The days dragged on... she heard nothing. Whatever she did, full concentration was impossible:

'How had the chairman reacted to my statement? Why hadn't I been contacted? What were the legal implications? Had I been successful, baring my soul to those in authority?

These questions and many more brought her sleepless nights. The waiting seemed endless...

'Bert Mussett had been chairman of the housing committee for 4 years, and a councillor at Southend for sixteen. A former mayor of the borough, he had chaired many other major committees and had earned tremendous respect from all who came in contact with him.

Would he now order an inquiry? Would he call a special meeting of the housing committee? Perhaps he might consult the town clerk. There were, obviously, legal implications that would need his guidance. The thought pulled her up sharply. I wonder if I went too far. No; it had to stop. I'm going to see it through whatever the cost.

Then, suddenly, another thought struck her... What would be the cost to me?

Out came pen and notepad. A few jabs at her calculator revealed a figure, which made her gulp. The salary and pension losses amounted to approximately £60,000. She was appalled: Am I doing the right thing? If I stay Muckley would make life even more intolerable and my health would suffer. 'Yes,' she assured herself, 'I have done the right thing.'

Two weeks had passed since Anne's meeting with Cyril Purrott. In that time she had seen him more often than had been the case for the past two years, but other than requesting that she change her mind about leaving, he had said nothing regarding what was uppermost in her mind; She wondered what the outcome had been?

Anne, for her part, was too polite to broach the subject, feeling that it was incumbent upon him to make the first move.

Now he approached her once more.

'Surely, Anne, you're not going to let all that experience go to waste. Couldn't you get a job with another local authority or even with one of the housing associations?'

'Mr Purrott, your concern for my future is most warming. Is there more than my future prospects behind your concern?'

'Well, Anne, I must admit it would make my life a lot easier if I could announce that you are leaving to take up a new post.'

'I bet it would!' Anne retorted, suppressing her anger, 'but I can't think of one good reason why I should. What's at the bottom of all this, Mr Purrott? Have you heard from the chairman yet?'

He seemed embarrassed. 'Err, well... yes, I have... actually.'

'And what did Mr Mussett say?'

'Mr Mussett just said "how sad."'

'"How sad"... is that all?'

'I'm afraid so, Anne. Although, did you know, he has since had suffered a slight heart attack?'

'Did you discuss our conversation with him?'

'Well, no, not really,' replied Purrott, now unable to conceal his discomfort.

Anne could not believe what she was hearing. 'So what

happens now? Is Muckley going to get away with it again?'

His voice had developed a slight croak. 'I just don't know what else I can do. I've left it in the chairman's hands. I am very sorry, Anne.'

Now completely bewildered, Anne made her way back to her section. She feared that her effort and sacrifice had been in vain.

She was sorry that Bert Mussett had had a heart attack, but it was beyond belief that he had dismissed the matter so lightly. *How could Muckley be so lucky?* Sensing the irony of the situation she smiled as she thought... *'What one might call a stroke of luck?'*

The final few days in the department passed slowly as Anne wound down towards her departure. She had adopted a philosophical attitude, reflecting on how Muckley had achieved his position by ruthlessness: she wondered why her efforts to expose him should succeed, however noble her intentions?

The last day of her twenty-four years in the housing department arrived. Anne was finishing the task of clearing out. The farewells to friends in the department had been made, some of them tearfully. It occurred to her that she ought not to leave without seeing the town clerk, even if only to say goodbye. She rang Rosemary, his secretary, and arranged to see him in an hour's time. Anne knew that he was aware of her long-standing complaints against Muckley. Subconsciously, she hoped for a last minute opportunity to clarify the situation.

Rosemary greeted her warmly. 'I was most surprised to hear that you are leaving us, Anne. I thought you had several more years to go.'

'Yes, Rosemary; so did I. It's a great disappointment to me, but I don't really have much choice. I shall miss you all very much.'

Rosemary looked puzzled. 'I don't understand.'

'You will, my dear, some day.'

Rosemary tapped lightly on her boss's door.

'Come in.'

She opened the door and peered in. 'Mrs Archer to see you, Mr Laws.'

'Thank you. Do come in, Mrs Archer. I'm pleased that you came to see me before leaving.'

Anne wondered if he meant it. She stepped inside. It was tastefully furnished, as befitted the holder of the highest office in local government. A profusion of well-tended pot plants gave the office a homely touch, and ornately framed pictures of renowned local buildings and attractions adorned the walls.

At the far end was a beautiful polished mahogany conference table which, Anne estimated, could have seated eight to ten people. A large oak leather-topped desk dominated the centre of the room, allowing the user a panoramic view of Victoria Avenue, the main thoroughfare leading into the town centre. How it had changed! Since the turn of the century large houses had sprung up along the length of the avenue; when the population of Southend had more than doubled in a decade from around 12,000 in 1891 to over 27,000 now. Southend councillors and officers were proud of their new civic centre, which had been opened eight years earlier by the Queen Mother. The building was one of the many tall office blocks that lined Victoria Avenue. Surprisingly, Fred Laws' office was the only one in the Civic Centre which had curtain-draped windows.

Fred Laws' legal status was emphasised by the impressive rows of law books packed closely on the shelves behind his desk. This was indeed the office of a very important man, the chief executive officer and town clerk: the man whose domain encompassed the awesome responsibility for every one of the council's hundreds of council employees. Official complaints against officers, councillors or others had to be lodged with him before being dealt with; the man whose authority extended to the control of all the council's property and premises. Of equal, if not greater, importance was his influence and power as the council's Legal Adviser. No project, plan or proposal could proceed without his approval.

Fred Laws looked very much the part. A little overweight, double chin, short neatly trimmed shiny black hair, and dressed very smartly in a dark pinstripe suit: the epitome of businesslike self-confidence. He had come a long way since being appointed assistant solicitor of Blackpool Corporation in 1952. Within three years of joining Southend Borough Council in 1959, also as assistant solicitor, he rose to become the deputy town clerk. In 1974 he was promoted to chief executive officer and town clerk. His bearing clearly indicated how much he relished his position of supreme authority.

'Do come in, Mrs Archer.' He directed Anne to a seat facing his desk and lowered himself into his sumptuous leather wing chair.

'Thank you, Mr Laws. I'm glad you are able to see me before I leave.'

'I'm pleased that you took the trouble, Mrs Archer. We've both seen this Council through some very big changes haven't we?'

'We certainly have, Mr Laws: some of them quite exciting too. You must be very pleased with the way things have happened for you.' replied Anne.

Fred hesitated, unsure whether her remark invited a reply. 'Well, yes, I suppose I must be, really,' he said casually, but realising instantly how much of an understatement it must have sounded.

As befitted his status, he was an excellent talker. Lucid in the manner of a Politician, one who speaks with such conviction that listeners become entranced by the apparent ease with which he discourses on all subjects. Now he was intent on winning Anne over by reminiscing over council matters.

Anne was not really listening; her mind wandered. She was certain that he knew why she was leaving, and yet it seemed that he was carefully avoiding the issue. His voice droned on. She desperately wanted to bring the matter up, but feared that she might be wrong. Afraid that he might condemn her for making such serious allegations against a man who, like himself, had served the council for so many years.

She became aware of a change in his tone. He was now speaking purposefully:

'Mrs Archer, I'm sure you'll be glad to shake the dust from your feet when you leave this place, but can I ask you, when there is an inquiry, as inquiry there surely will be, will you come back to give evidence?'

Anne could hardly believe what she was hearing. Her heart pounded. Struggling to conceal her excitement she replied slowly: 'Mr Laws, it will be a pleasure, a real pleasure.' It was pointless trying to say more; her voice had dried up.

'Good. Then may I wish you all the best for the future, whatever you do?' As he spoke he raised himself from his seat, offering his hand.

Anne responded to his gesture and they shook hands. 'Thank you so much, Mr Laws. I look forward very much to seeing you again.'

It was a different Anne Archer who left Fred Laws' office from the one who had entered. She was elated, excited by the prospect of all that his last few words implied:

'An inquiry, Is this going to be the decisive factor in finally exposing Muckley, is he going to get what is long overdue: official condemnation for all the misery he has caused?'

CHAPTER 3

Ron's wife, Patricia, was in the kitchen preparing tea. Her eldest son, Peter, sat at the table poring over his electronics book, deeply engrossed in computer technology.

Ron had settled comfortably in an armchair in the front room meticulously scanning the newspapers as usual before tea was ready. The world was in turmoil, trouble here, trouble there, but none of it directly affecting him. That is until he turned to a page announcing that the Callaghan government was intent on increasing the payroll tax by £1,000m. 'Patricia!' he called. 'Have you seen this?'

Peter, startled, looked at his mother as she gave him a knowing look before going in to her husband.

'What is it, Ron? What's the matter?' she asked, concerned by his tone.

He leapt from his chair and angrily thrust the paper towards her.

'What is happening in this country? How could they justify the imposition of such a crippling burden on employers, especially at a time of record unemployment?'

At these words Peter, knowing his father's excitable nature, and content that the disturbance was no concern of his, settled down once more, oblivious to all around him.

Patricia read the heading, peered at him intently. He was so excited, red-faced, anger shocking him into someone she was rarely confronted with.

'Ron dear, calm down. You'll have a heart attack.'

'So will half the country when this comes into effect. There'll be even more people on the dole. We are all too complacent, put up with anything. Surely, before it's too late, this must be turned round. It's not the right way. If I were in a position to do something I would fight this tooth and nail. I'd never vote for them. Too many are won over by matey rhetoric and promises of a bright future that are meaningless once elections are over.'

Her calmness soothed him, as it always did. Then he realised that he was venting his anger before the one person above all whom he could rely on, and he felt humble.

His mind cleared. She smiled at him. 'You know, you ought to be in politics, Ron. Really! Why don't you get down to the Conservative offices and join up... get things moving?'

She was playing with him, he knew that. Unwittingly though, she had fired his imagination.

'Come and have some tea, dear,' she said, gently pulling him to her and kissing his cheek. Placing an arm around him she guided him to the kitchen and sat him at the table.

Peter could see that they had lots to talk over and making his excuses put his tea on a tray and went into the front room.

'You've left your book here, Peter. Shall I bring it in to you?' his mother called out.

'No, it's OK, Mum. I think I'll see some television.'

Ron looked around at the things dear to him. Being happily married to this warm-hearted woman had stabilised him. The once-fiery spirit had diminished, but not entirely left him.

'You've given me food for thought Patricia. D'you know, I think I'll take you up on what you said.'

'Never mind food for thought... try this,' she said, smiling, placing his tea before him.

'Thanks. I'm serious. I'm forever complaining that nothing's being done politically to get us out of this mess. I feel like those old Kitchener posters, he stood up and adopt the pose of the man on the poster and pointing a finger at Patricia: "Your Country Needs You": extolling others what to do and yet stuck on a billboard.'

There are plenty of homes where the wife, one of the supposedly weaker sex proves to be the backbone of a family, whose word is respected above all others, whose intuition proves to be startlingly accurate at the end of the day. Weak men, strong men, have all been influenced: the whisper that is more audible than an ear-shattering roar.

Patricia was no exception. She and Ron were often involved in worldly affairs discussions, and he was constantly astonished by her clear vision. Family affairs were of course uppermost in the minds of both of them. Their children, Peter, Stephen, Philip, Carole and Rachel, had arrived in the course of ten years. Neither Ron nor Patricia had much spare time, he being a well-respected hairdresser by trade and she forever occupied with family matters and, at busy times, helping in the salon.

But somehow they never lost sight of their hopes and dreams, keeping level heads and always open with each other.

Patricia, for her part, respected Ron whatever mood she or he was in. He had proved time and again a loving husband, a true friend. He would never sacrifice his principles, never bow down in the House of Rimmon. And now, reading the signs emanating from him, she knew the time was ripe for earnest discussion.

Although Ron had always voted Conservative he had never participated to the extent of becoming a paid-up member of the Party, but he knew without doubt that he was going to action his feelings.

He and Patricia talked over the political events that had plunged the country into despair while Labour was in power: the weaknesses, ineptitudes, the enormous trade deficit, the demoralising effects of union strangleholds on people's way of life, and finally the latest outrage, one that was, unknown to them, to end Callaghan's premiership.

The following day, his enthusiasm undiminished, Ron drove into town. He stood outside number 11 Clarence Street and stared up at the sign above the converted shop front: Southend East Conservative Association. 'This is it', he said to himself. He felt a sense of excitement as he entered the front door and announced his intentions to the lady in attendance. Ron paid his subscription to the secretarial assistant, Kathleen who was responsible for signing in new members and eagerly took possession of his first Conservative Party membership card. Kathleen had served the constituency association for many years and she explained the procedure necessary for Ron to further his ambitions. The next step would be to see the chairman or secretary of the constituency Ward Committee in Shoeburyness who would tell him how best he could help.

Shoeburyness is the most easterly part of the borough of Southend-on-Sea. For many years and right up to the early thirties the main industry that supported the residents of this once small community was brick-making.

After moulding, the bricks were fired in kilns set up on the greensward, then, after cooling, were carried in wheelbarrows along wooden jetties to waiting barges. The loads that did not make it to the barges remained where they fell on the beach. Over the years, the tides continually buried and resurrected the bricks, and the legacy of this past industry remains at East Beach, which is constantly littered with brick fragments. Attempts by the Council to clear them have proved futile.

Ron lost no time. He immediately contacted the Ward Committee. Within a short time he was co-opted on to it. He got on well with the other members of the committee and was soon participating in the Branch's business and activities.

Five months earlier, at the May council elections, the Conservative candidate for Shoeburyness, Ron Bolton, had been elected with a comfortable majority, but rumours were rife following the elections that he had been planning to sell his house and move away from the district. The committee members knew how damaging the consequences would be if such rumours proved to be true. He was eventually confronted and confirmed that they were true. He would be moving a long distance away from the area within a matter of weeks. The members were very disturbed by his disclosure and they told him so; he should have mentioned the fact before he was selected to stand for the seat, because there would now have to be a by-election. Three weeks later he exchanged contracts on his home and promptly resigned as councillor for the Shoeburyness ward.

The selection machinery for a candidate immediately swung into action. Applications were invited from those wishing to be considered for selection. Members of the committee asked Ron whether he would like his name to go forward. He indicated that he had never actually stood as a candidate in a Council election before, but the idea was growing on him rapidly. The thought of taking part in the decision making process of running the town had a certain appeal that he now found difficult to resist. He eagerly submitted a formal application to the committee.

At this stage Ron was not aware of the effect his candidature and, if successful, his election to office might have on his family. Neither did he know for certain how he would fit Council duties in concurrently with running his business. He had moved his family from Hertfordshire into the four bedroom living accommodation of the West Road shop premises in January 1974. Although established for 50 years, it was a little run-down and old-fashioned. His 24 years experience in the craft was being dedicated to updating and revitalising the business. It was going well but there was still a lot more to be done before he would be satisfied.

There were 5 applicants for the vacancy. Interviews by the Ward Committee were to be held in the Shoeburyness Conservative Club. Drinks were handed out to the waiting nervous applicants followed by more later. Interviewing did not take long: two of the applicants had failed to turn up. Ron went in and was greeted warmly by the Committee. Because he was known to them, he felt at ease and had no difficulty in coping with the interview. The applicants were told that each of them would be telephoned by the Chairman once the Committee had made its decision.

Ron went straight home to wait with Patricia. Drinks were poured to steady the nerves. It seemed like a long wait, but they had hardly finished their drinks when the phone rang. Ron grabbed it eagerly, listened, and then quietly said 'Thank you'. He slowly replaced the receiver and turned to Patricia: 'I made it. I did it. I've been selected. I can hardly believe it... wowee! Amazing, isn't it? I shall be a Borough Councillor! Wonderful!'

'Oh, Ron,' said Patricia. 'Well done! But you've got to win first, of course! I'm so pleased for you. Congratulations darling.' She threw her arms round him. They held one another tightly. 'Another drink Ron: this time to celebrate?' Ron tried to calm down. While Patricia refilled their glasses he told her the rest of the telephone conversation: 'there's to be a Committee meeting next week, on Monday, to plan the election campaign. It gets under way immediately.'

There was so much to be done launching a by-election; the official nomination papers to be completed; the appointment of an Agent; the election address to be drafted and printed; an election committee room to be set up; the team of volunteer canvassers and leaflet distributors to be set up; a seemingly endless list of arrangements to be made.

The by-election was called for Thursday, 28 October 1976. The fervour and excitement of an election team at a by-election was an experience that Ron found quite breathtaking. Patricia remained calm. The children were very excited and a little overwhelmed at seeing their father's photograph on posters displayed all over the town and on the thousands of leaflets which they eagerly helped to deliver; each proudly wearing a blue rosette.

Election day arrived. Patricia was carried irresistibly along on the tide of enthusiasm. She had a little 1957 Austin A35 (the jelly mould) which she decorated with blue ribbons, like a wedding car, with posters and leaflets plastered all over it.

Peter had used his electronics skills to make a compact amplifier with two loudspeakers which he fitted on to the roof rack of his Father's car, alongside the poster display boards. Ron drove slowly around the streets throughout the day broadcasting his message to voters urging them to vote for him as the Conservative candidate.

Although previously the seat had a comfortable majority Ron was under no illusion. He had faced a great deal of resentment and criticism when canvassing. Many people objected to the cost of a by-election which could have been avoided if the previous candidate had disclosed his intention to move house so soon after being elected. The

Opposition candidates had tried to capitalise on the Conservatives' embarrassing slip-up, especially Bert McGaw, the Labour candidate, who was fighting to regain the seat that he lost five months earlier to Ron Bolton. The campaign workers knew that this would be no walk-over but everyone had worked hard and were determined to succeed.

The last-minute voters hurried to cast their votes as the closing hour of the polling station approached. At nine o'clock precisely the doors were closed. It was over. Weeks of electioneering were finally ended, the pressure lifted. Apart from a few remaining tellers' slips to be taken back to the committee room for a hurried assessment of the campaign there was nothing more to be done.

Counting of the ballot papers was to take place, as usual, at the Civic Centre. Ron, his agent, Patricia and three others (as permitted under election rules) together with the equivalent number of supporters of the other two candidates were gathered around the long rectangular board-room table in the large committee room when the ballot boxes arrived. Seated round the table were the official voting slip counters, mostly Council staff. Curiously, in the centre of the table was a pile of wooden clothes pegs. The chatter of the observers filled the air as they speculated on the outcome of the count.

The Returning Officer lifted the first ballot box on to the table and announced the commencement of the count. There was a brief hush. The box was opened and up-ended. Its contents cascaded into a heap which was then shoved to the centre of the table within reach of the counters. Each counter then scooped up a quantity of the slips, hurriedly unfolded them and stacked them into bundles of twenty-five. Now the purpose of the clothes pegs became clear:

they were used to clip each bundle of slips together for easy counting. The remaining boxes from the other three polling stations followed suit and their contents received the same treatment.

All the observers and candidates were required to monitor the work of the counters. Spoilt slips were passed to the Returning Officer, who called the candidates and Agents over to inspect them and decide whether to allow them or to exclude them from the count. The pegged bundles were then pushed back into the centre of the table and passed to the counting officers for checking against the registers of votes cast at the polling stations; the figures tallied.

The counters then took several bundles each, removed the pegs from them one at a time and divided the slips into separate piles, one for each of the candidates. The exciting part of the count had begun. The candidates and agents spread themselves around the table looking over the shoulders of the counters. A slip is placed in the wrong pile, three hands are thrust forward to point out the error, and the counter corrects it. At this stage it is impossible to estimate who is likely to win but it is beginning to emerge that the Liberal vote is lower than for Conservative and Labour. Speedy fingers rapidly work their way through the piles of slips. A counter abandons her finger stool, it is obviously easier without it. Drinks in paper cups stand perilously close to busy hands. The Returning Officer has calculated the percentage vote which is announced as being 38 per cent. Murmurs of disappointment rumble round the room at such a low turn-out. Empty ballot boxes are moved to the edge of the room. Some observers standing around the room are chatting excitedly, more concerned with expressing their point of view than with what is going on.

All the bundles have now disappeared from the centre of the table and the piles for each candidate are being counted into batches of 25 and are pegged together. The atmosphere is tense. Observers have stopped chatting; their attention is now directed towards the growing bundles of slips. The completed ones are tossed towards the Counting Officer at the end of the table and gathered in. His calm, detached manner is in sobering contrast to the tensions displayed by the election participants. In front of him is a wooden tray which is divided into sections each the width of the voting slips. He placed the bundles of slips into the tray, one section for each candidate. As the batches mount up in the sections the count has become a race in slow motion.

Ron and Patricia were caught up in the suspense and excitement building up in the room. The chatter was growing louder. By counting the number of pegs in the tray as the number of bundles lengthened, each candidate's progress was clear. It was still early in the count but it was becoming obvious that this was a contest between Conservative and Labour. The Liberal vote was now well behind, and Graham Penfold, the Liberal candidate, must by now have conceded defeat.

There were still quite a few slips on the table but Ron's bundles were distinctly taking the lead. Bert McGaw would need a lot of the uncounted slips to catch up. Was it possible? Ron's heartbeat quickened. He quickly glanced round the room at his colleagues: all were smiling. They knew. Sure enough, his section was now well in the lead. The air was buzzing with excitement. The noise was growing louder. Patricia gently squeezed Ron's hand and smiled at him. She also knew.

The Returning Officer placed the final bundles of slips in the tray, quickly counted the number of votes in each section and entered the figures on his results sheet.

'Ladies and gentlemen.' The room fell silent. 'I can now tell you the number of votes cast for each candidate is as follows: Ron Levy, 1,203 votes.' He paused until the rapturous cheers died down. 'Albert McGaw, 708 votes.' The cheers from Ron's team must have been audible at the end of the corridor. He continued: 'Graham Penfold, 325 votes.' The room erupted into even louder cheers and despite their obvious disappointment Graham's supporters joined in the applause. The Returning Officer had difficulty completing his duty. Without waiting for silence, he continued; 'I therefore declare that Mr Ron Levy is duly elected to serve as councillor for the Shoeburyness Ward in the Southend East Constituency of Southend-on-Sea Borough Council.

Ron's heart was thumping, fit to burst. Patricia hugged him: 'Oh, Ron, you've done it! Congratulations!' Suddenly good wishes were coming at him from all directions. He had never shaken hands with so many people in such a short space of time. The Returning Officer called for Ron's attention. 'Mr Levy, would you follow me, please, for the official declaration?'

Ron was led out of the room followed by Bert McGaw and Graham Penfold. in the traditional order of succession: the winner, followed by the second, third, and so on, through the foyer where Party supporters had been awaiting the result and who were now applauding and cheering loudly. The candidates were led on to the balcony of the Civic Centre where the Town Clerk, Fred Laws, made the official announcement over the loudspeakers to the handful of people in the square below. He shook hands with Ron first, followed by the other candidates, who then made the usual post-election pronouncements.

Returning inside from the balcony Ron was greeted eagerly by Councillor Norman Harris, leader of the Council for many years, 'Well done, young Ron! You did a great job. Welcome to Southend Council.' He turned to Patricia. 'You must be very proud of him. I'll bet he had plenty of help from you.'

'Well, just a bit. The children helped too.'

'So I heard. Anyway I shall look forward to working with Ron and I hope you can stand his attendance at all the meetings.'

There were many other members of the Council to meet and talk to before leaving the Civic Centre. It was a little after 11 o'clock when Ron and Patricia finally arrived home, exhausted but very exhilarated. Peter, Stephen, Philip and Carole had waited up to hear the result. They were so excited and there was so much to talk about. Rachel was tucked up in bed fast asleep; at four years old she was too young to stay up. She would hear all about it in the morning.

The following day Fred Laws telephoned Ron to make arrangements for him to call in to the Civic Centre to be sworn in as a newly elected councillor. A time was agreed for later that day.

Ron was shown into Fred Laws' office. They shook hands and sat down at his desk. 'Well, Councillor, have you recovered from the excitement?'

It felt strange to be called 'councillor', but Ron had a feeling that Fred Laws was revelling in the novelty of the situation, as he probably had done so many times before.

'The first thing I must ask you to do, Mr Levy, is to sign a declaration of secrecy. This requires you not to reveal anything of a confidential nature that will come into your possession from time to time as you carry out your duties as a councillor.' Ron was handed a sheet of paper which he briefly scanned and then signed.

Fred Laws took the document back and set it to one side. 'Now, this is a copy of the Council's Standing Orders. As you can see, it's quite a lengthy book. It contains all the rules, decisions, guidelines, minutes and statutory regulations relating to the running of the Council and the Council's obligations and responsibilities, legal and otherwise. You should find in its pages mostly what you need to know to assist you in carrying out your function as a councillor, but if ever you get into difficulties you can ring me and I will be pleased to help you.' He flipped through several pages as he spoke. 'Does that make sense to you?'

Ron reached across for the book. 'Yes, Mr Laws. I think I can understand that.'

'And this is your Council diary. You'll find this very useful. It contains the names, addresses and phone numbers of all the councillors: when they were first elected, all the past mayors. There's a rather interesting chronological data section going back many hundreds of years. Here's one that might appeal to you: "Battle of Benfleet, Danes defeated and driven across site of modern Southend to Shoebury by King Alfred's men." He turned a few pages. 'Looking at a more recent event: 31 October 1967. The new Civic Centre was opened by Her Majesty Queen Elizabeth the Queen Mother".' He handed the diary to Ron. 'You'll also find in there a list of the Council's chief and second-tier officers together with their telephone numbers. If ever you have a constituency matter to deal with you can speak to the appropriate officer, who you will find most helpful. I would explain, with respect, that it is not considered proper practice to speak to council staff below that level unless you are referred to them by the chief officer concerned. You will also find in there a list of the service committees and the names of all the councillors on those committees. There are eight all together: Amenities, Environmental Health, Highways, Housing and Estates, Personnel, Planning, Transportation and, finally, Policy and Resources which is made up mostly of the chairmen of the other committees.

The committees meet on a six-week cycle followed by the full council meeting which agrees, amends or refers back to any committee the decisions of those committees that it doesn't approve of. You'll find the dates of all the meetings for the municipal year entered in the diary, which should help you to plan ahead. Most councillors serve on two committees, decided by the P&R. That meets next week, and I expect a decision will be made then which committees you will serve on.'

Ron took a deep breath. 'Well, Mr Laws. That's quite a lot to take in and I am most grateful to you for taking so much trouble to help me understand it all.'

'It's part of my duty, Mr Levy, but I'm pleased to assist you in any way that I can.' He glanced at his watch. 'I still have some time to spare. If you like I'll take you for a look over the building: now, if you are free.'

'Thank you, Mr Laws. That would be most helpful, and very interesting I'm sure.'

Ron was then given a guided tour of the Civic Centre together with a potted history of the civic building complex: plans for such accommodation were being considered by the Council as far back as 1896. For nearly three quarters of a century the town's affairs were conducted from offices scattered throughout the Borough, mainly in converted accommodation. Co-ordination was difficult; efficiency was impaired.

Plans for a civic centre were commissioned in 1937 but war stopped the commencement of the building. Current restrictions and new Council requirements delayed further progress until 1956, when the town clerk, Mr Archibald Glen, submitted to the Council revised proposals. As a result, plans for a new Centre were prepared by the borough architect, Mr P F Burridge, and work on the site commenced in 1960: it was completed for occupation, at a cost of over million pounds, in 1965.

Two storeys high, the council chamber occupies the most important position in the Civic Suite. The chamber seats 90 members (councillors) in the arc of desks facing the dais. The public gallery, which runs all around the chamber at the upper level, seats 150 members, and has special provision for the press behind the mayor's dais. Also contained within the civic suite are; eight committee rooms; members' retiring Rooms; a small office for the Leader of the Council; Mayor's Office; Mayores's Room; two pleasantly furnished marriage rooms and an assembly room with kitchens, used for conferences, banquets, concerts and other community activities.

Moving on to the 16 floor administrative block was quite a contrast. Ron had often seen the building from the outside but from the inside it appeared even bigger. This part of the complex included a police headquarters, a court house, new buildings for the departments of the College of Technology and a large Civic Square around which the principal buildings are sited. Car parking had also been well catered for with underground and ground level spaces for over 600 vehicles.

Mr Laws was immensely proud of the fact that the Centre had received a number of awards for design and craftsmanship, including one from the Civic Trust.

Ron was overwhelmed by the immense size of the set up. The journey down in one of the four electronically controlled, high-speed lifts was spent wondering what he had let himself in for. In the main foyer Ron again thanked Mr Laws for his help and the tour. They shook hands and Ron made his way to the car park. He felt exhilarated by the prospect of being a member of the Council, but he had no illusions; it was going to take him a long time to know and understand the business of local government and his role within it.

The weeks following his election brought a steady stream of telephone calls from Ron's newly-acquired constituents. The problems that were brought to him were varied and numerous. There were complaints about noisy or anti-social neighbours: there were grumbles about delays with planning applications: objections to planning schemes; inefficient refuse collection; moans from tenants about the Council's failure to carry out repairs and maintenance; inadequate or non-existent street lighting; demands for pedestrian crossings on busy roads. So many of Ron's evenings were taken up with interviews and visits to sites that were the subject of complaints or to constituent's homes to see for himself the problems that were causing such discontent.

Many of the matters that Ron was expected to deal with were clearly outside the responsibility of the Council. He quickly became adept at identifying the problems that he could take up and the ones that needed referring to other authorities.

As Ron's notepad filled with the details of his case interviews, a pattern seemed to emerge that aroused his curiosity and which gave him some cause for concern. A worrying proportion of complaints were against the housing department. So many people felt that they had been dealt with unfairly or unreasonably. Whether this volume of calls had anything to do with his placement onto the Housing Committee he had no way of knowing. After all, his membership of the Housing Committee, together with the Personnel Committee, had been reported in the local papers. It was just possible that people had read of his appointments and decided to seek his assistance.

Many of the constituents' problems needed only clarification of the rules, a sympathetic ear or the suggestion that a little more patience was needed. The more complex matters needed advice or guidance from the housing department. Cyril Purrott, the Council's Chief Housing Officer, had suggested to Ron that he establish regular contact with his Senior Housing Officer, Lionel Golding, to deal with such matters.

Lionel Golding was a quiet, pleasant man in his early forties: Not apparently well endowed with the qualities to be expected of a person in his position, but tolerably competent: Unlikely to have risen to his present level in management without some assistance. Rarely unavailable when Ron phoned with enquiries, but with the usual retort 'I don't have the answer to that right away, Councillor. Give me a little time and I'll call you back.'

The demand on Ron's time and the impact on his family life were increased further by the committee meetings: Mostly in the evenings between six and 10 o'clock, sometimes running beyond 11 o'clock. The bundles of papers for each meeting were delivered a week or so earlier to be read through and understood in order for him to be effectively prepared for the meetings. Heavy agendas often took well into the night to get through all the relative documents. How obvious it seemed to Ron, at times, that not all the councillors had practised that important requirement!

The committee procedures appeared to be so very democratic; meetings open to the public; the press provided with desk, lighting and agendas; each item on the agenda debated by the committee members; clarification or explanation of the reports by the officers; questions asked; comments made; and finally, proposals put to the vote by the chairman who asks; 'Those in favour?' A show of hands and the matter is decided.

Full council meetings are different. This is where the

committee minutes are agreed or referred back to the committee for a different decision: A power-house of local government to be presided over by the Mayor, with the Town Clerk and the Deputy Mayor seated either side of him (or her). The council chief officers are seated at desks set at an angle each side of the Mayor's dais. For all the councillors, rows of desks are set out in semi-circles on the floor of the chamber facing the Mayor and Council officers. The aura of civic authority exudes a powerful presence.

The Mace Bearer solemnly enters the chamber, the ornate silver mace carried ceremoniously on his shoulder. In a loud, crisp voice he announces, as he has proudly done so many times, 'His Worship, the Mayor'. The chamber immediately falls silent. All councillors and officers rise. The Mayor, in scarlet and ermine robes adorned with the gold, silver and enamelled chains of office, accompanied in procession by the Deputy Mayor and the Town Clerk, follow the Mace Bearer through the silent chamber to take their seats at the dais. The mace is reverently placed on brackets on the ledge at the front of the dais between the dais and the table in the centre of the chamber which, traditionally, is occupied by a magnificent floral display. Not a sound is made. The councillors all bow to the symbol of authority. The Mayor reciprocates. The chamber sits. The council meeting commences.

CHAPTER 4

Thursday 11 May 1978

Jane Saxby rapped firmly on William Muckley's door. She was keeping an appointment for a preparatory talk with him about her forthcoming Final Part 1 Institute of Housing examination that she was to sit to gain her certificate in housing management. This was a decisive exam which, if successful, would lay the foundations for her future career.

Jane could hardly believe that a year had passed since she last stood outside Muckley's door waiting to prepare for the intermediate Part 1exam. She had fitted a great deal into that time, including marriage to John and setting up a home of her own. She had enjoyed her time at school and had worked hard to achieve good O and A level results: this was reflected in her successful first job application when she started work as a trainee housing assistant in Southend Council's housing department in 1974.

Although that first prep talk with Muckley was intense it had served to show that she was quite capable of passing the intermediate Part 1Exam, an achievement which she had accomplished with ease.

Jane felt equally confident about the forthcoming Part 2 exam. Her enthusiastic studies as a day-release student at Hackney College had fitted in comfortably alongside her duties within the department. She found the subject absorbing and was fascinated by all that it embraced: law; social science; psychology; and so on. 'Life is pretty good at the moment', she thought.

'Come in!' Muckley's voice was unmistakeable. It had an odd squeak which seemed out of character for a man of his stature and position. He was tall, rather slim, and he looked younger than his 50 years.

Jane strode into Muckley's office and settled down into one of the comfortable seats that were neatly positioned in front of his desk. It was a plain, modern office, uncluttered except for a few files dotted about. She noted the absence of any personal items and thought how clinical the room looked - a few plants, photographs and books would have made such a difference!

Muckley commenced the interview by posing numerous questions about her studies. He told her that he wanted to make sure that she had revised certain areas which he anticipated were likely to occur during the course of the exam. He clearly knew his job, and spoke knowledgeably. No suggestion was ever made of the questions being anything other than ones that might be reasonably anticipated. Jane was not surprised. Any top-notch training officer would know what was expected to arise in the exam.

But his questions this time were far too precise. Something was not right. Then it dawned on her with horror *this was the real thing!* from the actual exam paper! It must be. He was reeling off actual exam questions! Jane suddenly felt numb. He gave her no opportunity before starting out. And then 'Oh, no,' she thought. 'I don't want to know what you're telling me.' She felt helpless, unable to stop him. His voice droned on relentlessly. She scribbled down as much as she could of what he was saying, her mind frantically elsewhere. It was a long session, well over an hour.

Jane drifted out of Muckley's office in a daze: Unable to

recall how the session ended. She felt an urgent need to confide in someone. She sought her closest friend in the department, Pat Hunt, and took her into the ladies' loo, somewhere private. Jane told Pat in great detail what had happened in Muckley's office and asked her, if need be, if she would confirm what had happened; to simply say that she'd been in his office for that length of time, because it was extraordinary to say the least. She should never have been in his office for that length of time for any reason.

Pat was astonished. "Well, you weren't in there that long the first time, were you?"

"That's right," said Jane. "I just can't understand it."

"Whatever is he playing at?" replied Pat. "And what on earth are you going to do about it?"

Jane knew exactly what she was going to do. "Please don't tell anyone will you Pat."

Having received Pat's assurance, Jane hurriedly left the civic centre. She needed to speak to her husband. It would be unwise to contact him on an inside telephone.

The air outside was cool and felt good against her face, the civic centre heating had been uncomfortably high. She was relieved to find a phone box that had not been vandalised.

Within seconds the comforting sound of John's voice began to calm her. She could not conceal her anger as she blurted out what had happened. She knew very well what the consequences of Muckley's actions meant. It meant that she would not be able to take the exam at the time that she had expected to. She would have to wait for the next sitting.

Throughout their courtship and since their marriage seven months ago John had given her tremendous support and encouragement during her many hours' study. He was angry and alarmed by what had happened and agreed with Jane on the course of action to be taken - she must inform the Institute of Housing. This she did straight away, which was within half an hour of her meeting with Muckley.

The telephone was answered by Elaine Fordham, who was personal assistant to Dennis Crouch, Secretary of the Institute. Jane gave Elaine a brief account of what had happened and what her suspicions were.

'Right, you'd better come and see Mr Crouch as soon as possible. Let me look at his diary...now...how about...Could you come tomorrow morning at ten o'clock?'

'Yes, that'll be fine. It'll give me time to calm down before I explain it all to Mr Crouch.'

Jane was due to start study leave immediately following the Muckley interview so she was not expected to be at work for a few days. She wouldn't need an excuse for taking time off.

The following day Jane arrived at the offices of the Institute of Housing in London's Southampton Row. Her determination had not diminished, although she was feeling a little nervous. She knew that what she was about to do would have serious consequences and implications. She knew that the importance of the Institute to the housing profession was equal to that of the Law Society to the legal profession.

Elaine welcomed Jane eagerly and escorted her to Dennis Crouch's office. Jane wasted no time. After the usual formalities she settled down opposite him at his desk and proceeded to give a detailed account of the incident. He listened in silence. Very attentive, Elaine, sitting nearby, was mesmerised.

Jane was reading from the notes that she had made of Muckley's disclosures. The concern in Dennis Crouch's face was unmistakable. He interrupted her even though she had not finished. 'Let me see those, will you, Jane.'

She handed him the notepad. He anxiously flipped through several pages.

'Will you excuse me for a while; I want to check these against the examination paper.'

Dennis Crouch left the room hurriedly. Elaine chatted amiably, clearly trying to put Jane at ease. He was gone for no more than ten minutes, then he re-entered the room. 'Yes, I'm afraid that these are the examination questions.' He glanced at her notes again. 'Look, Jane, I don't want you to tell anyone about this, any of it, unless not doing so threatens your job. Would you mind?"

'Of course not, Mr Crouch. I'll do whatever you say.'

He continued: 'I am duty bound to report this incident to the Institute's senior directors. I'm sure they will want to take the matter up with Mr Muckley.' He paused. 'Jane, knowing what has transpired what have you in mind at present?'

'Well. I'm on study leave now for three days and then there are the three days for the actual exam, so I'm not expected back at the department for six or seven days.'

'You must realise, Jane, that I can't possibly let you sit the exam now.'

It was just as she had feared. She felt indignant. 'Of course not, I suspected that when I left Mr Muckley's office. That's why I was so angry. I just can't understand what made him do it.'

'Neither can I. But I intend to find out, Jane. What I want you to do now is to go home. Stay away from the civic centre. Continue with your usual arrangements as though you were going to sit the exam.'

Jane was puzzled. 'Yes, but what will happen after that?'

'Leave it to me. I take full responsibility for this and I'll do all that I can to protect you.'

Jane felt a little better but the situation was beginning to look somewhat bizarre. She left the Institute's offices in a rather confused state. She had little recollection of her journey home, vividly recounting events of the past twenty-four hours.

The following day a letter arrived by first- class post from the Institute of Housing. It read:

Dear Mrs Saxby,

This letter is to instruct you as a student member of the Institute of Housing, and in the circumstances we have discussed, to proceed with all your normal arrangements in preparing for the Final Part 2 of the Institute's Examination to be held during the week commencing 22 May 1978.

I, as secretary of the institute, accept full responsibility for these instructions which I would ask you to disclose in your own protection only if called upon by a person in authority to do so.

You will be informed as soon as possible of the Institute's decision following our talk.

The letter was signed by Dennis Crouch.

Jane read the letter several times. The grave implications began to dawn upon her. Dennis Crouch had kept his word; whatever happened from here on, this letter would cover her. She felt uneasy though. Dennis Crouch was, after all, instructing her to mislead her employers; but how would she explain her failure to sit the exam when she returned to work? She decided to sleep on it. With several days' leave ahead of her she resolved to enjoy the break and to see how she felt at the end of it.

Jane lived in the upper-floor flat of a large Victorian terraced house in Northumberland Avenue near Southend seafront. It was one of many such houses in the town that had been converted into flats with the benefit of a council home improvement rant and it provided Jane and John with their first home. The modestly furnished front room had bay windows which gave an unobstructed view in both directions along the street. The front entrance to the house, which provided shared access to both flats, retained the original door with its opaque stained glass panels.

Jane was content living in her little home and now she resented the intrusion into her normally peaceful life of all this intrigue and mystery.

Several days had passed since the meeting with Dennis Crouch. She was busying herself about the flat. Her door bell rang. She was halfway down the stairs when she glanced at the door. Through the glass panel she could see the shape of a tall man. She froze. 'It can't be,' she thought, trembling. Jane crept quietly back upstairs and looked out of the front window. Parked just a few yards along the road she saw Muckley's car. Fear struck her in a way that she had never in her life experienced. He was here! Although he had never actually done any thing to frighten her, didn't yell or anything, it was the fact that he was here, at her own home, and she was alone.

Jane remained silent - hardly breathing; waiting for him to go. Not daring to move, hoping he would think she was not at home. She felt very frightened. Eventually he gave up and left. A car started up and drove off. She felt sure it was his. She peered cautiously over the window-sill and gave a sigh of relief, but it was a long time before she regained control.

When John arrived home later Jane had still not fully recovered. He could see that she was upset and when she described the day's events he was furious.

'First thing tomorrow morning I'm going to see the Town Clerk to find out what the hell is going on.'

Jane begged him not to. 'Let's not do anything hasty. Wait until I go back to work. Perhaps things will have calmed down by then and I can find out what is going to happen.'

John agreed, reluctantly, and suggested that the situation called for a large gin and tonic. With tears welling up in her eyes, Jane nodded approval and hugged him tightly.

The following day Jane was surprised to receive another letter from the institute of housing. She sat down and read:

Dear Mrs Saxby,

I am directed by the President of the Council of the Institute and the Chairman of the Examination Board to inform you that following the events you reported to me on Friday 12 May, you are ineligible to sit the diploma examination (Part 2 final) in the coming week. Accordingly, your entrance fee will, if you so wish be transferred to the December examination.

They wish me to inform you also that prompt action has been taken by the institute to ensure that there can be no re-occurrence of the situation you have reported, and appropriate disciplinary measures have been imposed.

The institute is grateful to you for the information you have given without regard to your own personal interest. You will, I feel sure, treat the matter with the utmost confidentiality, but if it is the cause of any problems or embarrassment to you later on, please do not hesitate to contact me.

I am sorry that through no fault of your own you are denied the opportunity of taking the examination on this occasion.

Again, the letter was signed by Dennis Crouch.

Jane sank back in her armchair. 'Phew,' she thought. 'What have I done?' She read again several times the words that set her pulse racing ... *'appropriate disciplinary measures have been imposed'.* The statement made her wonder what on earth they must have done to Muckley. 'Maybe that's why he came here,' she thought; 'To sort me out? Surely not! That's more than his job's worth.'

Despite the conviction that her disclosure was justified, Jane was nonetheless apprehensive. Muckley's gaunt appearance through the glass panel, actuated by bright sunshine, had cast a sinister shadow, his blurred features contorted into a menacing figure.

What would have happened had she opened the door? How would she feel when eventually confronting him? Muckley deserved all that was coming to him, no doubt, but she knew that he would be a dangerous and wily adversary, as had been proved time and again when he had been upbraided over minor matters previously.

He had so much confidence in himself, an animal inner ferocity that had intimidated those around him and which would prove decisive when confronted with the latest allegations.

But Jane had to live with her conscience. Reporting him to the institute hadn't been deceitful: she had honestly stated what had occurred, what would have ensured her securing success in the forthcoming examination but which was blatantly dishonest. She couldn't understand Muckley's motives for wanting to ease her way, what did he hope to gain?

Talking this over with her John, it was decided that come what may she would see this through. Her fears eventually subsided, but later, when in bed with his comforting arm round her, they returned, and she lay for a long time in darkness alone with her doubts, despair, and finally determination, until weariness overcame her and she fell into a sound sleep.

The following morning Jane left for work with a heavy heart, still unsure of how she should broach the subject of not sitting the exam.

She needn't have worried. Mysteriously, someone had already given her excuses. Who had done so, she had no idea, but although this had broken the ice it was a lie.

She decided to keep quiet, keep things to herself, not tell

anyone until she had spoken with Mr Purrott.

She sat down at her desk and waited. She was fifteen minutes early and the staff would be in soon. Reaching for her handbag she took out a mirror and lipstick, she checked her appearance, then decided that she didn't need lip-gloss, but was shocked by her appearance. Dark rings under her eyes, pallid cheeks, and her hair wasn't right. Sometimes it seemed that whenever she was taut or nervous her hair tightened to her scalp, making her appear older and staid. She lightly fluffed her hair outwards, loosening the strands until satisfied that she felt freer. Just then a door opened along the corridor. Was it Purrott or Muckley?

The courage that comes naturally to women when confronted with snarling dogs or punching drunks came to her aid. This was it. Waiting only until whoever it was had settled down she pushed her door open, and hearing movements in Purrott's office, tapped on his door.

'Come in,' he called softly.

As she entered he said 'good morning, Jane,' apparently light-hearted, but his eyes told the truth. He was one of those people who are incapable of matching expressions to voices, quite unaware that their innermost feelings are forever revealed - guileless. He also had a stammer that became more pronounced in times of stress or excitement.

'Good morning, Mr Purrott,' Jane said.

He fiddled with his left ear, shoulders hunched, studying the grain of his desk, not daring to look directly at her but instead flicking his eyes at her in a mixture of apprehension and authority. Jane desperately wanted to relieve him of his obvious despair.

'This must be distressing for you, Mr Purrott, and I wish that this business with Mr Muckley hadn't happened, but I couldn't and will not be part of any deception. Whatever I attain must be through my own efforts, not through back-door scheming. You must understand that I feel strongly about this - I want it cleared up. I can't understand why I've been put in this position.'

Before she could say all that was in her heart, Mr Purrott interrupted her:

'Jane, I've, err, discussed the situation with the powers-that-be, and it has been decided to try to settle this amicably. Mr Muckley would like to see you and give reasons for his conduct. Have a chat with him. I feel sure that he will put your mind at rest.'

Then, from along the corridor, they heard footsteps that came towards the office but which stopped short. A door opened and closed. Muckley had arrived.

'Ah, that's Mr Muckley now. Shall I arrange for you to see him, Jane?'

Jane felt sick. So it all came back to Muckley: see *him* and chat with *him*. Once again he would be in control. He was the culprit and yet it would be him holding court as if she were the guilty party.

Her cheeks flushed angrily as she replied: 'Now! Let me see him now! Isn't anyone prepared to do anything? Let's stop pussyfooting for once. You are his superior. Are you delegating responsibility for his actions to him alone? This is tantamount to a Judge giving a criminal the authority to direct court proceedings. He is the guilty party, not me. Bring him in here, let's have witnesses. Are you aware that after I had complained about him he turned up at my house? What was that in aid of?'

'He did what?'

'Oh, it's all right, I pretended I was out. But he was there.

'Jane,' Purrott pleaded. 'Let me arrange a private meeting between you and him some time today.' Oh God, let it be' he thought.

'No. I shall see him now - not at his convenience but at

mine.'

Before he could reply she got up and left Purrott staring disconsolately as she marched out and rapped on Muckley's door. She heard him moving across towards his desk. Had he been eavesdropping?

His squeaky voice called 'Come in.' As she entered she expected to be confronted with his piercing eyes but for once they were averted as if he was planning something. It was as if she wasn't there, as if he was intent on dispelling her anger, so making her more pliable for when he would apply his coup de grâce. Instinctively she felt that he had overheard her conversation with Purrott, but she could not be sure.

Then he looked at her, shifty, cold-eyed and menacing.

Immediately, without even a 'good morning,' he launched into a tirade of shocked disbelief that a junior had had the audacity to question his methods. Wasn't he, as training officer, responsible for her, for pointing her in the right direction so that she would further her career? Wasn't she aware of the extent to which he had gone to for others as well as her? Wasn't it his duty to guide fledglings through their exams? Wasn't she aware of the standards expected by the council? It had all been a misunderstanding - one of those things that come about through over-enthusiasm on his part and ungratefulness on hers. His sole purpose was to help in any way possible. To have his good intentions thrown in his face was disgraceful. How many times had he guided juniors through until they passed, did anyone remember that? No, it had been because of him that standards were maintained, not despite him. Discipline was often objectionable, but necessary. She should be apologetic, not standing here accusing him of these ridiculous   In future, though, he would be more careful - it was obvious that he wasn't fully appreciated.

'You see, Mrs Saxby, it has all been a ghastly mistake. Just forget it, as I shall, OK?'

Her whole being was screaming at him: You two-faced bastard. You evil toad.

Aloud, she said: 'Mr Muckley, you must allow me to form my own conclusions. I know you were wrong, and so do you. But you haven't heard the last of this - I can tell you that. You are just covering up, as you always do. It's pointless trying to get through to you.'

He turned pale; he had expected her to crumple. He hadn't been prepared for this. She was going to fight him, and for once his brash bullying front had been breeched. Just those few words had given him an insight to her character. He had not succeeded in insulting her intelligence. She would be a formidable adversary.

Jane had had enough of this discussion. There was no point mentioning his visit to her home: she knew he would deny it.

As she left his office her immediate thoughts were of resignation. How could she continue working for a man who was so unscrupulous? She had heard all sorts of rumours about Muckley's behaviour during her 4 years with the department; he seemed to be disliked by everyone, she was beginning to understand why. The reason for Anne Archer's sudden and unexpected departure after more than 20 years of doing a job to which she was devoted was never made clear. There was some talk of early retirement but it didn't make sense; she was still fit and healthy. Was Muckley responsible for Anne's early retirement, had he ruined her career?

Jane was certain of this: something dramatic was going to happen over this present situation that would have an adverse affect on her ability to carry on normal working in the department. Her career training could not possibly continue with Southend Council under a cloud. It was an intolerable situation, one that forced Jane to make up her mind. It was time to move on.

In most areas of employment with local authorities it is relatively easy to change jobs within weeks: In housing it is different. There are only two main employing bodies: local councils and housing associations. It was imperative that Jane should continue her career training and she would need to find a job where she could do so. She started to scan the vacancy columns of *Housing Journal*. There were plenty of vacancies at varying qualification levels but because of the grade that Jane had reached she knew that she would have to be patient until she found a position suited to her present accomplishments.

In the meantime she would have to do the best she could to carry on as usual. It was going to be difficult; her heart was no longer in it. Her confidence had been badly shaken and what once had been a pleasant and challenging job had suddenly become meaningless.

During the next few days Jane felt sure that Fred Laws would call her. After all, the institute would surely have informed him of the incident and the fact that Muckley had been disciplined and he would want to know how Jane was coping. If Fred Laws really cared about the welfare of the council's employees, he would call her into his office to hear her side of the story. She wanted his assurance that she would not suffer because of her disclosure.

Nothing happened. Muckley was continuing all his normal duties as deputy chief Housing Officer, including his duties as the department's training officer. To all intents and purposes nothing had changed. If he had been disciplined, as the Institute had claimed, then it certainly wasn't apparent. It was uncanny, as though it had all been a dream. Jane wondered whether Muckley had got away with it. 'If that is so then he has some very powerful friends,' she thought. But of course this couldn't be the case. Give it time. Something was bound to happen soon. The days dragged: nothing.

During the next few months Jane attended several interviews but none of the vacancies she was applying for were really suitable. Then her hopes received an unexpected boost. An advertisement appeared in the *Southend Evening Echo* for a housing officer at the Utopian Housing Association's new development on the old Kursaal amusement site near Southend sea-front. She wasted no time in completing the application form and an appointment was arranged for the following week.

When she arrived for the interview Jane was astonished to be greeted by Anne Archer.

'Anne! What a pleasant surprise! It's lovely to see you. How are you?'

'Fine, and you?' replied Anne. 'I can't tell you how curious I was when I saw your application form on the boss's desk. I couldn't believe it.'

'Well, I'd heard on the grapevine some time ago that you were working for Utopian but it never crossed my mind that I would see you here on this occasion.'

'Yes, Jane. I've been here some time now. But tell me, why are you leaving Southend Council...or can I guess?'

'Oh, I must leave, Anne. Something terrible has happened. I couldn't possibly stay there.'

'Don't tell me, Jane. I bet it was something to do with Muckley.'

'You're dead right. The man's a monster.'

'Jane, I'd love to hear the details. Look, are you doing anything next Tuesday evening?'

Jane searched her mind. 'I don't think so.'

'Well,' said Anne eagerly, 'it's my birthday. Would you like to come round and have a drink with us? It just so happens that someone else is coming who I know would love to meet you and hear your story.'

Jane was puzzled, but she didn't press Anne to explain. She knew there were other applicants waiting to be interviewed. "Yes, Anne, I would really like to do that. Do you still live along the Eastern Avenue...oh, and what time?'

'Yes, I'm still there. Don't worry about a fixed time, around eight will be fine. And do bring John. I haven't seen him since the wedding.'

Her departure from the Utopian offices after the interview left Jane in a state of excitement and confusion.

Jane and John arrived at the arranged time. Anne greeted them both warmly and led them into the lounge. 'I don't know if you've heard yet from Utopian,' she said softly to Jane. 'But I'm afraid you weren't short-listed for the vacancy.'

'No. I haven't.' replied Jane. 'It's a pity, but I think I may have struck lucky, I had an interview with Basildon Development Corporation last Thursday and I've just heard that I've been short listed. It looks very promising, especially since I would be able to continue my studies for the Final Diploma Exam.

'Oh, that sounds hopeful, Jane. I do hope you get the job.' Apart from Anne's husband, Fred, there was only one other person present. Pleasantries and recollections of their meeting at the wedding were exchanged with Fred.

'Jane, I'd like you to meet Keith Bartell. Keith, this is Jane Saxby who I've been telling you all about. And this is her husband John. Keith is a reporter with the *Evening Echo*. His father plays golf with Fred. During their golfing Fred's been telling him all about my problems at the housing department and he wants to hear about your experiences."

'Hello, Jane, John. Very pleased to meet you. I understand, Jane, that you are also leaving the department because of Muckley.'

'I most certainly am,' she replied.

Whilst they talked Anne set about preparing drinks.

'Basically I've come here to see if there's a story in Anne's background to her departure. I understand that you've had similar problems. Are you prepared to tell me about it?'

Jane paused. 'Well, I wasn't expecting this. It's quite a surprise.' She smiled. 'It's just like Anne to spring this on me. Yes, of course I'll be glad to get it off my chest.' They settled down and Jane proceeded to tell him everything. She had brought the correspondence from the Institute which she showed to Keith. He made copious notes and from his reaction she knew she had an ally.

'It certainly was an incredible thing for a man in his position to do,' said Keith. 'Can you think of any reason why he would do it, Jane?'

Anne quickly interrupted: 'Well, I can answer that. You say why you think he did it, Jane, and I'll tell you why I think...'

Jane cut in: 'There are two possible reasons that come to mind. The nicest one I can think of is that he did it to ensure that I would pass, for his prestige, and the prestige of the department. What other motives he had, I can't imagine.'

'Strange, isn't it? Knowing him, it couldn't have been just that,' said Anne.

'I've thought about it many times,' said Jane. 'He certainly never asked for anything in return; and I do mean anything. So I can only presume that was his reason: he wanted it known that it was through his efforts that I had succeeded: a feather in his cap if I had.'

Anne expanded the theory a little further. 'You could be right, Jane, he wanted to bask in the reflective glory of getting you...'

Keith interrupted, probing a little deeper. 'Could there have been another reason?'

There was a thoughtful silence. 'Possibly,' replied Jane slowly, cautiously. 'He could have wanted in some way to have a hold over me. But then that doesn't necessarily make sense. If he did that he would be implying that...I mean...he had something to lose as well. 'She paused.

Keith gently encouraged her to continue: 'Well, Jane, every blackmailer has something to lose. It's a criminal offence, blackmail.'

She was beginning to feel uneasy, and it showed. 'Yes. I mean, he would have been, as you say, found out.'

'It's a question of who's got the most to lose,' replied Keith.

'Yes, quite,' said Jane. 'I spoke to John about it and I did hate... I mean, there are nastier connotations as well.'

His reporter senses were alerted. 'Did he at any time make an advance towards you?'

Jane hesitated. She was obviously uncomfortable with this: '... Once.'

Keith sensed that she was feeling nervous, reluctant to proceed. Quietly he asked her: 'would you tell me about it?'

'Well... it was... nasty. I hated it at the time. In fact it was the first...going back, I didn't mention this before because it's just a...I don't think it has any bearing on this and if it was from anybody else I wouldn't have cared. But when I went in for my first...'

Keith gently coaxed her: 'Ah, you're going back to the very first exam?'

'No, no, no.' replied Jane. 'Not my exam, the time of my coming marriage. When I was about to go on leave for my wedding and honeymoon and I went into his office and he wished me well... then kissed me.'

'Mmm. You told me that,' said Anne.

There was now a little anger in Jane's voice. 'He kissed me

on the lips - I hated it. Because to me he was...' She seemed unwilling to finish.

Keith gave her time to recover her composure. 'What do you mean, Jane?'

'I mean nothing more than that.' She feared that he was trying to make her say more than she wanted to say.

He sensed her resistance growing and decided to try a different tack. 'Do you think he got the message... that his advance made you cringe?'

Jane's reply was positive. 'Oh yes. He knew that he shouldn't have tried anything on. He certainly backed off.'

'What did you do then?'

'I left immediately.'

Keith wouldn't give up. 'He got the message from you... 'Keep your distance'?'

'Yes,' said Jane. 'But it would have been farcical if he'd wanted to try anything on. It was only three days before my wedding day. It would have been a very odd time to have done so.'

Anne could not resist the temptation to follow on: 'For a normal-thinking person, maybe, but are we talking of someone who thinks and behaves normally?"

Jane remained silent. Keith sensed that she had had enough of the interview: he knew it was time to end it. 'Well, Jane, that's quite a story. I think you handled the situation extremely well. It's quite outrageous that you should have been put through such an ordeal. And I've never before heard of a professional person holding a position such as Muckley has behaving in this manner. I'm very grateful to you, Jane, for telling me all about it. I do hope it wasn't too distressing for you. I think it's going to make a sensational story. What I'm going to do next is contact Muckley, try to find out why he did it. I shall also go to the Institute and have a word with Dennis Crouch.

Perhaps I can persuade him to explain why no action's been taken against Muckley.'

Keith stood up and stuffed his notepad into his pocket. He thanked Jane again and thanked Anne for her hospitality and for arranging the meeting.

When Keith had left, Jane and Anne looked at one another, both knowing that they were wondering the same; is Muckley at last going to be exposed? Will he finally be brought to account?

CHAPTER 5

Patricia was sitting quietly in the lounge reading when the telephone rang.

Since Ron's election the number of calls had increased, and although she had been prepared for this she nonetheless missed those quiet evenings that she and Ron shared towards the close of each day.

As she picked up the phone a woman's agitated voice blurted out: 'Ron? Is that Ron Levy?

'No, this is his wife. Can I help you? Ron isn't home yet, but he shouldn't be long.'

'My name is Mary...Mary Bates. I desperately need to talk to him.' The caller sounded so upset and out of breath that Patricia wanted to comfort her immediately.

'Mary, please calm down. Don't upset yourself further. Whatever it is, Ron will do all he can to help, you can be sure of that. You have my word on it.' She sensed the urgency and thought it best to invite Mary round in an effort to allay her fears knowing that instead of the loneliness of relaying her thoughts to a telephone mouthpiece she would be among sympathetic company, in direct contact with those prepared to help her.

'How far away are you?' Patricia enquired. On being given the location, she said, 'Oh, that's only round the corner from us, is there any chance that you could call in now? It won't be long before Ron arrives. In the meantime we could have a chat. Is that OK?'

'Yes, yes. I can come round now. I know where you are. Thank you for your kindness. See you soon, Mrs Levy.' She put the phone down leaving Patricia intrigued but determined to do all she could for her.

Patricia turned to the children. 'I've got to see someone downstairs for daddy, I want you to be quiet and behave. It shouldn't take too long.'

The entrance hall had a connecting door to the salon. Patricia went in, arranged the chairs and quickly checked that everything was neat and tidy. The salon had proved to be very useful for interviewing people away from the children and the television. She stood quietly for a moment, pensive. 'Oh God! I hope Ron does come home soon,' she thought.   'I wonder what the problem could be, the poor woman sounds so distraught.'

Within minutes came the sound of door chimes. 'That must be her.' On answering the door she was confronted by a wide-eyed woman who swallowed nervously as she spoke: 'Mrs Levy?'

'Yes. You must be Mary. Do come in... through here. Ron usually sees people in the shop. I hope you don't mind.'

'No, no,' Mary retorted. 'I'm just glad he could see me. Many people have spoken about Ron's kindness and his willingness to help people and I thought he might be able to help me.'

Mary was in her mid to late twenties. Small, slim, attractive, but looking drawn. She was rather timid and seemed to have lost interest in her appearance, which was a pity because with a little attention she could easily look quite stunning. Her hair was lank and in need of attention. It was difficult to tell if she usually had self-confidence: she certainly lacked it now.

'Well, as I said on the phone, he isn't here yet, but I'm sure he will be home soon. Would you like a coffee or something?'

Mary fiddled restlessly with the strap of her shoulder bag. It was something to hold on to: a comforter. 'No, that's all right, thank you.'

'Do have a seat, Mary. You seem very upset. Is there anything I can do?'

Mary lowered herself on to the edge of a chair. Patricia sat facing her.

'I'm not sure that there is,' she said quietly. 'I'm not even sure if your husband *can* help me.' As heat burned the back of her eyes, they brimmed over

Patricia's maternal instincts surfaced. She wanted to comfort this young woman as she had so often comforted her own daughters when they were upset. 'Would you like to talk to me about it first, would it help at all to do that?'

'That's why I'm not so sure... I don't know if I can talk to a man about it again... it's been going on for so long... they won't believe me... but they must... for the children's sake.' She stopped, wiping tears away, swallowing hard in an effort to control herself.

Patricia tried to reassure her. 'Mary, we have five children of our own. Ron is a wonderful father and he's very good at coping with problems. I'm sure you could speak to him, but if it will help you I'll stay with you when you see him.'

Mary stared at the floor, trying to regain her composure.

'Is it something you would like to tell me about first?' asked Patricia, gently.

Mary raised her head slowly, her eyes still moist. 'Please help me,' she pleaded. 'I don't know who else to turn to.'

Patricia was overwhelmed with compassion: What possible tragedy could have reduced this young woman to such misery?

'Look, Mary, I think you'd better tell me about it. We can

bring Ron up to date with the problem when he arrives. First of all, who won't believe you? You said "they" won't believe you.'

Mary replied immediately: This time there was anger in her voice; 'them up at the housing department. They say it's my word against my husband's. They won't let me have another house... but they must! I've got to get the children away from him.' She stopped abruptly, as though startled that what she had for so long suppressed was now coming into the open.

Patricia rapidly assessed the situation. Momentarily shocked as she was, she knew that she must keep calm and rational. Her intuition told her that a rather unpleasant story was about to unfold.

'Mary, tell me. Are your children alright? Where are they now?'

Mary was trembling. 'It's ok, my neighbour's looking after them while I'm here. My husband's out for the evening.'

'Let me get you something to drink, Mary, a coffee, perhaps?'

'Yes, please, Mrs Levy. Black, no sugar.'

'Right. You sit there and calm yourself. I won't be long. And please call me Patricia.'

Mary managed a faint smile as Patricia went to the kitchen. She returned a few minutes later with two cups of coffee.

'Now, Mary, are you ok?'

Mary nodded and took the cup eagerly. 'Thank you.'

'Do you want to continue?'

'Yes, I think so. I'm sorry. It just gets me upset talking about it. I'm alright now.'

'Mary,' said Patricia softly. 'What is it that they won't believe?'

'What he's been doing to the children.' Mary had steeled

herself to reply, but it came out more easily than she had expected. She was calming down now. It may have been the coffee, it may have been Patricia's kindly manner. Whatever it was, Mary was now ready to talk about it.

'How many children do you have, Mary; and what are their ages?'

'I have two girls and a boy: Michael is five; Susan, the youngest, is three; and Sharon is eight.'

'Tell me what you told them at the Housing Department.'

Mary visibly tensed, anger firming her voice. 'I told them he's been abusing the children, he's been doing it for a long time, I know he has, but always when I'm not there. And I can't be there all the time, even though I try to be.'

Patricia feared the worst. She didn't dare ask the obvious question in case her suspicions were wrong. She would have to be patient.

'How do you know what he's been doing, Mary?'

'Believe me, Patricia, I know. The children couldn't hide it for always. Every now and then they opened up. They told me things they couldn't possibly have made up. And their manner - their sparkle - has gone. They're sad... never laugh and play. They say he makes them do things to him, that he walks around naked with a towel hanging on his... 'Her voice faltered. She could not bring herself to finish the sentence. She turned her head to one side, lowering her gaze.

Patricia gave her time to be still: to choose her own pace.

Mary sighed and shifted in her seat. 'Oh, I don't think he's gone... all the way with them - you know what I mean. I don't think he's ever gone that far.' She stopped abruptly at the sound of keys jangling outside, and of the door opening.

'That'll be Ron now,' said Patricia, rising from her seat. 'Let me quickly tell him you're here. Just wait a moment, Mary. I know it's difficult, but try to relax, ok? Enjoy your coffee.'

Patricia hurriedly left the room and met Ron in the hall.

They greeted one another in the usual way. 'Hello, darling,' said Patricia, warmly. She kissed him lightly and snuggled her face into his neck.

Ron murmured approvingly. He gently caressed the curve of her back as he pressed her closer to him. Throughout their years together the chemistry that had bonded them since their first meeting was still there. 'Mm. Shall we have an early night?' he whispered.

Patricia drew back a little, smiled in mock disapproval and smacked his bottom playfully. 'You just dismiss such thoughts from your mind, you lecherous beast. Put your councillor hat on, you've got a problem to deal with.'

'Sounds ominous, what sort of problem?'

Patricia spoke quietly. 'Ron, I've got a young mum in the shop, her name's Mary. She's been here for about half an hour. She was very upset, but I think she's calmed down now. She says her husband has been sexually abusing their children. I don't think we should leave her alone for too long but, briefly, she's been to the housing department. She thinks they don't believe her and they're refusing to help her to get the children and herself away from him.' She paused and glanced anxiously towards the shop door. 'Look, you go up and say hello to the boys. The girls are tucked up in bed, have been for about an hour. They should be asleep by now. Then you come down and speak to Mary.'

Making his way towards the stairs Ron quickly took in the situation. 'Right, you go back to Mary. I'll be down in a few minutes.' He sprinted up the stairs as Patricia went back in to the shop.

He returned within minutes and joined them. Mary rose but he motioned her back as he walked over to shake her hand. 'Hello Mary. Patricia has told me briefly about your problem. Do you now feel up to talking to me about it?'

He sat down and produced a notepad and pen, assuring her that he would need to have the details in order to deal with the problem at the council offices, but that they would be confidential.

Mary put down the cup that she had been cradling. She warmed to him. Something in his manner dispelled any fears she had in relating intimate family details to a stranger. Something told her that he was someone in whom she could confide, and she repeated her story. Ron's reaction gave Mary comfort and hope. She knew that he would help her.

'How long has this been going on, Mary?' he asked,

'I can't be certain, but it must be at least two or three years. I've noticed the children getting worse ... more ... withdrawn, more unhappy.'

A list of questions flashed through Ron's mind but he decided to ask as few as possible at this stage. It would be best to reserve the more probing ones for later. 'Have you been to the police?'

'I didn't know if I should. It's not as though I discovered these goings-on suddenly. They came to light gradually: little by little during the past year or two. But every time I asked my husband if it was true... what the children said... he just grinned and said they were making it up, or imagining it all. I didn't know what to believe at first but the change in the children's behaviour convinced me it's true. I know it's true. It's got to stop. I must get them away from him. They are so unhappy. Sometimes they seem afraid.'

Her lips tensed as she fought back tears.

Patricia's heart went out to her and when she spoke her voice was hoarse with emotion. 'It's all right, Mary; take your time. Would you like another coffee?'

Wiping her eyes with the damp tissue that she had been clutching tightly, Mary gave a deep sigh. 'No, thank you. I'm ok... really.'

Ron paused with his note taking. He looked at Mary.

'I think I need a few more details, Mary. Do you feel up to continuing?

She nodded.

'Have you told anyone else, apart from the council?' he asked.

'Yes. The doctor was first. I'd been taking the children to him because I thought they weren't well. He was shocked... asked me if I could prove it. Well, I couldn't. But he did say it would explain their behaviour, the children's I mean. He put me in touch with Social Services. They came to see us a few times. My husband was there one of the times and they asked him about what the children had said, but he said they imagined it all and he got angry... said they should mind their own business and told them to leave the house.'

'What happened then, Mary. Did you see the social workers any more?'

She answered calmly. 'Yes, once more. They said they were satisfied something wrong was happening. They suggested I should see the council and ask them to re-house me and the children.'

'We know from what you told us earlier, Mary, that you did go to the housing department. But did you speak to anyone else before doing that?'

'The priest... at the catholic church. You know,.. the one on the corner of St. Andrews Road. I told him about it. But I think he already knew for a long time that something was wrong. He said he thought the children were looking unhappy. Then I told him everything. Somehow it seemed easier telling it for the third time. He said the social workers were right: That I should try to get re-housed away from him.'

Anger and pity welled up in Ron but he knew he must

contain his feelings.

'Are you all right, Mary? I'd like to ask just a few more questions. Can you cope with that?'

She nodded ... her face now expressionless.

'What actually happened at the housing department... who did you see there?'

The questions produced a positive response. 'I saw a young woman the first time, but she said it was too serious for her to deal with and she made an appointment for me to see the housing manager.'

'Who did you see? Can you remember his name?'

'Oh, yes. It was a Mr Muckley.'

'Did you tell him all that you have told me?'

'Yes, I did ... exactly the same.'

'And what was his reaction?'

Mary frowned, hesitated. 'It's difficult to describe, really. I thought it was a bit weird. Not the sort of man I'd expect to find in that high position.' She paused, became visibly tense. I tell you this, though. He made me angry. I'm sure he didn't believe me. I don't think he was interested, even when I told him the doctor, the social workers and the priest were convinced it was true. He said there was nothing he could do without some evidence to back up my story. He told me to get a doctor's report and one from the social workers and he would consider it again.'

'And did you get those reports?'

'Oh, yes,' she replied eagerly. 'The doctor wrote a letter saying that he was concerned for the children and for me... that he was unable to provide medical evidence of abuse to back up my story but that he believed the complaint. It was the same with social services. They wrote a report saying that they had interviewed us, and although they couldn't provide any actual evidence they were very concerned about the children and me. I even went back to Father

Patrick. He wrote a report on the children's well-being, and mine. He told me he did.'

'Mary. Am I right in thinking that these reports and letters were sent directly to the housing department?'

'Oh, yes. Then I phoned and made another appointment with Mr Muckley to see if they were all right... the letters, I mean.'

'Yes, Mary. I understand. What happened next? Did you see Mr Muckley?'

Mary's face mirrored her frustration and anger. 'I certainly did, but it was a complete waste of time. He told me what was in the letters but he said they weren't good enough. He said he wanted firm evidence. I told him that was impossible, but he said that without it he couldn't do anything for me because he didn't want it to look as though he was taking sides of either me or my husband.'

'I must admit, Mary, I find that quite astonishing. Whatever did you do next?'

Mary's voice shook. 'I'm afraid I got very upset, and I lost my temper a little. Well, it was more frustration, really. I told him I didn't believe him. That I thought he just didn't want to help me. I told him he was an unfeeling monster who didn't care about women or children suffering.' She hesitated, calming herself before continuing: 'I'm afraid I couldn't take any more from him. I knew I wasn't getting anywhere and so I stormed out of his office and came home.'

'Phew! I doubt if anyone would blame you for doing that, Mary. I was wondering ... '

Mary interrupted him, continuing from where she had left off: 'I needed someone to talk to about it. I went to see Father Patrick. He said he thought I had been treated unreasonably. It was Father Patrick who suggested I come and see you. He said he had heard that you helped a lot of people.'

'I'll certainly do what I can, Mary. What I really can't understand is why Mr Muckley refused so bluntly to help you. Although I must admit I have had a number of people come to me complaining of the treatment they have received from him.'

Patricia had been sitting quietly, listening. She wanted to help. 'Mary, I know that Ron will take up your case with the housing department, but I think you need some legal advice on your matrimonial situation. I know a very good solicitor in Southend. If you like, I'll take you there... give you some moral support. Would you want to take that step?'

Mary was a little overwhelmed. 'This is all very kind of you both. I am really very grateful. You're right, Patricia. I couldn't possibly stay with him... as his wife. You know, like a normal husband and wife. Not after knowing what he's been up to. I would like you to help me with finding a solicitor.'

Patricia was relieved. She knew how important it was for someone in Mary's position to do something positive. 'Right, Mary. First thing in the morning I'll get on to Jefferies and make an appointment as early as possible. Are you on the phone at home?'

Mary nodded and gave Patricia her number, which Ron wrote down in his notepad.

'Thank you. I'll ring as soon as I've arranged a date.' Patricia turned to Ron. 'Have you finished, dear? Is there anything else you want to ask Mary?'

He stood up. 'No. No. I think I've got enough to act on. I certainly won't delay on this one, Mary. I'm pleased you came to see me. I know it will be difficult, but try not to worry. I'll do all that I can to help you. Now, I suggest you go home to your children. They are going to need all the love and attention you can give.'

Patricia led her to the front door.

When she had gone Patricia went back in to Ron. 'What do you make of all that, and what on earth is wrong with Mr Muckley?'

He was deep in thought. Mary's story had disturbed him. 'Sorry, dear. What did you say?'

'I said, what's wrong with Mr Muckley? Why does he keep behaving in this way?'

Until this incident with Mary, and apart from attendance at housing committee meetings, he hadn't had a great deal of contact with Muckley.

'I just can't understand it.' he replied. 'I've certainly had lots of complaints about him in the past months, haven't I? I'm beginning to think there must be quite a problem with him.'

It wasn't so long ago that two young unmarried mothers had come to see him, on separate occasions. Both had been to see Muckley about their need for larger accommodation because of an expected additional child, both claimed they were told to go away and get an abortion. Ron hadn't approached Muckley about the complaint; it sounded too ridiculous to be true: but doubts were now creeping into his mind.

He glanced at the clock. 'Hey, look at the time. The kids will think we've left home.' Hugging her, he said, 'Come on, let's go up to them.'

'Hello - would you put me through to Mr Muckley please, this is Councillor Levy?... thank you.'

'Hello. Mr Muckley?'

'Yes, Councillor. What can I do for you?'

'Mr Muckley, one of my constituents came to see me yesterday. She was in a very distressed state. Mrs Bates. She told me that she had been to see you about ... '

'Yes, Councillor, I know who you are talking about. I did explain to her that we weren't able to do anything for her at present. She was unable to produce evidence of her claim that her children are being abused.'

'Yes, Mr Muckley. She told me you had said that. She also told me that you had received three reports, or letters, from her doctor, social workers and her parish priest who all confirmed their view that the children are being abused. Is that correct, Mr Muckley?'

'Well, yes. I do have those reports, but, as I told Mrs Bates, it wasn't really hard evidence. I would need something more positive than letters from those people otherwise it might appear that I was taking sides in a matrimonial dispute.'

'Oh, come off it, Mr Muckley. We're not just talking about a matrimonial dispute. We're talking about children who are being sexually abused by their father.'

'With respect, Councillor: alleged abuse. It is, after all, her word against his, and I understand that he denies the allegations.'

'Don't you think that's rather naive, Mr Muckley? Of course he would deny it. Wouldn't he be just a little stupid to admit to such serious allegations? In any case, how on earth is it possible to obtain absolute proof of such conduct? Surely you could have used your own assessment ability concerning the doctor, social workers and the priest, all three of them can't be wrong.'

'I can't answer that, councillor. I can only repeat that in my opinion there wasn't enough evidence for us to assist her with her request for alternative accommodation for her and her children.'

'Yes, Mr Muckley. That all sounds very pompous. But let me say this: my instinct tells me that the views of three professional people should carry a lot more credibility than you seem prepared to accept. I don't know why you are being so stubborn, but I think you are wrong.' The tone of Muckley's voice told him that he wasn't getting through to him, and, anger adding emphasis to his words, he almost shouted: 'Are you going to reconsider your decision, Mr Muckley?'

Silence. Ron was sure he heard Muckley gulp as, with a discernibly higher pitch to his voice, he replied: 'I'm sorry, Councillor. I don't see how I can. We mustn't appear to be taking sides ... '

'Yes, yes, Mr Muckley. I've heard all that. But I tell you this - I am not prepared to stand by and do nothing. Goodbye!'

Ron slammed the phone down, and immediately regretted doing so. It was not in his nature to behave discourteously. He picked up the phone again and dialled.

'Hello. Would you put me through to Mr Purrott, please? This is councillor Levy... thank you... Hello... Mr Purrott?'

'Yes?'

'It's councillor Levy.'

'Hello, councillor. How are you?' he asked cheerfully. 'I don't hear from you very often.'

'Well, I try not to bother you with matters that your officers can deal with easily. As to how am I... I am not very happy.'

'I'm sorry to hear that, councillor. Can I help?'

'I hope so, Mr Purrott. I've just had words with Mr Muckley about a constituent's problems. I think Mr Muckley has made a wrong decision and I would like to discuss it with you as a matter of urgency. But I think I would like to see you in your office about it. Can you see me today?'

'I'll certainly see you if I can, councillor. Let me look in my diary... I think I'm free... yes, I am. How about after lunch, say two-fifteen. Is that convenient?'

'Yes, that will be fine. The shop is closed today. It's my day off. Before you go, Mr Purrott, can I ask you to acquaint yourself with the case I want to discuss with you? It's about Mrs Mary Bates. I'm sure Mr Muckley will fill you in on some of the details - including my argument with him.'

I'm not sure I like the sound of that, councillor. Let's hope I can sort the matter out for you. I'll see you after lunch, then. Goodbye, Mr Levy.'

'Thank you, Mr Purrott. I shall look forward to that.'

Cyril Purrott opened his door, he had a sombre expression. 'Do come in, councillor.' He directed Ron to a seat facing his desk. His own chair, a large, sumptuous black leather one, which seemed much too spacious for him, making him appear even smaller than he was. Neatly positioned in the centre of his blotter lay a file; the name on the front cover being easily read from Ron's position, M Bates. Purrott opened the file, glanced at it, closed it, then looked at Ron.

'Well, Mr Levy. I've had a look at the case history and I've spoken to Mr Muckley about it. He told me about your disagreement; he said he tried to ring you back but your line was busy. He said he thinks there has been a misunderstanding.'

'Really!' replied Ron, unable to conceal his cynicism. 'And what do you think, Mr Purrott?'

'Well, I can see Mr Muckley's point. If we re-house Mrs Bates and we are wrong, we will have interfered in a matrimonial dispute - taken sides.'

'And if we fail to take action, Mr Purrott?'

Purrott shifted uneasily. 'Well... I...I... err ... '

Ron's impatience got the better of him. 'If we ignore this, Mr Purrott, the abuse and suffering will go on and it could end in disaster.'

'Well, yes...I suppose you could be right. Perhaps we had

better have another look at it.'

'For goodness sake, Mr Purrott. How much closer do you need to look? You've got all the information you're likely to get on the matter. Ron rose from his seat and leaned across Purrott's desk. It needs a decision now, he barked. Straightening up, he continued earnestly. Look, I must tell you that after speaking to Muckley this morning I phoned four of my colleagues on the housing committee. They all agreed that on the face of it something ought to be done for Mrs Bates as a matter of urgency. If I can't get a decision now, Mr Purrott, I'm going to ask the chairman to put the issue to an emergency meeting of the housing committee.'

Mr Purrott was not happy about such a move. It would override his authority. Ron knew that, but he was desperate. 'Look, Councillor,' Purrott said, 'I can see you are convinced about Mrs Bates, and I can agree with you about the consequences of getting it wrong. The only way we could do something immediately is if I speak to Utopian Housing Association. You know their new development on the Kursaal site is beginning to filling up now. I'm sure there are still some vacancies there. You may remember when we dealt with this in committee some time ago that this is a joint venture and we have a 60 per cent allocation on those units. Leave it with me and I'll get in touch with Colin George this afternoon.'

Ron breathed a sigh of relief; 'Thank you, Mr Purrott. I am very grateful to you. I'm absolutely certain it's the right thing to do. I'll wait to hear from you then. Perhaps you'll let me know as soon as you have an answer.'

'Yes, Mr Levy, I will.' They stood up and shook hands. Ron left the Civic Centre feeling emotionally drained, but convinced that help was on the way for Mary and her children.

Taking care not to raise her hopes falsely, Ron phoned

Mary and explained what action he had taken. His first salon appointment in the morning was at ten fifteen and he planned to call Utopian early to find out if Purrott had contacted them.

The phone was answered immediately: 'Utopian Housing.'

'Good morning. My name is Levy. I'm a member of Southend Council. I'm enquiring about a constituent of mine who is being referred to you by the housing department. Her name is Mary Bates.'

'That's Councillor Ron Levy, isn't it? I've heard about you. I am Anne Archer. Does that mean anything to you, Mr Levy?'

'Yes, it does. I recall a Personnel meeting not so long ago. Didn't you leave to take up another post?'

'Here we go again,' said Anne. 'That's what they wanted everyone to think, Mr Levy.'

'I'm sorry, Mrs Archer. I'm somewhat puzzled by your reply. Does it mean that that isn't what happened?'

'Oh, far from it, Mr Levy, far from it.'

'I'm intrigued. What is it all about, Mrs Archer? Oh, and please call me Ron.'

'And I'm Anne. I'd love to tell you, Ron, but it's rather a long story. Perhaps you'd like to come to my home some time. I'd be delighted to put you in the picture.'

'Well, Anne. I shall certainly take you up on that offer. I'll ring you later to arrange a date. Now, about Mary Bates...have you heard anything?'

'Oh, yes. Cyril Purrott's been on to us in a bit of a panic... said a member has demanded action on this case and he wants an urgent allocation offered. I presume that was you. Whatever did you say to him, Ron? It's most unusual for him to approach us in this way.'

'It's a very sad case. I don't know how much you've been told, Anne, but I spoke to Muckley about it and I was disappointed in his reaction. He bluntly refused to help Mary, which seemed unreasonable to me. I couldn't believe it.'

'Oh, I could. That sounds very much like Muckley. It doesn't surprise me at all.'

'Really! That sounds rather cynical. Is that consistent with your knowledge of Muckley?'

'Very much so: and it doesn't surprise me that you've clashed with him. I've been hearing of your exploits with the council. I'm only surprised that it didn't happen sooner. Oh, yes, my friend. They say that only cream and bastards rise. Well, Muckley certainly proved that, and he's not cream. Believe me, I could tell you some extremely interesting stories about our Mr Muckley.'

Ron was intrigued. 'I would like to hear more.'

Was she making a conscious effort to arouse his interest? He couldn't tell. But the bitterness in her voice whetted his appetite and he eagerly wanted to know more.

'I've got my diary here, can we fix a date?'

'Certainly,' she replied. 'I'm free most evenings, if that's all right with you.'

'Yes, Anne. That's the best time for me really, how about tomorrow evening, around eight o'clock?'

'Fine, I'll look forward to it. Oh, you don't know where I live, It's 169 Prince Avenue. About four hundred yards back from Kent Elms Corner, I think it might be a good idea for us to have each other's personal telephone numbers, too, don't you?'

'Yes, I do. Fire away then.' They exchanged numbers. 'Right, I'll see you tomorrow. And thanks for your help.'

CHAPTER 6

The following morning Ron came downstairs to find a large buff envelope on the doormat. It had been delivered by hand. He opened it immediately. To his astonishment it contained what looked like council documents, seven in all, relating to tenancy details. He looked for an accompanying letter. There was none. 'How peculiar,' he thought. 'Anonymous, eh!' He took a closer look at the name on the documents, then gasped in astonishment. 'Good grief, it's Muckley.'

He raced back upstairs. 'Patricia,' he called excitedly. 'You'll never believe what someone has put through our letterbox. Look, Council tenancy records.'

Sidling up to him, Patricia slid her arm round his waist and kissed him lightly on the cheek. 'Calm down, dear, and tell me about it.'

'Look. It's all about repairs … installation of a gas fire. I don't really understand it all. But the main point is that it's in the name of Muckley.'

'Let me see,' she said. 'That's odd. This one says "deceased ".'

Ron peered closer at the page. 'So it does. I didn't notice that. But it can't be right. Muckley isn't dead. Well, he didn't look dead when I saw him yesterday.'

Patricia dug him in the ribs. 'Funny! Just a minute, there's a date alongside the word "deceased"...1/4/74...that's three years ago. Look, there.' She pointed to the top of the page. 'Is that OAP?'

'Yes. Then it must be... his... father?'

'Who else?'

'So, who sent them to me... and why? I'm seeing Anne Archer tonight. I'll take these with me and ask her about them. She'll know what they mean.'

Patricia squeezed his arm. 'Good idea, Ron. Now I must get on with breakfasts or the kids will be late for school. And you've got the shop to open.'

After closing the shop Ron paid a hurried visit to the bathroom, quickly changed out of his working clothes and wolfed down a sandwich before preparing to leave for his meeting with Anne Archer.

Fifteen minutes later he turned into the driveway of 169 Prince Avenue, wondering what revelations were about to be opened up to him.

Anne Archer greeted him cheerfully with outstretched hand. 'Hello, Ron. I'm so glad you made it. Do come in.'

He was introduced to Fred, her husband, who poured drinks for them. It was a modest home, immaculately kept. Ron wondered who the elephant-lover was: there were dozens of elephant ornaments everywhere, of varying sizes, mostly black ones, the kind seen in many homes, usually souvenirs brought home by tourist visitors to Africa: very popular in the sixties.

Anne settled into what he guessed was her favourite armchair. 'Now, Ron. Where shall I begin?'

'Let's start with your departure from the department. On the phone you implied that you had left under unusual circumstances.'

Anne sat forward on the edge of her seat. 'That's right. I didn't want to leave. I loved my job. 22 years I'd been there, and I was forced to go by that creature Muckley. In today's jargon I think they call it "constructive dismissal".'

Ron listened to Anne's story, his mind reeling between astonishment and disbelief. Yet he had no reason to doubt her.

Anne continued. 'I tell you this, Ron. I wasn't the first to be forced out by Muckley. There was Jane Saxby, a young trainee housing officer. Do you know about her?'

He shook his head. 'No.'

'It was reported in the *Evening Echo* only last year. Didn't you see it?' It was obvious that he hadn't. 'It must have happened about the time you were elected.' She stood up and went to the sideboard, picked up a newspaper and handed it to him. 'It's all in here.' She poured another drink.

The bold headline said it all.

Examiner quits in row over test questions

A Southend housing chief has quit an official examination board after a complaint by a girl trainee.

Mr William Muckley says he resigned from the Institute of Housing's examination board because he did not see 'eye to eye' with the organisation.

The Institute says: Mr Muckley, who is still one of its members, committed 'an indiscretion'.

Mr Muckley, an assistant housing director at Southend Council, quit after a complaint by trainee Mrs Jane Saxby.

Pep talk

Mrs Saxby, of Benvenue Avenue, Eastwood, alleged that Mr Muckley offered her information about questions in a forthcoming examination.

She complained to the Institute, who interviewed her at their headquarters in London and asked her to keep the matter secret.

She later had to withdraw from the examination, due last May, and cannot now sit another test until later this year.

In a letter to Mrs Saxby, the Institute said 'disciplinary action' had been taken in the matter, but Mr Muckley says no action had been taken against him.

Mrs Saxby, 26, worked as a trainee housing manager for four years and was studying for the diploma in housing management.

Mr Muckley was her training officer.

Mrs Saxby said she was called into Mr Muckley's office for a pre-examination briefing.

'It is normal procedure to be called into your training officer before you are due to take an examination for a pep talk,' she said.

When Mrs Saxby was due to take the second part of the examination, there are three parts, she says that when she went in to see Mr Muckley he suggested she take notes.

'He said we would start with the law paper, which was one of five papers to be taken.'

Mrs Saxby said she was asked if she had studied certain areas, including subjects known as under leasing and distress.

She said: 'These are both unusual areas which could not be predicted and are far removed from the "chestnut" questions that regularly crop up in exam papers.

'While I was in Mr Muckley's office I became suspicious. I knew he had access to the questions because I knew he was a member of the examination board.

'But he was getting far too specific in his briefing.

He was missing out whole chunks of things I had revised already, feeling certain they would come up.'

Routine

Mrs Saxby said: 'I glanced at the paper Mr Muckley was reading from and I was able to read a list of figures and numbers which turned out to be questions. I could see the paper was laid out in exactly the same way as a question paper, although it was not an official question paper. I had decided to do something about this even before I left Mr Muckley's room. I realised that if my suspicions - that he was telling me in advance what my questions would be, were right, I would not be able to sit the May examination.

'Apart from my driving test, I have never failed an examination in my life and I wanted to pass on my own merits. I was furious.'

Mrs Saxby phoned the Institute and was asked to go to their London HQ where she met the secretary, Mr Dennis Crouch. Mr Crouch read the notes Mrs Saxby had taken and then went to check them against the examination questions.

Mrs Saxby said: 'He came back a few minutes later to tell me he regretted that these were the specific subject areas on which the forthcoming questions would be based. He said I would not be able to sit the next examination and I would get a formal letter confirming this.'

Mrs Saxby said the Institute wanted her to keep quiet about what had happened but, she says, she told them this was 'intolerable' and a week later told the Council's housing director, Mr Cyril Purrott.

Mrs Saxby says that after Mr Muckley had been interviewed by the Institute, he told her he 'admired' her integrity.

She added: 'I subsequently received letters from the Institute confirming that I could not take the May exam and telling me my fee could be transferred to the December sitting.

I was also informed that disciplinary action had been taken in the matter.'

Mrs Saxby said that immediately after the incident she 'felt like resigning'. But she left later anyway for a higher paid job at Basildon Development Corporation, where she now works.

Mr Muckley told the Echo 'it was normal practice to talk through an examination syllabus with candidates and 'put them on the right lines of more or less what is expected'.

He said that in Mrs Saxby's case he talked deeply to her 'on all aspects of the syllabus'.

He said, 'I gave her various hints, such as preparing yourself for an examination and being in a relaxed frame of mind. I told her what the examiners would probably be looking for. After each examination, examiners prepare reports on their findings and indicate clearly what they were looking for. I always make a great study of these and I talk at great length on these subjects. I don't honestly feel I gave Mrs Saxby any more information than any other student could have got after discussion with her tutors.'

Mr Muckley said that after Mrs Saxby contacted the Institute he was called to a meeting at their London office and told of her allegations.

He said 'It was indicated to me that perhaps on

reflection that sort of approach might not be the correct thing. I pointed out that it was one of my duties to assist trainees and my duty to my authority came first and in no way would I stop doing it unless instructed by my director. We obviously did not see eye to eye and I offered my resignation for personal reasons.'

Asked why Mrs Saxby was unable to sit the May exam, he said, 'The Institute took the decision, but I can only imagine they were being ultra-cautious.'

Breach

Mr Muckley said he was still a member of the Institute of Housing and still training officer at the Council's housing department.

Mr Crouch, the Institute's secretary, confirmed the Institute's talk with Mrs Saxby and the following interview with Mr Muckley.

He said, 'This is entirely a domestic matter. I think someone is guilty of a breach of faith.'

He said there was 'no total evidence' to support Mrs Saxby's allegations.

Asked why, then, Mr Muckley had left the Institute's examination board, he said, 'Perhaps it was an indiscretion, no more than that. In the eyes of our Council it was no more than an indiscretion, which anyone might have committed.'

Ron took a sharp intake of breath. 'Anne, that is astonishing. Unbelievable.'

She grinned. 'I hoped you might think so. But that's only a part of it.'

He looked again at the report. 'What date is this? October 26, 1978... last year! I didn't see this! I've heard nothing from anyone on the Council.'

'That doesn't surprise me in the least,' Anne replied. 'They all keep very quiet about Mr Muckley's antics.'

He was perplexed. 'But why? Don't they know he's been behaving in this way?'

'They must do,' said Anne. 'Or at least most of them must know. But none of them seem prepared to do anything about it. I can tell you, Ron, it's something that has frustrated me, and others, for years.'

Her remarks jogged his memory. 'That reminds me.' He opened his briefcase. 'I received these papers through my letterbox this morning. I think I know what they are, but I would like you to look at them and tell me what they mean.'

Anne took the papers and gave them a cursory glance. 'Oh, yes. I've seen those before. I know exactly what they mean and it makes my blood boil, I can tell you. She examined them more closely. You do realise that these are photocopies, Ron.'

Ron knelt down beside Anne's chair to look over her shoulder. 'I didn't, but I'll take your word for that'.

She selected one of the pages. 'Look, this one shows that William Muckley senior was first registered for rehousing on the 13 April 1967. At the time he lived at 93 Marlborough Road. That's a very nice semi in Thorpe Bay. They had lived there for years.'

Ron interrupted her. 'This is Muckley's father, I presume?'

'Yes. We always thought it rather ironic that Muckley should be in a position to arrange for his own father to be re-housed, and even more so that they should both have the same Christian name. Anyway, his father owned the house in Marlborough Road, so he was an owner-occupier. Now, we know that Council policy says owner-occupiers will not be considered for housing. Yet here you can see by this entry he was re-housed on the 26 June 1967 into one of the new flats at Southchurch Rectory Chase, number 28. Wasn't he lucky!' Anne placed the top page underneath the rest, which she spread out. 'These three pages are copies of the tenancy record card. Look, they show all the improvements, redecorating, fittings and so on that were carried out up to April 1974. That included a new gas fire, new light fittings, draining board, and so on. Just look at all these entries! We always said that Muckley senior had more done to his home than any other tenants could possibly have done.'

Anne turned to another page. 'Ah, now, this one is marked "Deceased 1April 1974". That's when he died. I remember that.'

Ron took the papers from her and looked again at the last page. 'Patricia and I wondered about that one this morning. This is quite serious really. But I wonder who sent them to me... and why?'

She smiled mischievously. 'I should think that's obvious. You've been acquiring a bit of a reputation for stirring things up in the Council. I expect someone thought you might do something about Muckley and his goings-on.'

'Hm, sounds plausible,' he said. But judging by the look on her face he thought it was just possible she knew who that someone was. It occurred to him, also, that there was a faint possibility that *she* might have sent them. But he decided not to pursue it.

Anne interrupted his thoughts. 'And are you going to do something, Ron... about Muckley's antics?'

Ron looked at the papers again, shuffled them. 'Well, I'm certainly very concerned with what I've heard. But I think I'd like to know the complete story before I decide what to do. And I have a suspicion, Anne, that you are quite eager to tell me.'

Her face spread into a wide grin. 'You can bet on it, Ron. You can bet on it.'

He returned to his seat, prepared to take notes.

'I suppose I should start at the beginning, but as we're

talking about people being housed who shouldn't be, let me tell you about two cases that happened recently. One of them lived just round the corner from you, in Richmond Avenue. Mr and Mrs Kenney, a young couple. They were buying their own house, coincidentally, with a Council mortgage. They got into arrears and applied to go onto the housing waiting list. Normally they would have been refused, for reasons that, being owner-occupiers, like Muckley senior, they weren't eligible but, for reasons that escape everyone else, Muckley took up the case and placed them on the list.'

Ron looked for flaws in her argument. 'Surely though, Anne, might not some people say that makes sense? If the Kenneys were in arrears, wouldn't they eventually be evicted? Then, as homeless people, wouldn't the Council have an obligation to rehouse them?'

'No not really. The system doesn't work that way. It fails to take into account the reasons for the arrears. The Kenneys might have been wasters, or bad money managers. Thousands of people get into arrears. If the Council had to register all of them, the list would be enormous. It would also open up the system to abuse; people could deliberately go into arrears in order to obtain Council housing.

'Don't misunderstand me, Ron. And you probably know that the Council has an obligation under the Homeless Persons Act to house people who are made homeless through no fault of their own. But the Council has very limited housing stock and if they have to register anyone who make themselves homeless, like the Kenneys... it wouldn't be possible to house those in genuine need. That is why it was necessary for the Council to adopt the policy of not registering owner-occupiers. And it must be wrong for any officer to act in breach of Council policy.'

Whichever way he looked at it he could not fault Anne's

argument or the principle on which it was based. 'Ok, Anne. I can accept that, but are there any exceptions to that rule?'

Anne fielded the question expertly. 'Yes, there are. The policy can be overridden on grounds of health or infirmity, or severe social distress.'

'That's interesting. They sound like the very grounds on which Mary Bates and her children could be re-housed. And yet Muckley refused to help her.'

'Purrott didn't tell us much about the background when he phoned us. I understand there were allegations of child abuse.'

'Really! I am *convinced* there was abuse,,, sexual abuse against the children. But you said that you could tell me about two cases. What is the other one?'

'Ah, that one was quite different,' replied Anne. 'It concerned a Mr and Mrs Welling whose marriage was dissolved. They lived in a Council house in Bunters Avenue, also in Shoeburyness, by the way. Mrs Welling departed the matrimonial home leaving behind Mr Welling and their children at Bunters Avenue. Mrs Welling went into private accommodation and subsequently relinquished her share in the tenancy of Bunters Avenue. Some months later, it can't have been more than three or four, she applied to be registered on the housing waiting list as a single person. She was registered on 31 May 1978 and was allocated a one bedroom flat in Cunningham Close, which she moved in to on the 19 June, a short period of just three weeks. Considering that the normal waiting time for this category is between three and five years, it could be said that she was extremely lucky.'

Ron interrupted. 'You certainly seem to have a remarkable memory for detail; but you said that this case also breached Standing Orders. How does it do that?'

'Well, this was a matrimonial case and in such situations

no one is allowed to be registered before the Decree Nisi is awarded. But this was wrong for another reason; it created two tenancies for one family. Remember Mr Welling continued to live at Bunters Avenue. There was something else rather odd about this case. The chairman was asked to authorise the allocation, which he did, probably without reading it. He would sign anything that Muckley put in front of him. I know he hasn't been chairman for very long but you must have formed an opinion about him: not quite the most intelligent member of the Council, would you say?'

'Absolutely, Anne. I often wonder how he became Chairman, but then he has been a councillor for many years. A former mayor. I assumed that he was given the chairmanship because it was Buggin's turn.'

Anne nodded vigorously. 'But do you see Muckley's cunning? He knew there could be no justification within existing policy for re-housing Mrs Welling, so he shifted responsibility to the chairman. That way he would be in the clear if it was ever questioned.'

'This is all very disturbing; but why does Muckley do these things and, more importantly, how on earth does he get away with it?'

She had pondered these and other such questions countless times. Her reply was laden with years of frustration. 'The answer to both questions must be the same, Ron. We don't know... we just don't know.'

Ron's astonishment compelled him to probe further. 'But surely, Anne, other members of staff must have been aware of what was going on. Didn't any of them complain?'

'That's a very good question. To understand the answer you need to appreciate the psychology of working in local government. You see, in order to make advances in your career there are two golden rules: pass as many exams as possible, and keep your eyes and mouth firmly closed. The department is littered with the dead careers of those who dared to speak out. You could say that mine is one of them, as you heard earlier. I could give you a list of many others, but I won't bore you.'

Ron scribbled away furiously, trying to keep up with her. 'One thing puzzles me in all this. Where does Mr Purrott fit in, didn't he know what was going on?':

'Ah, to understand that you have to understand Cyril Purrott.'

With a heavy sigh, she sank deeper into her chair. 'He was always a peace loving man: didn't like confrontation. If he knew about Muckley, and he certainly knows a lot more now than he did before my departure, he kept quiet about it. But, in fairness to him, Muckley made sure Purrott knew as little as possible. There was a saying in the department that "Nothing gets beyond Muckley's door that he doesn't want Purrott to see". Muckley used to vet all mail addressed to Purrott and decide which would be passed on. If a letter contained anything that Muckley wanted dealt with in his own way, he would reply to that letter and sign it by copying Purrott's signature exactly. So the writer of the letter thought that the reply actually came from Purrott.'

Shocked, Ron said: 'Just a moment, Anne. I write to Purrott from time to time on all kinds of matters. Are you saying it's possible that he doesn't always see my letters - or, worse, that any reply may not be actually signed by him, that the signature could be forged?'

Anne nodded: 'In a word, yes. Not only is it possible, but it's most likely. It depends on the subject matter.'

'But that's outrageous. Some of my constituency cases are very personal. They need to be dealt with by the Director. This is very serious: but how could I know which were signed by Purrott and those which were not?'

Anne leaned forward in her chair, eyeing him intently.

'You wouldn't, Ron. But I would. Muckley had a certain way of writing that was peculiar to him alone. He didn't have a very good education and it reflects in his composition.'

'You really would know whether it was Muckley or Purrott who signed a letter?'

She detected a challenge in his tone. 'I certainly would,' she replied with unwavering confidence.

Ron reached into his case. 'Well, I happen to have with me two files. One of them is about a Mr and Mrs Watson. Here it is. They wanted a transfer away from the Woolpack estate. I had a letter from Mr Purrott quite recently. I wasn't very happy with his decision, but I think I just accepted it. It gave me something positive to show the Watsons that I had done what I could for them.' He opened the file. 'Here's Purrott's letter, on top.' He passed the open file to her. 'Here, Anne, see what you make of this.'

Taking the file, she eagerly scanned the letter, then chuckled. 'Oh, yes. This is one of Muckley's creations. Without a shadow of doubt.' She passed the file back to him.

'You're absolutely certain, Anne?'

'Absolutely, and if you showed it to Purrott I'm positive he would agree, if he were honest, and I know that he is an honest man.'

'I may do just that,' he said sharply. 'Its astonishing.' looking at Purrott's letter again, he said angrily, 'I feel deceived, and I don't think I can let it rest at that. But tell me, Anne. How long has Muckley been with the department?'

She warmed to the question. The subject had affected her life immensely and she was anxious to tell all that she knew about it. 'Muckley's time with the Council goes back beyond his start in the housing department. He actually began by working in the Town Clerk's department in 1961 or 62. He even got *that* job by telling lies. You see, in those days no one could get a job with the Council if he or she had a criminal record, and Muckley *had* a criminal record. He was convicted of theft from a building site in Southend in 1954. It was reported in what was then the *Southend Times*... and I have a copy of that, which you may have.' Feeling stiff from sitting for so long, Anne eased herself out of her armchair, went to the sideboard and took a sheet of paper from one of the drawers.

'That is quite serious,' said Ron. 'But it was rather a long time ago.'

She handed him the paper. 'I agree with you, Ron. But he wasn't a youngster at the time. He was in his late twenties. But what was really funny about it was the excuse he gave at the time. He was caught red-handed, with his younger brother, by two police officers in Belle View Road, Southend. They had a roll of chain-link fencing which they had stolen from a building site in Ambleside Drive. Look, it's quite a short article... see the last paragraph: "Asked what they were doing, William Muckley replied: "Ah! Just the men we want to see; we found this and we were just going to phone you".'

Taking the paper, Ron laughed, Anne and Fred joining in.

'But seriously,' said Anne, 'you will see that in court they admitted the theft. Take it away with you and read it later.' She paused, pensive. 'Ron, there are so many things that I could tell you. It would take absolutely ages.'

He looked at his watch. 'Anne, I would very much like to hear them. But its past eleven o'clock and I think I'd like to call it a day. We must get together again.' He stood up. 'You've certainly given me plenty to think about. I have a feeling I'm going to be kept busy with this matter for a long time.' He kissed her lightly on the cheek, as he would his mother, and wished Fred good night. 'I feel as though I've known you for such a long time, Anne. I'm so sorry for all the distress that you've suffered. It must have been dreadful. And I'm really pleased that you have discussed this with me. You can be sure I won't let this rest until I have some satisfactory answers.'

After seeing him out, Anne returned to Fred. 'Well, dear. What do you make of him?'

Fred was a quiet man who rarely expressed a strong opinion on anything, except, perhaps, golf. 'I'm impressed,' he said quietly. 'He seems to have more common sense than that lot at the Civic Centre put together. I think he was genuinely interested and I reckon he will do something about it. But I suspect he's going to get himself into a lot of trouble.'

'I do hope he doesn't,' replied Anne. 'But I do agree with you.'

What once seemed a lost cause was brought back to life: hope renewed. There was a glow of optimism within her and she felt good. 'Perhaps this time something really is going to be done about Muckley.'

CHAPTER 7

August 1978.

Ron finally managed to persuade councillors Eddie Pollit and Arthur Daniels to see him. He was determined to justify his actions regarding the way the Institute of Housing had evaded the question of disciplining Muckley. Ron took with him the press cutting from the Southend County Standard.

It quickly became obvious to Ron that both chairmen were irritated. Surely the matter had been resolved. What was the point in going over old ground? Muckley had been cleared and had in fact resigned from the Examination Board over conflicting loyalties; the young Jane Saxby had left and was now furthering her career with another Local Authority; and surely that precluded more delving that was an embarrassment to their authority: end of story.

Ron realised he was not going to get anywhere with these two old codgers, and so he resolved not to bother with them again. He arranged another meeting for several days later, this time with Cyril Purrott. At that meeting Purrott seemed to show some concern that Muckley had forged his signature, assuring Ron that the practise would be stopped.

A few weeks later Ron received a letter from Arthur Daniels: An unconvincing response regarding the complaints against Muckley. Another cover-up. In reply Ron insisted that this wasn't good enough, he wasn't going to have the wool pulled over his eyes. It was necessary for

Muckley to be dismissed, thereby restoring confidence within the housing department.

Following that, Ron met the Town Clerk. In an uneasy atmosphere where Fred Laws had reiterated the committee's previous disquiet over allegations that had been examined and thrashed out, he said: 'Mr Levy, you have not given me any information of which I was not already aware. I've heard of these complaints some months ago, and I've discussed them with the Director of Housing. He told me that he had dealt with the matter administratively and agreed that there was no evidence to support disciplinary proceedings against any officer in the department. I must tell you, Councillor, that is still my opinion and I do not see that there is any other action that I should now take.'

This was not what Ron expected. But he sensed that Laws was resolute. There was no point continuing the interview. Gathering his papers, he stood up and politely thanked Fred Laws for his time. Disillusioned, he left the room; but it was early days.

Several months passed whilst Ron assembled details of other complaints against Muckley and the housing department. He then wrote to Fred laws describing the Welling and the Kenney cases, explaining how they breached Council policy and demanding that the matters be dealt with in accordance with Standing Orders.

Nothing was heard from Fred Laws, but two weeks later Ron received a letter from Cyril Purrott explaining that Mr Muckley had reported these two cases to the Chairman, who had approved their registration. Ron was not surprised. After all, Daniels would sign anything that was put in front of him. It probably made him feel important. In any case, committee chairmen do not have the authority to make such decisions: they should be dealt with by the committee.

Correspondence between Ron and Fred Laws continued: Fred repeatedly claiming that he had not been made aware of any breaches of Council policy; Ron insisting that there had been such breaches and that the complaints against Muckley should be dealt with according to the procedure laid down in Standing Orders. Despite his refusal to take such action, Fred did report the complaints to Norman Harris.

Several more weeks slipped by, Ron heard nothing. Weeks turned to months; a year; 2 years. What more could he do? He couldn't let it all pass: couldn't let Muckley get away with it. Yet, he felt helpless. Incredibly, complaints about Muckley's behaviour continued to be voiced over those two and a half years and still nothing had been done to reprimand him. Yet more complaints were discussed frequently among the Councillors, but none had been persuasive enough to galvanise the Town Clerk into action. Muckley seemed immune from them and the apathy finally culminated in Ron exploding into action. There would be no avoiding the issue, no more frustration. It was time to get it sorted out once and for all, come what may.

He retrieved the file and wrote to Fred Laws telling him that this time he was determined to have the complaints against Muckley dealt with properly and brought to a satisfactory conclusion. 'It's no good you saying "I am not aware of any breaches of the regulations",' said Ron in his letter. 'I am making you aware of those breaches in the detail of my allegations against Muckley. It is your duty to report my complaints to the Policy and Resources Committee, and it is my right to have the matters so dealt with.' He went even further: 'You said in your last letter that the Kenney and Welling cases had been authorised by the

Housing Chairman, Councillor Daniels. I have searched the Council minutes of the time and there is no record of such action having been taken by the chairman. As you will know, Mr Laws, all Chairmen are required to report decisions taken between committee meetings to the next meeting of their respective committees under Chairman's Action. This failure by the chairman is a breach of Standing Orders, and I request that you include this matter when reporting to the Policy Committee.' Ron concluded his letter with a very clear indication of his intentions: 'I tell you this, Mr Laws. If my request is refused I shall have the matter dealt with by a higher authority.' For some reason he felt compelled to send the letter by recorded delivery. Perhaps the matter was so serious that it needed official recognition of its delivery. Perhaps he didn't trust Fred Laws.

'Sending your letter to me by recorded delivery was, if I may say so, an extraordinary thing to do and I can only assume that you had a reason,' replied Fred. 'I do not know what that reason was but in certain circumstances letters are sent in this fashion for aggressive reasons and you have no cause to be aggressive with me nor, if I may say so, to tell me what my duties are.'

His letter continued, insisting that he had not been given any fresh matter of substance to investigate; that he had investigated the cases and found no cause for complaint; that so far as he was concerned there was still no prima facie case of misconduct by either an officer of the Council or a councillor which required him to report to the Policy and Resources Committee. Ron could not believe what he was reading. Hadn't he *made* Fred aware of misconduct, of grounds for an investigation? How could he possibly ignore the facts?

Ron was resolute; his retort firm. He wrote clearly describing how the Welling and the Kenney cases went against Council policy, and quoting verbatim the Standing Order that Daniels had breached in failing to report his action to the committee, and demanded that the appropriate action be taken.

Fred Laws' reply was equally resolute:

'So far as I am concerned, I cannot say it more clearly and so I repeat, your complaint, in my opinion, is without foundation. Mr Purrott and Councillor Daniels have acted quite properly and in accordance with the Council's Standing Orders and policy decisions. If you wish to take your complaint to some other authority you must do that but I am not, in the circumstances, prepared to take any action on what you have said to me so far.'

'Well, that's pretty final,' thought Ron. 'I'm not going to get anywhere along that route. The next step must be to inform Norman Harris, as Council Leader he must do something. He can't possibly allow this to continue unresolved.'

How mistaken Ron was! Harris's reply was no different from Fred's:

'I have now had an opportunity to investigate the complaints made by you. I wish to stress that this has been a detailed investigation of all the facts. I can find no evidence whatsoever to substantiate the complaints. The actions of both the Chief Officer and the Chairman are clearly quite proper and fully in accordance with the Council's Standing Orders and policy decisions.'

This was completely unexpected and was a great disappointment to Ron. But there was a glimmer of hope. Norman Harris wrote to Arthur Daniels informing him of his finding but advising him that he intended reporting the matter to the next Policy and Resources Committee, but briefly and without detail.

'I know you would rather that I did not do this,' he wrote,

'but I am bound to do so and it is, in any event, the only sure way to resolve the issue as far as the Council is concerned.'

A date was arranged for the meeting, 15 February 1982. Fred Laws had been instructed to prepare a report to the committee outlining Ron's complaints. But Ron wanted to be sure that the members of the committee were made fully aware of his concerns. And so he wrote to each member setting out in detail the history of the issues since his first encounter with Muckley's misdeeds, accusing him of corruption, maladministration and abuse of authority. Whilst describing the Welling and the Kenney cases Ron focused especially on how Muckley had arranged for his own parents to be re-housed; how he had engineered the departure of a number of excellent staff; that, in a report to the Housing Committee, he had presented figures of homelessness that differed widely from figures presented to the Department of the Environment. He described the matter of the forged Director's signatures. Muckley's departure from the Institute of Housing Examination Board and the dramatic effect the incident had had on Jane Saxby, and how, in his view, 'Muckley is unfit to hold office in this or any other local authority'.

The committee assembled on the due date. Fred Laws reported, ad nauseam, that he had investigated the Welling and the Kenney cases and in his view there was no evidence to substantiate the complaints. As a result of the further allegations that had been made by Ron in his letter to the members, the committee agreed that, subject to there being no independent legal proceedings, the Town Clerk was to investigate all the allegations in accordance with the procedure laid down in Standing Orders, and that he was to report to a Subcommittee comprising Councillors Norman Harris, Norman Clarke, George Elvin (Labour) and Philip Herbert (Liberal), prior to further consideration of the matter by the Policy and Resources Committee.

'Sounds suspicious to me,' thought Ron. 'Could be a delaying tactic, It could all come to nothing.' Understandably, he didn't trust them.

Six weeks passed and Ron heard nothing. He wrote to all the committee members again, this time expressing his fears that the matter was being suppressed. There had been no legal action from Muckley: no request for evidence of the further allegations that Ron had made. He took his time putting the letter together:

'Whilst I appreciate the appointment of a Subcommittee to receive an investigative report from the Town Clerk, I fear that the Sub-Committee could be prevented from meeting to discuss the matter by use of the sub-judice device. Therefore, either legal proceedings against me should commence immediately, or the Subcommittee should meet in the very near future to hear all the evidence, and Muckley should be suspended, perhaps on full pay, pending the outcome of the inquiry.'

Two weeks later Ron received a brief letter from Fred Laws informing him that Councillor Harris had asked him to call together the Special Subcommittee appointed to investigate his complaints. A meeting had been arranged for 3 pm on Wednesday, 28 April 1982 in the Civic Suite and Ron was invited to be present. His pulse raced. At last his complaints were to be officially recognised and dealt with. But there was a nagging doubt in his mind; this was not quite the way it should be done; not exactly in the order of things as laid down in the book. Still, at least he had got an inquiry. After a total four years of trying he was thankful for that.

The large committee room was crowded and buzzed with excitement. At the centre of one side of the huge table sat

Norman Harris: To his right, Norman Clarke, alongside him Councillors George Elvin Philip Herbert. To Harris's left sat Fred Laws, bundles of files in front of him. Next to him, Brian Fisher, Fred's assistant, designated to make notes of the meeting. The public gallery facing them consisted of four rows of seats running the length of the room. All seats were occupied. Only two councillors: Joan Carlile, 'Dear Joan', thought Ron, and Alan Crystal. The remaining seats were occupied by members of the public. In the centre front row sat Anne Archer; calm: expressionless. Positioned at the far end of the table sat Purrott and Muckley, both looking sombre. Next to Muckley was the NALGO representative, Andy Wallace. In the far corner of the room, alongside the public gallery, at a table permanently provided for the press, sat the veteran local reporter Del Flattley.

Ron made straight for Anne Archer. 'It's good to see a friendly face, Anne,' he whispered. They exchanged a few words of mutual support. He turned to face Norman Harris, needing to know where he was to sit. With his right hand Harris directed Ron towards the opposite end of the table to Muckley and Purrott. Harris smiled sardonically, 'Have you brought your solicitor?' he asked.

Ron was puzzled. The remark was unexpected, but it revealed Harris's attitude, it was unmistakably hostile. 'I didn't think I would need one,' he replied nervously.

'You will, boy, you will,' he retorted, relishing the smartness of his reply.

Ron glanced at Anne, shrugged, and made his way to the seat as indicated. He suddenly felt alone. The enormity of the task that he faced now bore down on him. But he was committed. Taking a deep breath, he placed his case on the table, removed his papers and set them out in front of him. He was ready.

Norman Harris tapped the table with the end of his pen,

as he always did, to call the meeting to attention. The room fell silent. Briefly announcing the purpose and format of the hearing, he turned to Fred Laws. 'Town Clerk, we have a copy of your report in front of us. Will you present it and explain its contents.'

'Yes, Chairman. But I would like you to read it in conjunction with the statement by Southend Branch of NALGO.'

Ron was alarmed. There hadn't been any mention of a NALGO report or statement. He should have seen it before the meeting. He felt vulnerable, fearing what was to come.
councillors, he told the meeting: 'The complaint, in short, is that Councillor Levy alleges that he has:

"evidence and information which clearly reveals a long history of corruption, maladministration and abuse of authority. This situation was instigated and is sustained by the assistant Director of Housing, William Muckley..."

'Councillor Levy considers:

"William Muckley to be unfit to hold office in this or any other authority".'

Fred put the letter down. 'I have been able to identify eight specific allegations or incidents used in support of the complaint as laid by the Councillor.' Now reading from his own report Fred gave persuasive answers to the complaints. When it came to the housing of Muckley's parents Ron was asked what evidence he had to support such allegations. It was the moment he had waited for. Out came the documents that he had nurtured for so long, the tenancy records. Sheet by sheet he explained their contents, laying each one down like a playing card, as a gambler does who knows he has a winning hand at cards, watching for the effect his move would have on his opponents. Their reaction was swift and startling. Even before he had laid down the final document there was uproar. Fred Laws jumped to his feet. Red faced, he exploded with rage. 'Where did you get those documents?' he demanded. 'I've spent months searching the department for that file. You have no right to be in possession of it. How did you come by it?'

Ron was stunned. 'The man's gone berserk,' he thought. 'The papers must be more important than I imagined.'

His thoughts were interrupted by Norman Harris. 'Let me see those papers, Councillor.' Ron passed them down the table. There was complete silence as Harris took the papers and turned towards Fred Laws. They both scanned them hurriedly, their whispers faintly audible in the hushed room.

Harris turned to Ron. 'This is very serious, Councillor. These are confidential files. How did you come by them?'

'I cannot be certain, so I'm not prepared to say. They came to me in the post.'

Harris persisted. 'Who sent them to you? You must know that.'

'Why must I?' snapped Ron. 'They were sent anonymously, so I can't say.'

Fred Laws continued protesting at what had happened, the loose flesh under his chin shaking with indignation.

'There must be more to this than I imagined,' thought Ron. 'This is a smoke screen. No one seems interested in the contents of the papers: That's what they should be looking at.'

Clarke, Elvin and Herbert pompously agreed that Ron should not have the documents, insisting that he should divulge how he got them.

Harris expertly steered the meeting back on course. 'Town Clerk, will you give the answer to the Councillor's allegations?'

Fred cleared his throat. Having regained his composure, he referred again to his report. 'Yes, Chairman. As you can see, at the time Mr and Mrs Muckley senior were housed there was a different system of allocation; applicants were given numbers which were put before the Housing Committee, without revealing their names. The committee then decided on the allocation on the order of priorities placed before it. Under that system Mr Muckley would not have been able to influence the housing of his parents.'

Ron's morale plummeted. Frantically searching for an appropriate response, he glanced at Anne. Her eyes flashed, she knew the answer. She wanted to tell him, but protocol precluded her from doing so. He felt helpless. If only he had seen a copy of that report before the meeting, he would have been so much better prepared. But that, probably, had been intentional. 'This would never be allowed in a court of law,' he thought. 'All this evidence would have been disclosed before a hearing. Fred, being a lawyer, would know that. It was a very clever move on his part.'

Harris's voice broke the silence. 'Councillor, you heard the Town Clerk. What have you to say?'

Ron tried to speak. No sound came. Before he could gather his thoughts, Harris continued: 'In view of what we have just heard I think you should withdraw the allegation. Are you prepared to do that, Councillor? In the circumstances I don't think you have any option.'

Ron didn't want to withdraw his allegations. But this explanation was convincing. He didn't want to appear unfair. Doubts crept in. Perhaps he had got this part wrong after all. The room was quietly expectant. All eyes trained on him. Involuntarily and barely audible, he answered 'Yes.'

Whispers rippled round the room. Anne Archer looked at him, slowly shaking her head. Muckley and Wallace exchanged expressions of satisfaction.

'Thank you, Councillor,' said Harris. But there was cynicism in his voice, not gratitude. 'Now can we turn to the allegation that Mr Muckley's departure from the Examination Board of the Institute of Housing was, in Mr Levy's own words, "a disciplinary measure for revealing the contents of an examination paper to a female member of staff who was a candidate for the forthcoming examination". Mr Laws, will you take us through this one?'

'Yes, Chairman. I telephoned the Secretary of the Institute, Mr Dennis Crouch. I explained to him the substance of Councillor Levy's allegation. He told me that there had been no disciplinary action taken against Mr Muckley. He also said that Mr Muckley had resigned from the Examination Board for personal reasons.' Fred extracted a document from the files in front of him, turning several pages. He continued: 'Members have a copy of Andy Wallace's statement on behalf of Mr Muckley. On page four you will see both the Institute's and Mr Muckley's replies to that allegation. I quote the Institute:

"It was impossible for Mr Muckley to have revealed the actual questions because he was not privy to the details of the papers until after the examination was held. The practice of the Institute is for the Board to appoint its examiners to decide on the format of their respective papers. These papers are then passed by the Institute's Secretary, an individual of unquestionable integrity, to printers and are kept in sealed packets until they are opened in the examination rooms throughout the country.

'The Institute was satisfied that there was no possibility of Mr Muckley having revealed the actual nature of the questions but was concerned about his role with them in the light of his work as a training officer. He resigned from the Board of the Institute because of that concern. He has letters from the Board and from his local branch expressing their regret that he found it necessary to resign and confirming their confidence in him.

With an air of smug confidence, Fred almost threw the document on the table. 'That, Chairman, I would suggest, positively disposes of Councillor Levy's ridiculous allegation.'

Norman Harris also looked pleased with what he had heard. 'I agree with you, Mr Laws.' Murmurs of approval emanated from the other members of the committee. Harris turned to Ron. 'Well, Councillor, that sounded pretty conclusive. Are you prepared to withdraw that allegation as well?'

'Certainly not.' Excitement rose in him. He knew that this time he really did have a trump card. Now the tide was turning. He picked up Jane Saxby's letter. 'I find the Institute's comments very curious. I have a letter here addressed to Mrs Jane Saxby from Mr Dennis Crouch. He says, and I quote:

"I am to inform you that prompt action has been taken by the Institute to ensure that there can be no recurrence of the situation you have reported, and appropriate disciplinary measures have been imposed".'

The room erupted with a babble of loud voices and laughter.

Harris conferred anxiously with Fred Laws before calling for silence. 'Mr Levy, may I see that letter? This is very serious.'

Ron handed the letter across the table. Harris and Laws read it and passed it to the other members, giving them time to read it before continuing. 'Mr Laws, if this is true are there grounds for taking disciplinary action?' asked Norman Clarke.

Before Fred could reply Philip Herbert said. 'I think it would be unwise to deal with this item until we have had discussions or information from the Institute.'

'I agree entirely,' said Norman Clarke. 'The Institute of Housing does not come out of this very well, and professional standards are less than I would like to see. There is clearly a conflict of evidence, we need more evidence from Mr Crouch and Mrs Saxby.'

Herbert was not going to be denied the last word. 'That's how I see it. We're not really in possession of enough information to make a decision.'

Ron began to sense victory. Harris looked uncomfortable. 'Gentlemen, I propose to instruct the Town Clerk to write to the Institute for clarification of the conflicting evidence. Despite that fact I think there is insufficient evidence and the complaint cannot be substantiated.'

Clarke, Herbert and Elvin grunted their agreement.

There was a discernible murmuring of disapproval from the public.

Ron was getting a clear message: it didn't matter what evidence he presented to this inquiry, they were not going to find against Muckley. There seemed little point continuing. He was not going to achieve his objective.

The rest of the meeting didn't seem to matter. It ended with a resolution that cleared Muckley, something to the effect that the Subcommittee found no evidence to substantiate the complaints and allegations made against him. Fred had done a good job. Ron had no idea what was in his report, or Andy Wallis's statement. Harris and the other councillors had been persuaded that Muckley was innocent. Whether anything worthwhile would come out of the Institute matter remained to be seen. Ron had his doubts.

He left the meeting demoralised. Had all his sacrifices and persistence really been to no avail?

Joan Carlile and Alan Crystal were outside the room. 'Oh Ron. I'm so sorry for you,' said Joan. 'It's monstrous what happened in there. Muckley's as guilty as hell, and they know it. Well, I can tell you, Ron, you have my full support in all this.'

'Mine too,' added Alan enthusiastically. 'We may be poles apart politically, but I agree with what you have tried to achieve. I think it was very brave of you to go this far on your own. I don't know what the next move is, but after this I'll do what I can to help.' He reached out to shake hands. 'In the circumstances, Ron, I think you did a good job. I'm only sorry it went the way it did... well done.'

'Thank you both. Your support means a lot to me,' Ron replied. 'And I know there are others who share your views.' He kissed Joan lightly on the cheek and hugged her. 'I must go home now. I've got some thinking to do.'

'Well, whatever you do after this, Ron, God will give you strength I'm sure.' said Joan with genuine conviction.

Anne was waiting patiently for him at the end of the corridor. 'I see you've got some worthy supporters. It doesn't surprise me at all. I'll walk with you to the car park,' she said. 'What a charade! That was no inquiry that was a clearing-up operation. You've no idea the self-control it took to keep silent when they gave that nonsense about Muckley's parents. When they said Muckley took no part in recommending applicants, that wasn't strictly true. In those days a list of applicants' registration numbers was put to the committee for approval. There were no names, just numbers. And Muckley was certainly in a position to put his parents' number on that list, nobody would have known who it was. The moment you were forced to withdraw the complaint I could have wept for you. It was so unjust.'

Ron stopped walking. He turned to face her. 'Thank you, Anne.' He hugged her. 'If only I had seen those reports before the meeting. It would have been so different.'

'Of course it would,' she replied. 'Why do you think Fred Laws never gave you copies? He's not daft. He knew exactly what he was doing. There was no justice at that meeting.'

'That's how I feel,' he said wearily. 'Thank you for your support, Anne. I'd like to talk it over with you some time. Right now I want to get home to Patricia.'

I can understand that, Ron. You get off home and ring me when you feel up to it. Goodbye, and take it easy.'

As expected, Patricia was comforting and sympathetic. She threw her arms around him and held him tightly. 'Oh Ron. I am sorry: After all your hard work and dedication. How could they?' She drew back from him. 'I just can't believe it,' she said. 'How could they dismiss so much against Muckley? Surely they must have realised there was something wrong, that you weren't making it all up. It's almost as though Fred Laws is protecting him. There's something wrong about all this... something sinister. I have a deep instinct about it. You mark my words. There's more to this than meets the eye.'... She paused, gently brushing her cheek against his. 'I know it's a little early, but let me get you a drink, you look as though you need one.'

'You could be right... about there being something more to all this. But I can't think what that could be. What happened at that meeting was shameful. It has made me very angry. I feel as though I ought to do something immediate to register my feelings.'

'Here, try this. It might help you to think.'

'Thank you, dear.' The golden liquid sparkled invitingly; she knew how to pour his scotch. He took a generous sip. 'Mmm. That feels good.'

Patricia took his arm. 'Let's go into the kitchen. We should get a few minutes' peace there. The children are upstairs watching the television.'

They sat at the table. He held her hand. 'I know I've already decided not to stand for re-election this year. And you know the branch committee fully understood my reasons. But I've never put those reasons in writing.

Perhaps this is the right moment to do just that.'

She squeezed his hand gently. 'Sounds like a good idea. But who would you write to?'

'I'd have to think about that.' He scratched his chin through his beard, as he so often did when thinking. Inspiration suddenly hit him. 'I've got it! Why don't I actually resign from the Council. I know it would be academic because the new candidate has already been chosen. But it would enable me to say why I want no more to do with the Council.'

'Sounds good to me,' said Patricia. 'You can get it off your chest and let them know what you think of what they have done.'

'Brilliant. I'll do it now.' He jumped up and went to his study.

Fifteen minutes or so later he returned. 'I've done it... short and sweet. Tell me what you think. He handed her the letter. She took it eagerly and read:

You will have been aware for some time now of my intention to resign my seat as the elected member for Shoeburyness, for the principal reason that I am dissatisfied with the way in which my complaints against the Housing Department have been dealt with.

Since the Policy and Resources Sub-Committee meeting today to consider my complaints I am even more dissatisfied and it is my intention to take further action in the matter.

Consequently, I hereby resign my seat as the elected member for the Shoeburyness Ward Constituency of Southend District Council to take effect from this day 28 April 1982.

Patricia handed the letter back to him. 'Well, Ron. In the circumstances I think it's very restrained. You could have been a lot more forceful. But it's good. I see you're sending copies to Harris, Elvin and Herbert. That's wise. You can be sure they'll know that you have done it.'

He smiled. She also didn't trust Laws.

'You go and post that, and don't forget the copies. I'll get the children's tea. They must be ready for it now.'

Eight days later: Thursday 6 May, Polling day. Ron now had no stomach for elections. It felt strange not to be involved, but he was pleased to be out of it.

The telephone rang. The caller introduced himself: 'DC Kevin Macey, Southend police. May I speak to Mr Ron Levy?'

Ron was puzzled. 'Speaking.'

'We've received a complaint from Mr Fred Laws, the Town Clerk, about your allegations against a Mr Muckley. I need you to help me with my inquiries. Would you mind calling in to the station sometime today?'

Ron quickly overcame his surprise: 'Err... yes. I think so. I mean, no, I don't mind... let me have a look at my appointment book. Yes, I can. Does it matter what time? Yes, two o'clock is fine, Mr Macey. I'll see you then.'

He hurried out to the kitchen. 'Patricia, I've just had a call from Southend police,' he said excitedly. 'They want me to go and speak to them about the inquiry last week: They want to know more about my complaints against Muckley.'

'Good heavens!' she replied. 'It can't be that important, surely. Perhaps they take it more seriously than the committee did. When are you going?'

'This afternoon... 2 o'clock. I've no bookings until 4 o'clock, I should be back by then. This is marvellous. Perhaps the police would like to look into Muckley's conduct.' The prospect of such an event quite lifted his spirits.

Ron arrived at the appointed time. Kevin Macey came to meet him in the front lobby and escorted him upstairs to an interview room, accompanied by DC Jim Lewis. Macey directed Ron to sit at a small table and seated himself opposite him. Lewis was seated at the opposite end of the room.

'Mr Levy.' He looked serious as he glanced at the bundle of papers in his hands. 'Mr Laws has given me some details about the meeting last Wednesday. He tells me that you produced some documents which he claims were missing from the Council files. Are these the papers? Do you recognise them?'

'Yes, they're the ones,' he replied.

'Would you like to tell me about it, Mr Levy?'

Ron explained all that had happened since the first complaints about Muckley... about his frustration at Fred Laws' refusal to accept that there was anything wrong and his refusal to investigate the matters.

Kevin Macey listened patiently. 'So how did you come by these papers, Mr Levy?' he asked sombrely.

Ron didn't like the question. It seemed almost menacing. 'They came through the post,' he replied nervously.

'How... in what way?'

'I don't follow you,' he replied.

'Were they in an envelope, and if so, what kind of envelope?'

The question caught him off guard. He had to think. 'I believe it was a buff envelope. Handwritten, I think.'

'What size was it?'

It seemed an odd question. How could it matter? Was it a trick question? Ron searched his memory. Then he glanced at the papers. He noticed there was no fold in them. 'It was a large one... A4.'

Kevin Macey did not look happy. 'Well, Mr Levy. I don't believe you. And I'm going to keep you in custody whilst I carry out further inquiries.' He stood up.

His mind was in turmoil, near panic in his voice, Ron asked, 'Why would you do that? I don't understand. I can't stay. I've got appointments this afternoon in the shop. Can I make a phone call?'

'No you can't,' Macey replied firmly.

Ron was escorted unceremoniously from the room, down some stairs, through corridors into a room with painted brick walls. There was a table to one side with papers on it. A single filing cabinet stood in a corner. At the far end, an exit with steel bars, through which could be seen a wide passageway - he wondered where it led to. The only occupant of the room turned as he heard the three men enter. From his belt hung a bunch of large keys, which jangled as he moved.

Macey spoke. 'Hello, Ken. This is Mr Levy. I want him detained for a while. I'm conducting some inquiries. It shouldn't be for too long.'

Ken was obviously the gaoler. He told Ron to sit at the table, and then purposefully eased himself into the chair facing him. Macey and Lewis stood watching impassively.

Ken picked up the pen and neatly squared the form in front of him. 'Right, Mr Levy, let's have some details.'

Hardly aware of what he was saying, Ron answered the questions: name, address, date of birth, occupation; the questions seemed endless. Suddenly the tone changed. 'Now Mr Levy. I want you to stand up and empty your pockets.'

Ron thought 'This is madness, I shouldn't be here. I'm not a criminal.' He slowly placed his possessions on the table in front of him. The gaoler listed the items on the form.

'Now stand to the side, please.' Ron did as he was told. 'Remove your shoes and stand with your feet apart.'

'Whatever for?' asked Ron nervously, still not believing that this was happening.

The reply was terse. 'Just do it... and raise your arms sideways.' Experienced hands ran down his arms, his sides and his legs. He felt humiliated, embarrassed. 'Now take off your glasses.'

It was the last straw. He was not going to submit completely. 'I can't. Without them I get headaches.' Despite feeling pleased with his quick thinking Ron hated telling lies but he was now outraged and was determined to retain some dignity in this absurd situation. Ken paused. He seemed unsure about Ron's reply. 'Hmm. All right, you can keep them on.' Unhooking the bunch of keys, he turned to Macey. 'Ok, Kevin, time to put him away.' The two officers nodded and left the room.

'This way, please, Mr Levy.' Now, his mind in absolute turmoil, Ron was led towards the exit through the steel bars. The keys rattled as one was selected to open the door, along the short passageway, then a left turn into a long corridor. Grey-painted steel doors, each with a hinged viewing panel, lined the corridor. His captor stopped, opened one of the doors, and held it back for Ron to enter. He froze as he peered into the small cell. This was a nightmare. He felt numb, sick. His knees trembled. Tears welled up, but he fought them back.

'Inside, please, sir... now.'

'Yes... of course.' Reluctantly, he stepped through the doorway. It felt cold. There was a bunk against the facing wall below a high window of translucent glass bricks, letting in only light. To the left was a partially screened lavatory. He jumped nervously as the door crashed shut behind him, echoing round the cell.

Anne Archer arrived for her hair appointment at four thirty.

'I'm sorry, Anne,' said Patricia. 'I'm afraid Ron isn't back yet. The police phoned this morning and asked him to go along to the station to help them with some inquiries: Something to do with the meeting at the Council offices last week. Ron told me you were there. He was very upset at the outcome.'

'He wasn't the only one, my dear. It was quite disgraceful, a thorough whitewash. Ron was like a lamb to the slaughter. It was such a shame. Mind you, it was brilliant the way he produced those papers. They all went mad. I had to laugh. Anyway, that's enough of that. What's happening to Ron?'

'Well, I've phoned the police station twice in the last half hour to find out how long he's going to be, but they won't tell me anything. It's very mysterious. I'm getting rather worried.' They had been talking for 15 minutes or so when the doorbell rang. 'Excuse me, Anne, I'll just get that.'

It was Macey and Lewis. 'Mrs Levy?'

Patricia nodded.

'I'm Detective Constable Kevin Macey and this is D C Jim Lewis. May we come in?'

Patricia's heart sank. She stood aside to let them in. 'Is it about my husband? Where is he?'

'Mr Levy is at the station,' said Macey. She gasped as he said; 'We want to search the house.'

Despite her confused mind, Patricia kept calm. 'Have you got a warrant?'

'Mr Levy is in custody, and so we don't need one.'

'My husband's not in custody... he's only gone to help,' she snapped, nervously.

Macey's reply was as positive as it was contradictory. 'He is. He's in custody and we've come to search for papers.'

Rachel came down the stairs dressed ready for Brownies. She was frightened. She heard what had been said but at ten years of age she could not have understood what was happening.

She grasped Patricia's hand, as children do when seeking comfort.

'What's... custody, Mummy?' she asked, looking up at Patricia.

'It's all right, darling. It just means that Daddy has to stay at the police station for a while to help these gentlemen find things out.'

Rachel squeezed her mother's hand tighter. Uncertainty in her voice, she asked, 'Will he be home soon? I don't want to go to Brownies.'

Patricia drew her little girl to her and comforted her. 'I'm sure he will be, darling.' Patricia turned to Macey. 'Is that right, Mr Macey? Will her daddy be home soon... before Rachel gets home from Brownies?'

His tone mellowed at this vision. Perhaps he had children. 'Oh, I expect so. This shouldn't take too long.'

She gave Rachel a reassuring hug. 'There you are, dear. You go off to your Brownies. There's nothing to worry about. Daddy will be here when you come home. Is that all right?

Rachel nodded, moist eyes reflecting her confusion. OK, Mummy.' She kissed Patricia on the cheek, said goodbye, and slowly walked out of the door.

Patricia took a deep breath. She believed they could not search without a warrant but was worried that they might think she had something to hide if she stopped them. And so she let them search. Macey asked where Ron kept his papers. Leading them to his desk and filing cabinet, she said: 'This is where he works... where he keeps all his papers to do with the Council.'

They rummaged through the pile of papers on the desk. 'What are we looking for, Kevin?' whispered Lewis.

Macey closed the filing cabinet and glanced again at the piles of papers. 'I'm not really sure.' He turned to Patricia.

'Did he get any packages, or large envelopes delivered?'

It was an absurd question. 'The Council is always sending him packages... papers to read for Council meetings. Other people send him papers, cases for him to take up. Unless you can be more specific, I'm not sure I can help.'

He hesitated, thought better of further explanation. 'At this stage, Mrs Levy, I can't. I think I'm finished here for the moment. We'll be off.' He turned and made his way to the door.

Patricia followed, unable to conceal the distress in her voice. 'Just a minute: What about my husband... what's going to happen to him; when is he going to be released?'

Apparently unconcerned at her plight, he opened the door and shrugged. 'I really can't say at the moment. I've got further inquiries to make. You'll have to phone the station.'

Closing the door behind them, she turned to Anne. 'Well. I wonder what all that was about?'

Anne smiled sardonically. 'I should think it was all about the Muckley files. But I wonder why they didn't ask outright. Did you know what they were looking for, Patricia?'

'Oh, yes. I knew all right. But they didn't ask. And all I could think of was Ron being locked up. I didn't want to say anything that might make his situation worse. Although I don't see how it could. But I still can't understand why they would arrest him. He hasn't done anything wrong.'

Anne racked her mind for an explanation 'The police can only act on information received. They acted on something that Fred Laws told them, so... whatever did he say for them to take such drastic action?'

'I wonder. But I doubt if we'll ever know,' replied Patricia.

'I wonder,' said Anne. 'Fred Laws was very angry at the meeting. I've never known him to lose his temper before. He was livid. Mind you, he *is* a very clever man. I do wonder if it was contrived. After all, there was so much confusion that nobody asked the meaning of what was in the papers.'

'Yes. Ron told me. It did seem a little strange. But then Ron has been pestering Laws for a very long time... constantly complaining about Muckley and the housing department. Perhaps the surprise of producing those documents was the last straw.'

'I tell you what else is strange, Patricia. Kevin Macey... he came in here, walked past me several times and didn't seem to notice me. He didn't ask who I was. It was quite amusing. I was thinking, "If only you knew".'

Patricia smiled. 'Yes, I wondered about that.'

Anne glanced at her watch. 'Goodness me, look at the time. I'd better be off. Oh, by the way, what about Ron's other appointments?'

'Yes, I had thought about that before you arrived. I told the girls he wasn't sure when he would be back. They're sharing his bookings amongst themselves. They'll manage. I'm afraid that's the last thing on my mind at the moment. Oh. You didn't get your hair done.'

Anne dismissed Patricia's concern. 'Don't worry about it. I can do something with it when I get home. You just concentrate on Ron's problem. And if there's anything that I can do to help, you just phone. Will you do that?'

Patricia hugged her. 'Of course I will, Anne. And thank you so much for your support.'

'Right then, I'd better be off. I'm sure I'll see you soon. And keep in touch.'

As soon as she had gone, Patricia phoned the police station, still no news. She felt alone... helpless. The children would be wondering what was going on. Rachel would soon be home from Brownies. She needed someone close to her, to confide in, to share her fears. Her brother Roy lived at Wakering, she would give him a ring.

'Oh Roy. Thank goodness you're home. Ron's in trouble. He's been arrested. I don't know what to do. Please help me.' Unable to hold back any longer, she broke down and wept.

'I'll be there in a few minutes.' He said, sensing the urgency, and longing to comfort her. 'You just hold on. I'll be there.'

By the time he arrived Patricia had regained her composure. A few dabs of face powder had softened the redness of her cheeks. She hated losing control, but she felt better for the release of her pent-up emotions.

Roy had brought with him Gill, his eldest daughter. Gill and Patricia were very fond of each other; had always been good friends, especially in troublesome times.

'I've come to give you some moral support.' Gill said warmly: 'And to help where I can.' The school teacher in her had surfaced. 'Why don't we go into the kitchen... make some coffee. Then you can tell us all about it.'

Patricia's family already knew of Ron's difficulties with the Council. She told them what had happened at the meeting and the events leading to his present predicament.

'That's crazy,' said Roy. 'Let's phone the station again and find out when he's going to be released.'

'There's no point,' she replied. 'I phoned them after I called you. They just won't tell me anything.'

'That doesn't make sense,' he said impatiently. 'Why don't we go to the police station; stay there until they do tell us. I had a feeling we might end up doing that... it's why I brought Gill with me.'

'Oh Roy, you are thoughtful. I'd like to do that. I feel so helpless here... so... remote from him.'

They finished their coffee and left.

Ron heard again the faint metallic rattle of keys followed

by the squeak, squeak of crepe shoes on the polished concrete floor. The footsteps stopped outside his cell door. A key turned noisily in the lock. The door swung open.

'Right, Mr Levy. You can come out now.'

He gave a sigh of relief. He had been in the cell for almost three hours. 'Freedom at last,' he said.

'I'm afraid not,' replied the gaoler. 'Mr Macey wants to see you again. This way, please.'

Ron's heart sank. He thought, 'This is ridiculous. How much longer must this madness go on?'

He was led back to the interview room. Macey and Lewis were already there.

'Sit down, please. I want to ask you some more questions. I want you to think again about those papers; where they came from. Who sent them to you?'

'I've already told you. They came through my letterbox. Oh, and I forgot to tell you, they weren't actually posted... there was no stamp on the envelope... it must have been delivered by hand. And I don't know who did that. Although on reflection I suppose it could have been a member of staff.'

Macey would not give up. 'Well, why do you think they were sent to you... why not another councillor?'

'I've had a lot of publicity lately, about my complaints of the housing department. I expect whoever brought them thought they might help me.'

'Could you have taken them... the files?'

'Certainly not; I wouldn't have access to such files. Mind you, as a Councillor I probably would have had a right to see them anyway.'

'And when you received them, did you not realise they might have been stolen property?'

'Not at all...I could see they were photocopies.'

Macey was getting impatient. 'All right, let's try another

angle - when you first saw the papers, what did you make of them? What did you do?'

'Well, I wasn't really sure what they meant. I mean, I could see that they were tenancy records, and I could see that they were to do with Mr Muckley. But I didn't really understand them. I'd never seen these kind of documents before. I needed to speak to someone who knew about them.'

'And did you speak to someone?'

Ron hesitated. He didn't want to bring Anne into all this but he knew it was now too late. 'Yes. I know a lady who used to work in the housing department... a Mrs Archer. I took the papers to her, she explained them to me. It was then that I realised their importance.'

'Could she have sent them to you?' he snapped.

The question was anticipated. 'I doubt it. She had left the department long before the papers were sent to me.'

Macey was unhappy with the answer. 'She could have taken them before leaving, and given them to you later.'

'That's a bit far fetched, and hardly likely,' replied Ron, irritated by the questions.

Macey persisted. 'But possible, you must admit.'

'Mm... possible yes, but as I said, hardly likely.'

The questioning continued: pointless questions that seemed to lead nowhere. He stood up. 'I'm still not satisfied, Mr Levy. I can't let you go yet. I still have further inquiries to make.' He rang for the gaoler and Ron was escorted back to his cell.

'You've been in custody now for almost four hours, Mr Levy. I have to offer you something to eat and drink. Do you want anything?'

Ron had no recollection of replying, but a few minutes later the gaoler returned with a large plastic mug of warm, sweet tea and two ham rolls on a plastic plate. The ham, which protruded from the sides of the rolls, had dried and curled up. His ordeal had not robbed him of his appetite and he ate hungrily. He hadn't taken sugar in his tea for years, but it was a welcome drink to wash down the rolls. When he had finished he sat back against the wall, resuming the position he had adopted during most of his incarceration. Sitting; T thinking; mulling over all that had happened. Joan Carlile's words repeatedly echoed in his mind and a strange peace came to him; a peace that he had not felt before. Closing his eyes, he longed for his freedom.

Anne Archer felt better for her change of clothes and for washing her hair. But she was troubled. She could not erase from her mind the rapid developments since the hearing. She desperately wanted to help Ron and Patricia, but she could think of nothing. She was busying herself about the house. It was the only way she could cope. A loud knock at the door released her from her thoughts.

She opened the door and immediately recognised Kevin Macey.

'Mrs Archer?'

'Yes,' she replied, struggling to conceal her surprise that he hadn't recognised her.

'I'm Detective Constable Kevin Macey and this is DC Jim Lewis. May we come in?'

Anne led them into her front room. 'We're investigating a complaint from the Town Clerk about some Council documents. Do you know a Mr levy... Ron Levy?'

'I do.'

'And how long have you known him?'

'Two or three years, I would say.'

He thought, 'this one's not giving much away.' Opening his case, he produced the papers and handed them to Anne. 'Have you seen these before, Mrs Archer?'

She gave the papers a cursory glance. 'I certainly have. Several times,' she replied, handing them back to him.

'How is that?' asked Macey.

'I'm sure you know by now that I was a Council officer in the housing department for many years. I had access to these files, along with thousands of other files, in the course of my duties.'

'When did you retire from the Council?'

Her hackles rose. 'I did not *retire* from the Council... I was forced to leave four years ago.'

Her reply momentarily stunned him, but it was irrelevant.

'And when did you last see these papers?'

'This is a loaded question.' she thought. 'I can't tell you exactly, but it would be about...' she paused, searching her memory. 'It must be more than a year. I can't remember exactly.'

'And in what circumstances did you see them?'

'Ron Levy brought them to me. He wanted me to explain them to him.'

'And were you able to... to explain them to him?'

'Oh, yes,' she replied with relish. 'I know all about Mr Muckley and the housing of his parents.'

'Do you know how he came by the papers?'

'Yes, I know that too. But where is Ron now?'

'He's helping me with my inquiries. He's being held at the station.'

Anne turned on him angrily. 'Well, he shouldn't be. Muckley's the one you should be investigating. He's been causing misery in the department for years; breaking the rules: deceiving people. Did you know he has a criminal record? He's been getting away with it all this time because no one was prepared to stand up to him until Ron came along. He's the only one who had the guts to do something about it. He sacrificed his political career because he was not prepared to stand by and do nothing. I tell you this, Mr Macey. Ron's got more principles and courage in his little finger than all that lot at the Civic Centre put together. And you tell me he's locked in a cell... it's shameful.'

A brief silence followed her outburst. She looked into his eyes, searching for a reaction. His face was expressionless.

'I didn't tell you he was locked in a cell. But you obviously know. However, it matters not.' He quickly glanced round the room, located the telephone. 'May I make a call?'

'You certainly may.' she replied, standing aside.

He picked up the phone and dialled. 'Hello, Kevin Macey here. Put me through to Ken, will you.' He waited. 'Hello Ken. I think I've got as far as I can on this business with Mr Levy, for the time being anyway. Let him go, will you? Bail him for a month... yes, right away...thanks.' Replacing the phone, he turned to Anne. 'Thank you, Mrs Archer. That'll be all for now. Thank you for your help.'

'It's a pleasure, Mr Macey. Believe me it's a pleasure.'

As soon as they had gone she phoned Patricia.

'This is Gill, her niece. She's not here at the moment. Can I help?'

'This is Anne Archer. I...'

'Oh hello Anne. I've heard about you from Ron. Patricia is still at the police station with Roy.'

'Oh, what a pity,' replied Anne. 'I wanted to give her some good news: Ron's being released right away. But since she's at the station she probably knows that by now.'

'Oh Anne. That is good news. We can expect them home soon, then... right, I'll tell her you called. Thanks. 'Bye for now.'

Patricia approached the desk sergeant again. 'Officer we've been here now for almost an hour. We've been told nothing. Surely I'm entitled to know what's going on... why can't I see my husband?'

Before the sergeant could reply the sound and movement of a side door opening caught her attention. She turned to see Ron emerge. He looked pale, dazed. She hurried to him, held him close. 'Oh Ron... at last. Does this mean you're free?'

He kissed her. 'Apparently,' he replied, uncertainty in his voice. 'I've got to come back in a month's time.'

Roy had joined them. They shook hands. 'Hello, Ron. It's good to see you, mate. We've been very worried. They wouldn't tell us anything.'

'Thanks, Roy. Thanks for coming.' Sliding his arm round Patricia's waist, Ron kissed her again. 'Come along, darling. Let's get out of this place. I'll tell you all about it later.' They headed for the exit. Outside, he paused, took a deep breath. The air smelled good and fresh. 'I want to go home.'

CHAPTER 8

'EX-COUNCILLOR HELD IN CELLS' shrieked the headlines of the *Evening Echo (7 May 1982).* Ron felt the blood drain from his face. This further humiliation was intolerable.

Seeing his alarmed state, Patricia moved closer to him. She peered over his shoulder and gently clasped his hand to steady the paper. 'Oh, my God. Is there no end to this?' she said, despairingly.

They read the report together in silence:

> A former Southend Councillor today claimed he was held in police custody for several hours, searched and subjected to a long cross-examination.
>
> Former Shoebury Tory Councillor Ron Levy went to Southend police station by appointment last night to assist police investigations into allegations over missing documents from the council's housing department.
>
> Mr. Levy said "It was the most dreadful experience of my whole life, particularly being held in solitary confinement in a police cell for four hours.
>
> "It was frightening. I was put in a cell. I was searched. My property, including my watch, was removed. Even my shoes were removed."
>
> **Suspicion**
>
> Police were called to investigate by Town Clerk Fred Laws after Mr Levy was sent copies of documents missing from Council Files.
>
> Mr Levy, of West Road, Shoebury, said the police

were only doing their job.

But he added: "The situation is entirely wrong. I was held on suspicion of being in possession of stolen property... bits of paper, documents.

"I was treated like a villain. It was rather drastic treatment.

"I'd brought certain allegations in an endeavour to clear the air. I should not have been treated in this way."

Mr Levy, who resigned from the council last month, criticised Mr Laws' action in calling for the police to probe the missing documents riddle.

He said: "I feel it's disgraceful that he should do this.

Ex-councillor Levy declared: "I am innocent. But while I was held by the police, even though I had gone to the police station quite voluntarily, my home was searched by other police officers."

He said he wanted to know why Mr Laws had not revealed the documents were missing from the housing department files until after he, Mr Levy, had presented photocopies sent to him in the post.

Voluntarily

He added: "Why didn't he reveal the documents were missing before the enquiry opened? Why didn't he report the matter to the police immediately?"

Southend Police Chief Supt George Dollby said Mr Levy came to Southend police HQ voluntarily. He was later allowed to go home and was not charged.

He said: "The investigation is still proceeding. Mr Levy was treated in the same way as anyone else."

Mr Laws called in the police following investigations by a special sub-committee set up by the council's policy and resources committee into complaints made by Mr Levy against a council housing official.

In the course of the enquiry copies of the missing documents were produced by Mr Levy as part of his case. Mr Levy said the documents had been posted to him and he could give no details of their source.

Mr Levy added today: "I must stress I went to the police headquarters voluntarily. I've not been charged and the investigation is proceeding."

The council's sub-committee found that the eight complaints made by Mr Levy were unsubstantiate

'This is dreadful,' murmured Patricia. She held him close to her. 'Don't let it get you down, Ron. You can't beat them. They're too powerful. You're better off away from it all.'

He sighed deeply, responding to her warmth. 'That's all very well. I don't like turning my back on...'

His words were shattered by the shrill ring of the telephone. It was the first of several calls that were to show him just who on the council he could truly count among his friends. 'Hello, Ron. It's Joan Carlile. I've just been reading the paper. I had to phone you to see how you are. I think it's absolutely disgraceful what they did to you. There was no need to do that.'

'Thank you Joan, that's very thoughtful of you. I'm still in a bit of a daze. I just can't believe it all happened. And ironically, on election day, too.'

'Well. I want you to know that my thoughts and prayers are with you, Ron. You were in the right and I support you all the way.'

'Thanks Joan, that means a lot to me. I don't know where I go from here. I think I'm just going to put it behind me and gather my thoughts. Have a break from it all.'

'You do just that, Ron. I'm sure it will do you good. I'll

leave you to your thoughts and I'll speak to you later. 'Bye for now.'

The calls followed in quick succession. All with similar messages of support and good wishes: Anne Archer, Councillors Allen Crystal, John Croft, Chris Hudson, numerous constituents whom Ron had helped; and friends.

It was Chris Hudson who was most vociferous about the events, the school teacher in him coming across clearly in his voice and manner. 'Muckley's as guilty as hell and Fred Laws knows it. You were being punished, Ron, for what you did at that kangaroo court. I saw Fred's face when you produced Muckley's parents' tenancy records. He was livid. I've never seen him lose control like that. What puzzles me though, is why he said nothing in his report about the so called missing files, and why none of that lot on the committee didn't have the savvy to ask him why he hadn't mentioned those missing files. No, Ron, you got very close to the truth and they didn't like it. They were out to silence you and they crucified you. Make no mistake about that.'

Ron hadn't thought of things in quite that way. Perhaps he had been naïve in believing that he could bring about an end to such abuses within the council. He was grateful for Chris's strong support. Such words of comfort began to restore his self confidence.

Chris continued, 'I know you're no longer on the council, Ron, and I'm very sorry about that. But if that lot at the Civic Centre think they're safe now that they've got rid of you they are mistaken. I'm going to continue where you left off. As far as I'm concerned Muckley hasn't got away with it, and Fred Laws may live to regret what he did to you.'

Anne Archer took some time to recover from her shock and distress at Ron's imprisonment. She was not prepared to leave matters as they stood. She knew there was no point continuing the struggle at council level, the obstacles along that route were too numerous and difficult. It must go to a higher level.

Teddy Taylor was Member of Parliament for Southend East and had built up a good reputation for his constituency work. He had never been afraid to deal with matters of concern and injustice. Anne still had friends within the housing department and she had heard of Muckley's further misdeeds since her departure from his department. The latest scandal revealed he had been having an affair with Christine Holiday, headmistress of Thorpe Bay primary school in Southend. Apparently, he had arranged for a council house in Shoeburyness to be allocated to her and then promptly moved in with her. From there, the lucky couple had moved to a very desirable new housing association property in Baxter Avenue, after being nominated by Southend Council's housing department. Muckley's wife had been left in the matrimonial home and was eventually offered a council house so that the home could be sold. Ann had also kept the press cutting about Muckley which had been published in the local newspaper in 1957 before he had applied for a job at Southend Council. The story described how he had been caught red-handed stealing materials from a building site and was convicted of theft. At the time of Muckley's application it was a strict rule with local councils that a person with a criminal record would not be considered for employment with them. The only conclusion that could be drawn from this is that he made false statements in his job application in order to secure the job.

Teddy Taylor was most interested in these latest revelations. He had followed the saga from a distance and had discussed the situation briefly from time to time with Ron. But most local council matters were outside his remit as MP and he needed to be careful not to appear to intrude in these problems. However, he realised how serious these latest allegations were and he knew he had to do something. He would write to Fred Laws. Anne had hoped for more drastic action from Teddy but she settled for that as a start in the hope that the enquiry into Muckley might be revived.

Teddy was as good as his word. Fred Laws had recently written to Teddy in reply to a previous letter about Ron's complaints to the Subcommittee. Fred had explained in his letter how the Committee had dealt with those complaints. This was an opportunity for Teddy to ask Fred about these latest stories, which he described in detail in a letter to Fred dated 17 May 1982:

'I have been distressed by the number of phone calls I have received over the case since it was reported in the local paper that Councillor Levy intended to speak to me, which I can tell you in confidence that he did last Friday.

It would help to clear my mind if you could let me know whether these latest allegations are accurate and were known to the Council before they dealt with the case in the way that they did. I agree with you, as you pointed out in your letter, that there is a real danger of my getting unduly involved in an internal Council matter, but I just do not know what to do when people continually contact me with these most alarming allegations. I would greatly appreciate your comments on the questions I have raised on the strict understanding that I will not be following it up with other similar letters.

The only other interest I have taken is to write to the Chief Superintendent of police at the request of Mr Levy to enquire if they intend to press charges against him. Mr Levy has obviously been through a great deal and I am really quite concerned about the effect on his health of the issue which he clearly believed was an error of judgement.

On the same day that Teddy wrote his letter, Fred Laws carried out the instructions of the Subcommittee and wrote to Dennis Crouch, secretary of the Institute of Housing, saying:

You may remember that in October 1978 I wrote to you about a newspaper article which appeared in the Southend Evening Echo about Mr Muckley and some alleged impropriety in relation to an Institute examination. I attach a copy of that newspaper report to remind you.

We discussed the matter at the time and I was satisfied from what you told me that I need take no further action. Unfortunately some further complaint has been made by a Councillor against Mr Muckley in relation to quite separate matters but in the course of the enquiry the examination incident was quoted again as an example of unsatisfactory behaviour.

A subcommittee of my Council met on 28 April 1982 to consider these complaints, none of which was found to be substantiated, but I was asked to make further enquiries about the examination incident. This was because a letter was produced from you addressed to Mrs Saxby, the trainee in question, which said words to the effect that the Institute had taken disciplinary action against Mr Muckley, which was not my understanding at the time and seems to be inconsistent with the letter you wrote to Mr Muckley, a copy of which is attached.

My Members would like clarification of the position and to know whether it was the Institute's intention to discipline Mr Muckley or whether, alternatively, you accepted his resignation with some reluctance.

In the course of quite a long discussion on this incident, my Members were informed that Mr Muckley would not have had access to examination papers. I wonder if you could kindly indicate what the procedure is and what role the

Examination Board fulfils in relation to the preparation of examination papers. In other words, do you agree that Mr Muckley would not have had access to examination papers so as to be able to disclose them to Mrs Saxby?

Two days after dispatching this letter to the Institute Fred sat down and prepared a reply to Teddy's letter. It was a difficult letter to draft because he was now tiring of the whole business and began to wonder if it would ever go away. He cursed Muckley for bringing this burden upon him and cursed Levy even more for being such a persistent nuisance. Fred's irritation was reflected in the manner of his reply:

I am sorry you are still receiving complaints about Mr Muckley and it is a difficult situation.

So far as Mr Levy is concerned, I cannot help. He is now experiencing the inevitable consequences of his actions, and whereas at one time a full retraction and public apology may have got him out of trouble, I think now it is too late for that.

As to other complainants I hope you can dissuade them from putting about vicious and scurrilous stories because that is what they are. I shall certainly take no notice of any complaint not supported by some real evidence.

Specifically, I have already heard of allegation 1, it is quite spurious. Mr Muckley has no criminal convictions. The second and third allegations are new to me. Mr Muckley was, of course, accused quite falsely of improperly arranging for his parents to be housed and even Mr Levy withdrew that charge. *Now the man is accused of fixing up his wives and mistresses. As to Mrs Holland, we do not know her and the address quoted does not exist. However, it is not difficult to deduce what name and address should have been quoted. That case I am quite satisfied was properly handled some time ago, a homeless lady was re-housed for a short period at a privately owned house, leased to the Council. Mr Muckley does not live there nor did he live there at any time. Mr Muckley's wife still lives in Southchurch, has never been offered a Council House nor nominated for a tenancy of other accommodation as a Council sponsored prospective tenant.*

It is quite clear to me that these last two allegations are tittle tattle spread by people jumping to conclusions out of spite. I hope you feel able to ask any other complainants for their evidence and if there is none, show them the door.

With Fred Laws firmly rejecting allegations against Muckley, despite the supporting evidence of those allegations, Muckley was regaining his confidence: his invincibility remaining intact. Pushing his luck even further he contacted his NALGO solicitor, Penelope Grant. Informing her of Ron's persistence in making allegations against him he instructed her to write to Ron and try to persuade him to end his vendetta against him. This she did in no uncertain terms in a letter which contained a strong threat of legal action if he failed to desist:

I have been consulted by Mr Muckley in connection with allegations which you have been making against him since 1979. In particular I have been referred to a letter dated 11 February 1982, addressed by you to all members of the Policy and Resources Committee of the Council, with copies to the Director of Housing and Estates and the Town Clerk.

This letter concerns most serious allegations of maladministration, corruption, abuse of authority, forgery, and dismissal from the Institute of Housing Examination Board as a result of misconduct.

These allegations were without a shred of truth, and the Committee of Inquiry held in public to examine them completely exonerated Mr Muckley.

Notwithstanding this, I am informed that you have

continued to persist in repeating these allegations and have recently referred them to a local MP.

You will appreciate that there is a serious risk that by your repetition of these unfounded accusations, serious damage may be caused to Mr Muckley if any third party should give any credence to them at all.

I am writing therefore to ask for your immediate assurance that you will not repeat any of the matters contained in your letter of the 11 February 1982, and will let the matter rest following the full inquiry which you originally demanded. In addition, my client expects without delay a full retraction and public apology from you in respect of the allegations you have made which have been clearly demonstrated to be unfounded. If you fail to give me the assurance and make the apology and retraction which I have requested, I shall have no alternative but to advise Mr Muckley of his legal remedies. If you are in any doubt about these and the seriousness of your position I would strongly urge you to take independent legal advice on the matter. In the meantime I must warn you that all his rights are expressly reserved.

If this letter was intended to frighten Ron into submission, Miss Grant certainly knew nothing about his character. If anything, it was more likely to have the opposite effect. It was a red rag to a bull. Ron gasped in astonishment at the sheer audacity of the man. He read it through again, almost in disbelief, laughing to himself as he did so.

Ron showed the letter to Patricia. Her reaction was similar to his but there was a note of caution in her voice. 'The man's fooling himself. He might get away with all this with his friends on the Council, but with his history I doubt that it would get into court.' She gently touched his arm, her expression changing to that of concern. 'But I am a little worried, Ron. I don't like the way this is going. It's beginning to take over our lives. I just wish it would all end.'

He drew her to him and hugged her. He didn't like to see her so unsettled. She was by nature a peaceful person with an intense dislike of conflict. But she respected his motives, knowing that he had not been drawn in to all this willingly. His principles were too strong to allow such wrong-doing to go unchallenged. But her mind was troubled. Something told her that it didn't make sense. Anxious, she drew away from him, gently rubbing her tired eyes. 'There's something I don't understand, something that doesn't fit. What's behind it all? Why are they coming down so hard on you? There's got to be something big... some reason. What Muckley did wasn't really so serious as to justify this reaction, this suppression. Yes, he broke the rules. A council house here, a favour there. Get rid of anyone who stands in his way, but to go to such lengths to try and silence you. My instinct tells me again there's more to this than meets the eye?

They both stood in silence for a few second, deep in thought. Ron gave a deep sigh and shrugged. He never before had much reason to think about a woman's intuition but Patricia's words stirred him. 'I think you may have a point. I have wondered sometimes why I should be made to feel like the guilty party. Why such strong forces are trying to make me give up. But I just can't imagine what could be so big as to justify such behaviour.

Ron returned to the letter, striking it with the back of his hand 'I can't possibly do what Miss Grant asks. It would amount to an admission that everything I did was wrong. I can't do that. And I must say so...publicly.

A few days later the *Southend Evening Echo* carried the latest episode under the headline:

Ex-councillor refuses to retract claims

A former Southend councillor has been called on

to retract allegations of maladministration and inefficiency he made against a senior officer in Southend's housing department.

But Mr Ron Levy, who resigned as a Tory councillor in April says he is determined not to withdraw what he said: I spent three years of my life and sacrificed my political career, and I'm not going to throw away those sacrifices.

The call for a retraction came from the local government officers NALGO.

The Institute of Housing had been presented with a very difficult dilemma by Fred Laws' letter. Dennis Crouch knew that he must be careful not to make any more conflicting statements. He could not deny the letter to Jane Saxby which said that disciplinary action had been taken against Muckley, and yet how could he explain his letter to Fred Laws claiming that no disciplinary action had been taken? Such a challenge would test the limits of his ingenuity. This time his reply had to be truthful. He had delayed long enough. Six weeks after receiving Fred's letter he replied, begging Fred's forgiveness for taking so long saying:

The disciplinary action taken against Mr Muckley in 1978 was to insist upon his resignation from the Council of the Institute, and this he was prepared to tender. My letter of 18 May 1978 which followed was deliberately set on an even tone in order, so far as possible to avoid any perpetuation of the affair such as now occurs.

I believe that the Disciplinary Panel of the Institute would have dealt with Mr Muckley more harshly had it not been for the fact that, in their view, certain evidence pointed to the possibility of collusion and conspiracy against Mr Muckley. However, the Institute was not in a position to corroborate or expand that evidence so as to establish the true facts. May I say, however, that what you have told me about recent events must give rise to similar doubts, and you will presumably bear this in mind during your investigations.

So far as the examination papers are concerned, it is a function of the Examination board to vet and approve question papers submitted by the Chief Examiners concerned: Mr Muckley would have been in possession of a set of papers, and these would have been returned to the Institute on completion of the work of the Board.

Fred Laws was well aware of the serious implications of the Institute's reply: Dennis Crouch had been untruthful when he previously wrote saying that disciplinary action had not been taken against Muckley, and Muckley had lied in his statement to the Subcommittee when denying that he would have seen the examination papers. But how was Fred to report this development to the Committee? It would certainly confirm that this part of Ron's allegations were correct. It might even bring into question the remainder of Muckley's statement. How many other lies did it contain? Fred was furious with both Dennis Crouch and especially with Muckley for placing him in this very difficult position. It would look bad for him and the council. And what would Ron's reaction be? Would he be encouraged to intensify his demands for a proper enquiry?

Despite these revelations from the Institute Fred knew he must report back to the Subcommittee as instructed, and he accordingly arranged for a meeting to take place on 2 August 1982. He wrote to Ron advising him of the date and asked him if he would be attending the meeting. At the same time Fred informed Penelope Grant of the date, sending her a copy of Dennis Crouch's letter. Fred wrote:

At the meeting the Sub-Committee are only concerned with Mr Levy's allegation that Mr Muckley revealed the contents of an examination paper to a trainee in the department, Mrs Saxby. Mr Crouch's letter appears to repudiate the version given on Mr Muckley's behalf by officers of the NALGO branch at the previous meeting. The Sub-Committee is particularly concerned at the statement in the "NALGO paper" that it was "impossible for Mr Muckley to have revealed the actual questions because he was not privy to details of the papers". According to the Institute this is untrue.

I must also mention another matter to you which will not be mentioned by me or any members of the Subcommittee at the meeting, and I am referring to the attached press cutting and the Item headed "Stole on the spur of the moment". If anyone else should attempt to raise this matter now or at any time later I will, of course, object most strongly, having referred to the Rehabilitation of Offenders Act. I thought, however, that you should be aware of the matter even though I shall resist by all possible means any reference to it.

Having also been instructed to check with Jane Saxby the accuracy of the story in the *Evening Echo*, Fred arranged a meeting with her to hear her version of the incident. After the meeting he wrote down the details of his discussion with Jane which he titled:

'NOTE FOR THE FILE'

28 JULY 1982. Saw Mrs J Saxby by appointment at the offices of Tower Hamlets Housing Department, 217, Commercial Road. I explained about the inquiry into the complaint about Mr Muckley and asked if the newspaper report dated 26 October 1978 was substantially correct. She said it was. Mrs Saxby handed me copies of three letters sent to her by the Institute of housing concerning sitting for the examination.

In answer to my specific questions she could not

understand what possible benefit there might be to Mr Muckley as a result of what he did. There was absolutely no question of him being paid money for this information. She reported the matter because she was angry that he had prejudiced her sitting for the examination. She held no grudge against him and she had not told anyone other than those she was bound to tell about the incident. She said her interview at the time with Mr Muckley had lasted one and three quarter hours, an incredibly long time which I pressed her about. She said they were talking about the examination but they were interrupted during the course of their discussion. She was quite, quite sure he was quoting from a draft examination paper.

With this final part of his inquiry completed, Fred was ready to prepare his report for the Subcommittee. He was about to set about this task when he received a letter from the Director of the Institute of Housing, Peter McGurk, which was to dramatically and unpredictably alter the course of events. The tone of Mr McGurk's letter was unexpectedly intimidating:

Mr Muckley has been in touch with the Institute notifying us that Southend Borough Council intend to carry out an investigation into his involvement with the Institute of Housing's examinations in 1978.

My predecessor wrote to you in strictest confidence on 25 June indicating the Institute's view of the position at that time.

Following my conversation with you of Monday 26 July I would like formally to express my concern on behalf of the Institute that your Council have decided to carry out an investigation into a matter which in my view and the view of our legal advisers involves only the Institute and its member. As far as the Institute is concerned this matter has been fully investigated and has been dealt with.

I would be interested to know the legal basis on which you intend to carry out this enquiry, the objective of it and the alternative courses of action that are available to your Members following the completion of the enquiry.

I wish to object in the strongest possible terms on the action that your Council are taking and would wish to notify you that our solicitors have been instructed on this matter.

Your further comments would be appreciated prior to the scheduled meeting of your Committee in order that the Institute can consider further the position.

This was quickly followed by a telephone call and a letter from the Institute's solicitors stating in no uncertain terms that if Fred Laws read out to the Subcommittee Peter McGurk's letter, which had been marked "in strictest confidence", it would be a breach of confidence actionable in law. Stating that they did not wish to take out injunction proceedings against him, they asked Fred to confirm that he would not read the letter to the meeting.

Ron had no knowledge of the letters and discussions that had been taking place between the Institute, their solicitors and Jane Saxby. Had he known, his reply to Fred's request about his attendance at the forthcoming meeting might have been different. But Ron did not believe that there would be a fair hearing and saw no point in attending the meeting. He felt that it would be a whitewash and he wrote to Fred Laws telling him so.

The meeting duly took place. Fred reported Ron's refusal to attend, and the reason. He described the difficulties surrounding his inability to report the Institute's explanation and their threat of legal action. He said that there was really very little more that the Council could do in the matter. An impasse had been reached and there was no way round it. The Committee had no alternative but to resolve that "having regard to the conflict of evidence, and the withholding of information by the Institute of Housing, they were unable to reach a conclusion as to the allegations". The Committee also wished to place on record its objection to the letter from Mr Levy alleging that there had been "an extensive whitewash" which they totally rejected.

When news reached Ron that the Institute had thwarted his one certain opportunity to prove misconduct by Muckley he was angry. His instinct told him that what the Institute had written must be quite devastating for them to insist that the information must be kept secret.

He would have given anything to know what was in the letter, but he knew that there was no way that he was going to find out. The Institute had come out of this very badly and as far as Ron, and others, were concerned they had acted dishonourably. But what was to be done about it? Should anything be done about it?

An unexpected telephone call from John Croft steered Ron towards a possible course of action. John had phoned to commiserate with Ron about the outcome of the meeting. How it seemed, again, that Muckley had 'got away with it'. John explained that he had been in touch with Teddy Taylor to find out from the Secretary of State for Local Government about a councillor's rights of access to Council documents. Lord Bellwin had replied on Michael Heseltine's behalf stating that the courts had held that "a councillor has a common law right to inspect such documents belonging to the authority as he might reasonably and necessarily require to enable him properly to perform his duties as a councillor." John also had some exciting news. Paul Foot of the *Daily Mirror* had been in touch with him expressing a very keen interest in the goings on at Southend Council. Someone had been sending Paul Foot information about Muckley's behaviour and he was planning a series of articles about the Council.

What John had said raised Ron's hopes that the matter was not, after all, going to just fade away. It also gave him an idea. He could see Teddy Taylor about the Institute business. Perhaps Teddy could find out what they said in their letter to Fred Laws.

Teddy was very helpful. He arranged a meeting between himself, Sir George Young, Minister of State for Local Government, and the Director of the Institute of Housing to discuss Ron's complaint. In a letter to Ron giving details of the meeting Teddy confirmed that the Institute had admitted that disciplinary action had been taken against Muckley but could give no rational explanation for telling the Council initially that Muckley had not been disciplined.

Ron was very pleased with this development. He now had something positive to go back to the Council with. This latest information, including the details about Muckley's access to the exam papers and the report of his criminal conviction should convince the Council that Muckley was guilty at least on the allegations regarding the Institute. Ron doubted that he would get very far writing to Fred Laws and so he wrote to the leaders of the three political parties of the Council telling them of the action he had taken and asking them to reconvene the Sub-Committee to consider this "important new evidence."

During the following three weeks there was a flurry of correspondence between Fred laws, Peter McGurk and Ron. Fred wanted Ron to hand over his "important new evidence" fearing that Ron wanted to open up the whole enquiry again, Ron insisted that he wanted to present the evidence himself without restrictions, and the Institute was furious that, once again they had become the focus of unfavourable attention in Southend.

A date was fixed for a hearing on July 28 1983. But Fred

would not move on the question of restricting the evidence that Ron wanted to present to the committee. Agreement could not be reached on the issue and the meeting was cancelled.

Chapter 9

Several months had passed since the cancellation of the July 28 meeting: During that time Ron and Patricia had decided to take advantage of the period of inactivity in this seemingly-endless saga, and were relaxing in the shop, as they occasionally did when they needed a quiet place away from the children for some quality time together in peace: a place where they could discuss things, sometimes over a glass of wine, without interruption: this was one of those occasions.

'Well, it's certainly been a distressing time, Ron. I've been thinking a lot recently about where we go from here. Even, dare I say it, perhaps moving away from this place; to a place where we could start anew and put all this misery behind us, if that's possible.' She held her breath...waited for his reaction.

'Well,.. I have to say the thought had crossed my mind. It would be quite drastic. We would have to discuss it with the children... see what they would think.'

'Of course darling, I've given that some thought, too. Peter has turned 21 now, and we know he's been thinking about getting his own home.'

Peter had been going steady with his girl friend, Jose, and they quite liked the idea of getting a house on Canvey Island. Philip had been working in his spare time as a bottle-boy at the Bass Charrington off-licence opposite the shop since he was 13, and had been working full-time as a trainee manager since he left school two years ago. It had been made clear to him that it would not be long before he would be promoted to Manager at another branch, which usually came with accommodation.

Stephen, now 19, was working in the IT industry and would probably like to have his own place, following in Peter's footsteps. Carole, at 15 will very likely have left school by the time the move could take place. She would be able to decide what she wants to do then. Rachel, at only 10 years of age, would certainly be still young enough to need to move with her Mum and Dad.

'Yes, that's right, Ron. We must talk it over with the children, but I don't think they've fully recovered from the shock and upset at what happened to you. Let's give them a few more days to settle. It'll give us a chance to explore the market for selling the property. And you're no longer being on the Council means that there are no ties to obstruct a move.'

'Yes I must say that being free of that commitment is a great relief to me. But of course, we would have to think about where we would want to move to.'

Patricia replied instantly and enthusiastically. 'Oh, it has to be Colchester, surely.'

About 10 years ago Patricia's sister and brother-in-law, Doreen and Allan, had moved from Cheshire to a small village just on the outskirts of Colchester called Boxted. The move had brought them within visiting distance from Shoeburyness. During the many such visits over those years Ron, Patricia and the younger children, Peter was always too busy with his electronics, had explored Colchester Town and had taken a great liking to it: From now on their visits would grow to have a much greater purpose and meaning.

Without hesitation Ron agreed that Colchester it must be.

The following day Ron would begin the process of placing the property on the market.

Ron and Patricia raised their glasses and brought them together in celebration of what they knew was the right decision. They put their glasses down and held each other close in a joyful, timeless hug, until the door from the flat slowly opened and a little voice quietly asked: 'Mummy, Daddy, will you be coming upstairs soon?

Chapter 10

On the 9 October 1983 Paul Foot's first story about Southend Council appeared in the Daily Mirror. It was headed:

"Mr Muckley's ins and outs"

Mr and Mrs Brown got a shock when they heard that a council housing boss had moved into their house, which they had let through the council.

The Browns were off to Wales for a year, so they asked the council if it could provide a suitable "short life" tenant for their three-bedroom semi in Shoeburyness, near Southend.

Mr Brown said he dealt with the then assistant director of housing at Southend, Mr William Muckley.

Yes, said the council. It had just the person: a deputy headmistress of a local school.

That was fine by the Browns, and the deputy headmistress and her two daughters moved in the day the Browns left.

Not long afterwards Mr Brown heard from a neighbour that the deputy headmistress - Mrs Christine Holliday - had been joined in the house by Mr Muckley.

Mail

After Mr and Mrs Brown went back to their house a few months later, mail for Mr Muckley kept arriving.

"There was more for him than there was for me." Mr Brown remembers.

"There were application forms for American Express, porcelain, pottery - you name it. He must have been using the address for some time."

Mr Muckley denies ever living at the Brown's house. "I did not live there." He says baldly. He had "no idea at all" how his mail could have arrived at the brown's house.

Asked where he was living at the time he replied "that's none of your business".

He agrees that his department suggested Mrs Holliday for the Browns' "short let" but denies being personally involved.

He is now living with Mrs Holliday in a house she has bought in fashionable Hockley.

Mr Muckley, the senior official in the housing department, has been a controversial figure in Southend for several years.

In 1978, Mrs Ann Archer resigned as senior housing officer in the housing department after 23 years service to the council.

Replies

"I was prevented by Bill Muckley from doing my work as senior lettings officer," she said.

Mr Muckley replies that Mrs Archer was not a lettings officer. But her letter of appointment clearly promotes her to "senior welfare/lettings officer".

In the same year, Mr Muckley resigned from the council of the Institute of Housing after a complaint by a young woman in his department.

Mrs Jane Saxby, then 26, complained that Mr Muckley had called her into his office shortly before she was to take an important Institute of Housing exam, and "leaked" the questions she would be asked.

Mr Muckley was a member of the Institute's examining board.

Mr Peter McGurk, now the director of the Institute of Housing, says: "Muckley was interviewed by senior people in the Institute and, following that, he left our council. I think it is true to say that disciplinary action was taken; though it is true to say that the formal disciplinary procedure of the Institute wasn't used."

From 1978 a series of complaints about the lettings policy of the council under Mr Muckley was made by Tory councillor Ron Levy.

Mr Levy listed cases where good council houses had been let to people who did not seem to be at the top of the council's waiting list.

Mr Levy's persistence led last year to a public enquiry into this

Among the complaints was the fact that Mr Muckley's parents had been re-housed in a council flat after moving from private property.

Mr Fred Laws, town clerk and chief executive of Southend told me "it was proved that there was no substance whatever in the complaints which were gone into in detail, one by one".

Protest

Mr Muckley's solicitors demanded an immediate retraction and apology.

Mr Levy made neither. Nothing happened.

Mr Levy refused to stand for the council last year, in protest against its housing department.

Mr Muckley has many powerful supporters in

Southend.

Mr Fred Laws, for instance, defends him stoutly. "Some extremely defamatory, mischievous and, as far as I can tell, quite untrue allegations have been made against this man," he says.

This week there is even greater proof of Mr Muckley's popularity. He is to be "chaired "as the new Worshipful Master of the Crowstone Lodge of the Southend Masons.

Paul Foot's story caused great consternation among many people in Southend. There were angry protests and denials from Muckley, Laws, councillors, council officials, even Martin Brown questioned the accuracy of the story.

Ron and Patricia thought the article was hilarious, light-hearted. Perhaps even just a little mocking: Yet the events were serious, and there must be legal implication. This time, would Muckley sue Paul Foot as he had threatened to sue Ron? After all, if the story was untrue he would have every right to take legal action and could claim enormous damages.

Ron could hardly wait to telephone John Croft. John babbled excitedly. 'I think Paul Foot has done a wonderful job. It's about time this business was brought into the open. Perhaps something proper will be done about it now.'

Ron agreed with him but he was puzzled. 'Who gave Paul the story? He seems to have got hold of a lot of information.'

Before he had finished speaking Ron heard John chuckle quietly. 'Who, indeed?' he replied. 'But just you wait. I think we are going to hear a lot more from Paul Foot. I do believe he has taken a liking to Southend Council. There's a lot of mileage to be had from the Muckley affair and I think Paul has got the bit between the teeth.'

John was to be proved right. Less than three weeks later, before the storm over his first article had subsided another story appeared in the Daily Mirror, this time with an equally cynical heading:

Lucky for some

More about Mr William Muckley, senior housing official in Southend, and Worshipful Master of the town's Freemasons.

Three weeks ago I told the story of Mr Muckley's move to live with headmistress Mrs Christine Holliday in comfortable semi-detached house let to her by the council's housing department.

Now I hear that when Mrs Holliday left the semi, she was lucky enough to get a brand new flat in The Clusters, a sought-after block near the town centre.

The Clusters is owned by the Springboard Housing Association. The Reverend Ken Start, Springboard's director, tells me that Mrs Holliday had been nominated for the flat by Southend Council.

"We expect the council to make enquiries about housing need in these cases," he says.

The Reverend assured me with some force that he and his association had not known that Mrs Holliday was connected in any way with Mr Muckley.

"If we had known that it might have made a great deal of difference," he mused.

Rev. Start confirms that the flats at The Clusters are in high demand.

"Any accommodation we have has a long list of people waiting for it," he says.

He says that Mrs Holliday lived in The Clusters for about a year. She now lives with Mr Muckley in a house they have bought in fashionable Hockley.

Mr Muckley refused to discuss whether he lived with Mrs Holliday in her flat at The Clusters.

"I have nothing to do with council nominations to housing association flats," he told me.

This latest onslaught to his character revealed an astonishing degree of tolerance by Muckley. He had not started legal proceedings following Paul Foot's previous article and there was no indication that he would do so with this latest one. It was difficult to understand why. After all, if what Paul Foot had written was untrue there was a clear case of libel, and Muckley would have a very strong chance of succeeding in the courts and winning substantial damages.

If Muckley was to do nothing about Paul Foot, there were three councillors who were not prepared to let the matter pass without some kind of response. John Croft demanded to see Fred Laws to discuss the situation. A meeting was held on 3 November 1983. Norman Harris and Joan Carlile also attended. There was an air of deep concern over the Daily Mirror articles. All four present at the meeting agreed that the stories brought the town into disrepute and something must be done to try and end them, or at least officially refute them. Fred explained that he had examined the files relating to the matters referred to in the articles and could find nothing to criticise, describing the stories as "a pack of lies."

The following day Fred Laws wrote to John Croft confirming the main details of the meeting and quoting the facts as he saw them. He concluded his letter by saying; "I gave you the other information in my possession about this issue and the surrounding circumstances and I told you as I tell you now that I regard the stories written by Paul Foot as "a pack of lies."

In reality, this is just what John Croft had hoped for. Fred Laws had fallen into a trap. If the complaints against Muckley were not to fizzle out there needed to be a dramatic development which would ensure continuation of the efforts to bring him to book. Fred had provided that development. John knew that some kind of official recognition of Muckley's conduct was needed to counteract the protracted cover up by Southend Council. John's next step had been carefully planned. If Laws had admitted that Muckley had done wrong, a renewed enquiry would have been demanded. If, as expected, Laws had rejected these latest allegations then a complaint would be lodged with The Press Council; now The Press Complaints Authority. After all, if what Paul Foot had written really was "a pack of lies" then he had done Southend Council a serious misjudgement and he should be compelled to retract his words and apologise. If, on the other hand the articles were judged to be truthful that would provide a powerful weapon with which to continue the battle. On the tenth of November 1983 John Croft wrote to The Press Council enclosing a copy of Fred Laws' "pack of lies" letter and copies of Paul Foot's articles.

The procedures for dealing with complaints against a newspaper were thorough and lengthy. The first step was to send a copy of John Croft's complaint to the editor of the Daily Mirror, Michael Molloy. Mr Molloy replied expressing grave concern:

Before we can reply to this matter in detail I would be grateful if you would let me know each and every allegation in Mr Foot's article which is alleged to be a lie. You are no doubt aware that to describe a journalist as having written "a pack of lies" is about as defamatory a statement as you can possibly make. Should these allegations be repeated in public Mr Foot may find it necessary to take such proceedings as he may be advised in order to restrain them.

John had not expected to be involved in the submission of documents and letters when lodging the complaint but he was determined to see it through. This meant further correspondence with Fred Laws who was most unhappy that John had shown his letter to the Press Council. In his reply Fred sent to John copies of letters from Mr Brown and Mrs Muckley, together with a note of a conversation he had had with the Rev. Start, all were unhappy with the publicity and the content of Paul Foot's articles.

The Editor of the Daily Mirror, Michael Molloy, gave a detailed written explanation and rejection of the allegations and enclosed with his reply copies of two further articles by Paul Foot, which had been published since the complaint was lodged with the Institute. The first article went under the Heading:

More home truths

More news of happy families in my favourite council, Southend. I hear that Mrs Jane Hawes is living happily at The Clusters, a desirable new residence owned by the Springboard Housing Association.

Mr and Mrs Hawes were nominated for the tenancy by Southend Council where Mrs Hawes' brother, David Poulton, is the welfare officer in the housing department.

Readers may recall that another successful applicant to The Clusters was Mrs Christine Holliday, who went to live there with her sweetheart, Mr Bill Muckley, Southend's senior housing officer, in 1981.

The Rev Ken Start, director of Springboard Housing Association, tells me that his association knew nothing of Mrs Hawes' relationship to Mr Poulton.

Mr Bill Muckley tells me he knew nothing about it either.

"These people were nominated correctly in accordance with housing need" he said.

The second article was headed:

"TURNED DOWN FLAT / strange case of a housing chief and his wife's new home"

You may have heard the one about the housing director whose wife got a council nomination for a nice new flat?

It happened, needless to say, in my favourite council, Southend.

When the council sent off its list of nominations to the Utopian Housing Association in September, there on the first page was the name of Joan Thoroughgood, 45, Arlington Road, Thorpe Bay.

Joan Thoroughgood is the maiden name of Mrs Joan Muckley, wife of Mr William Muckley, the town's senior housing official and Worshipful Master of Southend Masons.

45, Arlington Road, a £60,000 detached bungalow, was their marital home for many years before Mr Muckley left it in 1979.

If Mrs Muckley had got a housing association flat, the Arlington Road house could have been put on the market. They were still married when the nomination was made. The "decree nici" for their divorce came later.

Signed

Worshipful Master Muckley explains: "That name was included in that batch issued from this department without my knowledge. It was signed by me, but I sign hundreds of letters that go out each day. Obviously I don't have time to check."

I asked him whether he might have noticed his own former address on the first page of the nominations.

"No, I did not," he said.

Two weeks ago, the chairman of the Utopian Housing Association, Mr Collin George heard that Joan Thoroughgood was Joan Muckley.

He complained to Southend's town clerk, Mr Frederick Laws. Mrs Muckley's name was taken off the list.

As you may remember from earlier articles here, Mrs Christine Holliday had better luck. She left her husband in 1979, was nominated by the council to a lovely flat owned by another housing association, where she was joined by Mr Muckley.

Mrs Holliday now lives with Mr Muckley in Hockley, a fashionable suburb.

I had a letter the other day from Penelopy Grant, solicitor for the local government workers union NALGO.

Puzzle

She complained about "inaccuracies" in my articles about Mr Muckley. Mrs Holliday, she wrote, had been housed by Southend Council because of "urgent need".

This puzzles Southend housing experts, since the home where Mrs Holliday left her husband was not even in Southend.

The solicitor's letter by the way, asked for an apology and damages for Mr Muckley. He got neither,

The Press Council's report ended with its adjudication which was:

The allocation of houses let by local authorities is

a matter of legitimate public interest. The circumstances dealt with in Mr Paul Foot's articles in the DAILY MIRROR were sufficiently unusual to warrant enquiry and comment.

Despite requests, the complainant has not identified to the newspaper or the PRESS Council any inaccuracy reflecting on Southend Council or its officials in the articles and the Press Council is not satisfied that they were misleading. Nor does it find that the articles were unfair.

The complaint against the DAILY MIRROR is therefore rejected.

John Croft read the three short paragraphs through several times. Each time feeling more excited at the implications of the report. It was more than he had dared to hope for. He immediately phoned Ron to tell him the good news. 'You've just got to see this, Ron. It's wonderful. If you've got time I can bring it to you now.

Ron's exhilaration on reading the Press Council's report was beyond measure. 'That's fantastic, John. At last, I've now got official recognition that I was right all along. That lot at the Civic Centre can't possibly deny me that now.

'That's what I thought. But what about Fred Laws? He doesn't come out of it too well, does he?

'Too true,' replied Ron, his excitement clearly subsiding, 'I think it shows that he protected Muckley, but I still can't understand why. He certainly went to extraordinary lengths to prevent the truth coming out.'

'Yes, and made you suffer enormously in the process.' Replied John angrily. But what are you going to do about it?

Ron paused briefly, his thoughts ahead of John's question. Well, I think this exonerates me, without any doubt. And I think the council and Fred Laws owe me an apology. I shall not be wasting any time seeking both. I do thank you, John, for going to all this trouble. You did a brilliant job.'

'It was a pleasure. You know I'm as anxious as you are to sort this business out and get to the bottom of it all. The truth must come out. The public has a right to know that truth.'

When John had left, Ron and Patricia held each other closely. Patricia broke the silence. 'What are you going to do, Ron?

He picked up the report, holding it as though weighing it in his hand. 'First of all I'm going to read this thoroughly. This is a powerful argument and I'm going to use it to clear my name.'

Patricia was worried. There was caution in her voice. 'Do be careful, darling. Fred Laws is a wily old fox. I can't see him submitting easily.'

He hugged her again. 'Always the wise one: I'll be careful. I do love you.'

Three weeks later, after a great deal of soul-searching Ron wrote a carefully drafted letter to Norman Harris:

As you know, Mr Laws' action following the council's 'enquiry' into my allegations against Mr Muckley resulted in my distressing five hour incarceration in a police cell and my family's equally distressing search of my home by the police whist I was in custody. Since this action could not possibly contribute anything productive to the "enquiry" Mr Laws' action can only be interpreted as malicious and vindictive. This, together with his unprofessional conduct in the matter, hardly gives credence or dignity to the high office that he holds.

Needless to say, these occurrences discredited and dishonoured me unjustly and left me devoid of any opportunity to regain my honour and credibility, especially as I was unable to match the administrative resources that were available to Mr Laws.

The recent judgement by the Press Council, following its own thorough investigation into publication of related matters in the Daily Mirror, clearly vindicates me and justifies removal of the slur on my character. Consequently, the time has now come for me to receive a full apology and a retraction of the defamatory comments directed at me by the Committee of Enquiry and, subsequently, the full council.

Ron read his letter through several times to make sure that it said all that he wanted it to say. He was well satisfied. As Leader of the Council it was up to Norman Harris to take the necessary action.

Norman Harris did none of the things that Ron might have expected him to do. But he did reply promptly to Ron's letter saying:

You ask me to bring your letter to the attention of the Conservative Group and the Council. I am not a lawyer but it would seem to me that your letter is undoubtedly libellous of Mr Laws. If that is so, I should be guilty of an offence if I passed your letter to any one except Mr Laws.

I can comment on your reference to the Press Council. The report of that Council is entirely irrelevant to the enquiry into the allegations that you made.

Ron hardly had time to digest what Norman Clark had said when he received a letter from Fred Laws which contained a threat that was to trigger a long drawn-out legal contest. Fred pulled no punches, his anger clearly revealed in the text:

As you know, Councillor Harris has shown to me your letter to him of the 17th August. It is a quite disgraceful and defamatory letter which I cannot ignore. My present employment and future career depend upon my professional competence and integrity and I will defend my reputation against groundless attack regardless of the source.

I cannot let you escape the consequences of describing my conduct as malicious, vindictive and unprofessional whether or not you understand what had occurred and what you are saying. If, therefore, you do not apologise and withdraw this contemptible letter by Friday of this week I will start proceedings in the High Court against you without further notice.

Ron was visibly shaken by Fred's vitriolic letter. He took it to Patricia who read it with growing alarm. 'Oh Ron. This is very serious. What are you going to do?

He sat down, the letter trembling in his hand. 'I don't know yet. I haven't got over the shock. I don't see how he could do that...take me to court: It would cost a fortune. And look at all the evidence: All the stories in the Mirror. He didn't need to call the police. He could have called me in, talked it over; asked me properly how I came by those papers. He was furious with me...he wanted to get...'

Patricia tenderly laid her calming hand on his shoulder, gently placing her index finger on his lips. 'Ron, take it easy. You're babbling...shock reaction. You must think this through carefully. It might cost us a fortune, too. A fortune we haven't got.'

He stood up and held her close to him. 'You're right, darling, of course. I know we couldn't afford to defend a legal action. But I'm convinced he did it to punish me for all the trouble I caused him. If I do what he demands it wouldn't be true. I really can't see him going to such an extreme.'

Patricia drew away from him. 'I'm worried. Ron. I believe you, you know I do. But will a court of law?

Ron was slowly stroking his beard, thinking deeply. 'Hmm. Who knows? It's a bit of a gamble. Perhaps this is the conclusion I need. It's very extreme, I know, but where do I go from here if I throw in the towel now. It would all be in vain, all for nothing. And if I fought and won, the impact would be enormous.'

Patricia's feelings were unchanged. 'I realise all that, Ron. But I'm frightened. I don't want it to come between us. To ruin what we have.'

He drew her to him again and kissed her tenderly. 'I won't let it do that. I love you,' he whispered.

Patricia hugged him tightly. 'And I love you...so much. Just ... please be careful.'

'I will, darling. I will.'

Three days after receiving Fred Laws' letter Ron replied complaining about the tone of the letter and giving a clear indication that he did not intend apologising or retracting.

Ten days later, 17 September 1984, the first legal salvo was fired at Ron. A letter from Drysdales & Janes, Fred Laws' solicitors in Southend, informed him that they had been instructed to issue proceeding but were to give him a final opportunity to retract and apologise.

Ron did neither.

On 17 September 1984 Fred Laws issued proceedings against Ron claiming damages for libel.

CHAPTER 11

Paul Foot's cynical laughter rippled through the richly carpeted corridors of the *Daily Mirror* building in High Holborn, causing occupants of other offices to turn their heads in wonder at what new revelation had reached the ears of the notorious scribe.

'He's done what?' bellowed Paul, when he had regained enough composure to be understood

'He's suing me for libel. I had a letter from him yesterday... dated 17 September 1984' replied Ron, nervously.

Paul sensed Ron's unease. 'Now why on earth would he do that?'

'Well, according to the letter from his solicitor he wants to defend his professional reputation...'

Before Ron could finish the sentence Paul, again, burst into barely-controllable laughter. This time he must have been heard in the street. 'Professional reputation?' he spluttered, 'after all that has happened in Southend during the past few years? He can't possibly be serious.'

Ron could not have agreed more with Paul's sentiment. It seemed quite a ludicrous thing to do. 'That's exactly how I feel, Paul, but I have the writ here in front of me and I don't really know what to do.'

Paul shifted the phone to his other ear. Ron's obvious anxiety had pulled him up sharply to the reality of the situation. 'Well, my friend, the first thing you need to do is to find yourself a good lawyer. And I know... the very man. James Nichol. He's with an extremely good firm of solicitors here in Holborn, Seifert, Sedley and Williams. If you like I'll have a chat with him for you... fill him in on the background.'

'Thanks a million, Paul. That would be very helpful, although I'm not sure about the cost of all this. I know that legal actions like this can be quite expensive.'

'Oh, I think you'll find Jim quite accommodating. This is the sort of case he likes. I'm sure he'll understand your position. Anyway, you have a chat with him and see what he comes up with. Leave it a couple of days so that I can speak to him. I'll just give you his number.

Paul's ear was still hot from Ron's call as he put pen to paper to compose the next episode of the Southend saga: It was short and deliciously barbed, giving him a gem of an opportunity to use Fred's name in a play on words for the heading;

Mr Laws goes to law

Sparks are flying at my favourite council, Southend!
Chief Executive Fred Laws is suing former Tory councillor Ron Levy for
Libel. What's more, Southend ratepayers will be paying his costs.
It seems Mr Levy wrote a letter to the council leader about an inquiry into the housing department.
Mr Laws wrote back to Mr Levy: "It's quite a

disgraceful and defamatory letter which I cannot ignore."

Well blow me! This chap Laws is the one who wrote to another Southend councillor describing my articles as "a pack of lies."

The Press Council couldn't find a lie anywhere.

I could say that Mr Laws' letter was "a disgraceful and defamatory letter which I can't ignore."

But I won't. That would be too pompous by far.

Ron's hopes were given an encouraging boost on his first contact with Jim Nichol. A meeting was arranged in Jim's office, he wanted Ron to bring every letter, document, file, report, copies of council minutes, press reports - everything even remotely connected with the case.

Jim's office occupied a single room in a rambling Victorian building in High Holborn. It was a small office, too small judging by the mountains of files and boxes that littered the room. Not a square inch was unused. Jim carefully sifted through the pile of papers that Ron had placed on his desk. Asking questions here, seeking explanations there. Carefully identifying each paper with a yellow sticky notelet on which he pencilled various comments and dates. On the large, faintly ruled pad beside him he started listing the documents and making meticulous notes. 'He's thorough', thought Ron.'

There were long periods of silence broken only by Jim's occasional remarks and questions as he waded through the pile, at times shaking his head in disbelief, or was it disapproval? The sound of rapid typing, occasionally interrupted by the shrill ring of a telephone, filtered through from the outside office. While Jim continued his task Ron cast his eyes over the contents of the room. It appeared to be in a mess. But he suspected, like himself with the papers in his own study at home, that Jim knew where everything was. 'order in chaos' was the phrase that came to mind. His eyes focussed on a long row of lever arch files on a high shelf to his right, each with the same heading and numbered 1-16. If they were all full there must have been thousands of documents. Something about the headings stirred his memory: 'Bridgewater Four'. It rang a bell from the distant past, but he couldn't immediately think why. It bothered him slightly, knowing it should mean something to him. His thoughts were interrupted by a sharp, confident, rap on the door. Jim's secretary, Linda, peered in, enquired if coffee were needed. Jim eagerly accepted the offer which he extended to Ron. Linda disappeared as quickly as she had appeared, quietly closing the door behind her.

Jim threw his pencil onto the notepad, removed his rimless glasses and rubbed his eyes. 'Seems like a good time to break and discuss the situation, Ron. It seems to me something strange has been going on at the council for a very long time. You appear to have stumbled onto a situation that doesn't immediately make a lot of sense.'

He leaned back, stretched his legs and cradled his head in his hands. 'It seems to me Ron that this letter that you wrote to Norman Harris is, at first sight, quite libellous. But we have to explore the state of your mind at the time of writing it... your motive for writing it. Understandably, you must have felt that there was no need for Fred Laws to inform the police about your possession of the council files: that it was a bit heavy handed. It certainly seems that way to me. He needn't have done that. He could have called you in and said something like; "Come on Councillor, what's it all about? How did you come by these papers? They are obviously photocopies. Do you know what happened to the actual files? Do you really not know who sent them to you?" He's a clever man; he would have known that there was little the police could have done. He would have known that the police would need to question you and that in all probability they would want to search your home. Now, we could claim what's known as 'qualified privilege'. Which means, in layman's terms, that because of your position as a councillor, and your understanding of the system of local government you made those comments in the context of your position: it's a long shot and it may not be enough. What would really help your defence is if you could find a similar situation where Fred Laws had become aware of a possible criminal offence, within the council, which he did not report to the police. That way we could justifiably claim that he singled you out and treated you the way that he did for reasons other than the professional ones that he claims, and that he used the police to get back at you for causing him so much aggravation; so much trouble and extra work.

'Sounds good to me' thought Ron. The coffee arrived. For most of his life Ron had felt that coffee smelled much more delicious than it tasted, especially when passing a shop where coffee beans were being roasted and ground, the tantalising aroma drifting on the air, reaching out, defying anyone to resist its call. This time it was different. It tasted delicious. He sipped eagerly at the rich brown liquid. Linda leaned across the desk as she passed a cup to Jim, her black skirt hugging her trim figure, confirming London's reputation for having some of the most glamorous secretaries in the world. Ron fixed his eyes on the document that Jim had selected for discussion. But he could not ignore Linda's delightful perfume that left a reminder of her visit.

Jim continued. Despite his youthful appearance, he couldn't have been more than 32-33, he seemed to have a good grasp of this area of law. He explained, in simplistic terms, the process leading up to the actual trial. The Summons had already been served. Then there would be the Plaintiff's (that is Fred Laws') Statement of Claim which sets out the effect of the offending letter of alleged libel on his reputation and so on. This would be followed by what is known as 'discovery' which means that every document that the Plaintiff or the Defendant intends to use at the trial must be disclosed to both parties; which also means that either side has a right to ask for a copy of any document that the other side has in their possession or has access to. This would be followed by the Defendant's Reply to the Statement of Claim which would form Ron's defence of the action. When all the document preparations are nearer completion Counsel's opinion is sought which assesses the likely chances of success, or otherwise, of the defence argument. Then of course, it would be down to the Judge and the Jury.

'So, as I said to you earlier, what I want you to do is go away and do some research, find some evidence that Fred

Laws had been made aware of offences that he did nothing about: that he failed to report to the police. Keep looking through your papers and any correspondence you have, however remote from this matter. In the meantime I'll go through these papers again in greater detail, put them in order and start preparing your defence argument. If the case goes ahead the time will come when we will need to get Counsel's opinion, that's when the costs start to take off. But we'll deal with that nearer the time. My own costs I can keep to a minimum, I can see that you're not well off. But I must warn you that this could drag on for some time and it could cost quite a bit of money. It could depend on how anxious Laws is to actually get into court. I understand from Paul Foot that Southend Council have agreed to pay Fred Laws' legal costs. That's a bit naughty, I think I'll write to them and ask them if they will pay your costs as well.' He grinned cynically and started to shuffle the papers into a single neat pile. 'It's a long shot but may be worth a try.' He stood up, stretched, and moved to the front of his desk, extending a hand to Ron. 'Let me know immediately if there are any developments and don't write any more letters or do anything without consulting me first.'

Ron stepped into the outer office. Linda was seated at her typewriter. She looked up and gave him warm smile as she bade him goodbye with brief a wave.

On the bus journey back to Waterloo Station Ron found that he had no great regard for this capital city that visitors from all over the world came to gaze on in wonder. He hated the underground with its scurrying crowds, and long escalators probing deep below the surface. It made him feel vulnerable, trapped; much safer above ground.

Ron was lucky. A train for Southend was waiting on platform 13. He was the first in the carriage and immediately claimed a seat by the window, his back to the engine. The train soon filled with commuters who ritually settled down and prepared for their journey home, folding newspapers, opening books or making small desks of their briefcases. As the train pulled out he pondered all that had happened since first arriving in London that morning. He knew that ahead of him loomed an enormous battle. He knew it was not going to be easy. He wondered how it would affect his family and his finances, how Patricia would react. Despite the small pangs of fear and uncertainty that crept in he drifted into a light sleep.

Stories about Muckley and Southend's housing department continued to appear in the local press and the *Daily Mirror*. On 5 October 1984 the *Southend Evening Echo* reported that John Croft had told the Council Meeting that there was a 'conspiracy of silence' hanging over the housing department regarding his complaints to the Press Council over the stories in the *Daily Mirror*. He was angry that no official statement had been made by the council to refute The Press Council's judgement.

John was supported in his argument by Chris Hudson who said that he had received scores of letters, many of them disturbing. 'We have had a torrent of suspicion for a year or more. Why this conspiracy of silence?' he had asked. 'We should be suing the *Mirror*.'

Norman Clark, now leader of the council, dismissed the

two councillors' complaints saying: 'There is no cover up. There has already been an all-party public investigation and a great deal of time spent considering evidence, much of which was rubbish.'

Three weeks later another of Paul Foot's articles appeared in the *Daily Mirror*, this time under the heading:

Moving story of the Muckley wives

If you're following the saga of my favourite council, Southend, why not compare the fates of the two Mrs Muckleys?

Mrs Muckley the First has to leave her home against her will. Her ex-husband, Mr William Muckley, Southend's chief housing officer, has sent his lawyer to the High Court to get a possession order against her.

The judge, Mr Neil Taylor QC, refused him the order, but insisted that the two-bed roomed bungalow where Mr and Mrs Muckley lived for 7 years should be sold at once.

Mrs Muckley does not want to go. But the terms of her divorce with Mr Muckley last year include the sale of the house, and the division of the proceeds.

Mrs Muckley applied for a council house. She was told she was not eligible. She hung around hoping her ex-husband would allow her to stay but is now obliged to look for a much smaller house.
She is very depressed. She has to live on
£60 a week.

Mrs Muckley the Second used to be married to a post office engineer in neighbouring Rayleigh, Mr

Peter Holliday, she had a mortgage on their house there.

One Friday evening, Mr Holliday came home from work to find the home stripped of all its furniture and carpets, and a note from his wife to say she'd left.

The furniture van crossed the boundary between Rayleigh and Southend, and went straight to a very desirable house in Shoeburyness, which had been let to Mrs Holliday by Southend Housing Department. Mrs Holliday and her daughters were joined there by Mr William Muckley, then assistant director Southend Housing Department.

He spent the nights there and visited his wife in the lunch hour.

Not long afterwards, Mrs Holliday was nominated by Southend Housing Department for a brand new housing association flat in the town centre. Mr Muckley spent the nights with her there, too.

Then the couple bought their own house, got married, and are living happily ever after on a combined income of about £600 a week.

Mr Muckley said very crossly: "I'm not going to discuss my personal affairs with you."

Then, on 31 October 1984, a story appeared in the *Evening Echo* which caused widespread surprise: the heading said it all;

Housing chief to retire early

Mr Bill Muckley, head of Southend housing department, is to retire soon.

Tory leader Councillor Norman Clarke said today: "Under the council's new structure there will be a drastic re-organisation of the housing department and the job held now by Mr Muckley will disappear."A new chief officer will be appointed for the new department.

Mr Muckley is 59 and, in common with other council officers with the required service, should be able to retire on pension.

Councillor Clarke added: "There is no question of a golden handshake."

Mr Muckley was involved in a series of investigations by a committee set up by Southend Council.

Allegations concerning the conduct of the housing department were made by ex-Tory Shoebury councillor Ron Levy.

Mr Muckley was cleared of allegations.

Recent attacks on the housing department by the *Daily Mirror* led Southend Tory councillor John Croft to complain to the Press Council, but the complaint was dismissed.

Mr Muckley was not in his office today and could not be contacted by the *Echo*.

'Housing chief'? thought Ron. He whistled in astonishment. Well, well. So they promoted him to Director of Housing. Despite the huge cloud of suspicion hanging over him for so many years, regardless of all those allegations of misconduct, they upgraded him to chief officer. And now... they sack him: astonishing; and what an amazing coincidence, Ron had just heard that Fred Laws had resigned as Town Clerk, with effect from the very same day. 'Could this be the rats leaving the sinking ship?' Ron asked himself, with a wry smile.

 Paul Foot could not resist this new gem that Ron had passed to him. He wrote another story about his 'favourite' council to add to the growing list. This was written under the heading:

Exit Mr Muckley

Mr William Muckley, chief housing officer at my favourite council, Southend, Essex, has been made redundant. Mr Roy Peacock, who took over last week as Southend's chief executive, told me he has handed Mr Muckley a statutory notice, and Mr Muckley will be leaving the council on January 27'

Mr Peacock says this is part of a "general reorganisation of property services. One can't have too many chief officers. Mr Muckley is the senior officer nearest to pensionable age and he accepted that his name should be top of the list for redundancy."

Did Mr Muckley's redundancy have anything to do with the articles I have written since October last year about him and his department?

"That is not a matter on which I could express an opinion," said Mr Peacock, after a long silence.

P.S. Mr Muckley was promoted to chief housing officer in July.

This was getting better all the time. Ron gleefully cut out the press stories and filed them ready for his next visit to Jim Nichol. Jim did write to the council, albeit tongue in cheek, suggesting that they might also pay Ron's legal costs, especially since this legal action against him resulted from his work as a councillor. As expected, the council would have none of it and rejected the request in a terse letter.

It was now mid-November. Nothing was likely to happen before Christmas and Jim suggested that Ron take a break and leave matters until the new year, but to continue looking out for any further papers and press cuttings.

Then, on January 30 1985 a shock headline appeared unexpectedly in the *Evening Echo.* A friend had brought the paper into the shop and shown it to Ron. At first glance he thought it referred to Muckley but as he read on he realised it was someone else. By the time he had reached the third paragraph he was trembling and perspiring. This was brilliant. It could turn the tide for him. Unable to conceal his excitement, he rushed out into the kitchen to show Patricia. 'You must read this,' he blurted, 'I haven't read it all yet but… just the opening… it's unbelievable… fantastic.'

Patricia was preparing the children's tea. She stopped what she was doing and grasped his hand. 'Calm down, Ron. I've told you before you'll burst a blood vessel. Let me see.'

'Right. OK. But I think we'd better sit down. My legs feel wobbly.'

They sat together at the table, sharing the paper, both expressing disbelief and astonishment as they read the article. The headline was bold and to the point:

HOMES PROBE: MAN FIRED

A senior official in Southend Council's housing department, responsible for the administration of council housing grant scheme, was sacked today.

He was dismissed by Southend's Town Clerk and Chief Executive Officer, Mr Roy Peacock.

The dismissal followed a detailed police investigation into the administration of the home improvement grants scheme.

On Monday it was announced a man had been charged and papers relating to the police probe forwarded to the Director of Public Prosecutions.

The man already charged was not a member of the council staff.

At the same time it was announced an official in the housing department had been suspended on full pay, pending an enquiry.

Now the council's investigation is complete.

I understand the sacked official has been in local government for 30 years, 10 of them with Southend Council.

Mr Peacock said he was prevented from naming the employee. Police also refused to name him.

Triggered

An Essex Police spokesman said: "The investigation is continuing and other people have yet to be interviewed."

Police action was triggered following information presented by Councillor Reg Coppley, leader of the council Labour group, to the Town Clerk concerning the operation of the home improvement grant scheme.

After preliminary investigations the council called in police.

The council says the police investigation is confined to the housing grant scheme administering section. No other activity of the town's housing department is involved.

Following the retirement of Mr Bill Muckley as housing manager, the department is without a chief officer.

Southend Council is now advertising for a new Director of Property Services who will also become responsible for the administration of the housing department and control of all property owned by the council.

There have been over 20 applications for the job. A short list is being drawn up.

The story was breathtaking. The breakthrough that Ron could not possibly have expected: and certainly more than he could have hoped for.

'Phew, that's incredible.' said Patricia, pointedly. 'But what's it all about? There must be very strong evidence of a criminal offence for the police to act as they have.' She shook her head disapprovingly. 'D'you know, I was right. I knew there was something big behind all this business with the housing department. I said they came down too hard on you for trying to get an enquiry. What you were complaining about was small fry. Yet they tried to stop you.

There just had to be more to it than appeared on the surface.'

Ron interrupted: 'Yes, darling. I think you must have been right. I should have trusted your intuition. I just couldn't imagine what it could be. But this... this is... I must get more information about it. I must tell Jim Nichol straight away. I'm sure it will help my case.'

'Yes, and I must get on with the children's tea. Judging by the noise they're making up there they are probably waiting for me to call them for it.'

'And I must get back to the shop. My customers will think I've deserted them.'

Difficult as it was to concentrate on his work Ron managed to finish his last customer. He couldn't remember attending any of them since he had returned to the shop. His memory had effectively buried them beneath the excitement of these latest revelations. Like driving through a town and not remembering doing so, as sometimes happens.

That evening Ron phoned around. Anne Archer had heard rumours but hadn't been able to find out exactly what had happened. Chris Hudson was aware that the police were investigating but he could not get any details; the enquiry was still at a very early stage and was extremely confidential: it seemed that no-one at the Civic Centre was prepared to discuss the matter. He was mystified and very concerned. He promised to phone Ron immediately if he heard anything new. John Croft was equally uninformed. Ron would have to be patient and await developments.

The following day Ron phoned Jim Nichol and read the

Echo report to him. 'That's pretty damning, Ron. It could show that you were on to something. And, as that story reveals, it was something very big, very serious. But I'm not sure exactly how it is going to help your defence.'

Ron was momentarily lost for words. His spirits had plummeted along with his newly found hope. When he spoke his throat was dry. 'But how can that be? Surely it shows that there was criminal activity going on in the housing department...that I was justified in demanding an enquiry... a proper enquiry... that I was right... that there was a cover-up.'

Jim sensed Ron's distress and tried to calm him. 'All that may be true, Ron, and you'll be congratulated and praised for your fortitude and integrity. But it need not necessarily show that Laws acted maliciously in setting the police onto you. What I'm saying is it would be difficult to convince a jury that he did so just with this story. If you remember I did say that you need to find a situation, a reportable offence that he was made aware of but which he then failed to report to the police. That way we could possibly show that he singled you out when he reported you to the police.'

Again, Jim broke Ron's silence. I know how disappointing that must sound to you, Ron, but we have to be realistic. Yes, it's a brilliant story which will, without a doubt, help to justify your actions. But the other side's lawyers will demolish it in court.' Jim softened his tone. 'Look, Ron, there's no hurry, this is going to take a long time before it comes to court, but I'll need to see you to start putting the papers in order and preparing your discovery list: I'll certainly need the report you just read to me. Perhaps you could send me a copy, I'll read it through again to see if there is anything useful in it that I can use.'

Jim was right. It did all sound very disappointing. And that disappointment came across in Ron's trembling voice when he told Patricia of Jim's reaction to these latest developments. He began to have doubts; to wonder whether it was all really worth the struggle and the stress. As always, Patricia was calming and reassuring. 'Why don't you switch off for a while; Give yourself a break from it all. Jim said there's no hurry. Spend some time with me... with the children. It'll do you a power of good. You can return to it later with a fresh mind. Perhaps to decide how far you want it to go.'

Her appealing, almost pleading tone was irresistible. Ron gave a deep sigh, drew her to him and held her closely. He kissed her tenderly. 'You are absolutely right, darling, and I love you very, very much.

A mysterious cloud of silence had descended upon the police investigation. No further press reports. No word from the council. Rumours were rife but no information was available. Then, on the evening of 18 March 1985 Ron received a telephone call from Allan Goble, a builder from Westcliff-on-Sea. 'I don't know if you remember me, Ron. You helped me out with a planning problem about eighteen months ago.' Ron rapidly searched his memory but the name did not ring a bell. 'It's about this business in the housing department, the home improvement grants fiddle.'

Ron's heart skipped a beat. 'Yes,' he croaked, his voice barely audible. 'I read a little about it in the *Echo* some weeks ago but nothing since.'

Allan continued. 'I know you've been trying for a long time to uncover the goings-on at the council and I know it's been difficult. I've got some information which I think may help you. The property behind the police investigation is number 26, Park Road, Westcliff. It's a three-story Victorian house. About a year ago I was asked to quote for converting the building into two flats. I didn't get the job and I gave it no more thought. But a few months later, October it was, I was given some papers that made me very angry. I've got them in front of me now. The papers are copies of a Home Improvement Grant Notice of Approval for 26, Park Road. But when I saw the amount, the estimated costs of the conversion, I nearly fell of my chair. It was for £23,253. It was the same job I quoted for in March and my estimate was for £11,650... almost double my price. It was an obvious fiddle: a big one.'

Ron's heart pounded harder against his chest. 'That's staggering.' He croaked. 'The thieving bastards. And they covered it up all this time. But what did you do about it, Allan?'

'Well, I would have got in touch with you but I'd heard you wasn't on the council any more, and so I got in touch with Reg Copley 'cause he's my ward councillor. I told him about it and showed him the papers and we took them to the Town Clerk, Mr Laws. Nothing seemed to be happening and Reg Copley got in touch with Mr Laws a few times, but it seemed that he didn't report it to the police...'

'He did what!' shrieked Ron, his heart now beating almost unbearably. 'Would you repeat that, Allan.' he begged, his throat now even more constricted.

'Mr Laws didn't report the complaint to the police. Apparently it was only reported to the police after Mr Laws left and the new Town Clerk took over.'

Ron rambled on excitedly. This was incredible; exactly what he needed; A truly wonderful, unexpected gift. 'Forgive me Allan. I'm completely astounded. You don't know how valuable this information is to me. Would you put all that in writing, with a copy of the grant papers?'

'Of course I will. I don't see why they should get away with it. I know you'll do something about it. In any case, they used me and I don't like that.'

'Allan, that is really fantastic. I'll never be able to thank you enough. You've saved my life.'

Allan was a little overwhelmed by Ron's reaction. 'Don't worry about it. I'm pleased it's going to help you. I'll drop you a line straight away. If I can help with any more information give me a ring. Good luck.'

There was an unusual hint of excitement in Jim Nicol's voice. 'That's wonderful news, Ron. If we can prove that Fred Laws failed to report the matter to the police, I think we are home and dry. It would be a powerful argument. But I don't think we should be over confident. We'll need to find out from the police themselves who actually reported the complaint to them. You say this builder is prepared to put the details in writing.'

'Allan Goble. Yes he said he would do it right away, but I couldn't wait to tell you about his call...'

Jim interrupted him. 'Well I can understand that. It sounds too good to be true. But I'll need to see the papers. I'd like

185

you to send them to me as soon as you receive them. Then I can examine them before we meet. We must do that soon. Can you fix a date now… say in a couple of weeks?'

'I'm sure I can. I'll just get my diary.' A date was arranged, and Ron was reminded, again, about bringing any other relative documents, notes and press cuttings.

The next call had to be to Anne Archer. She would be astounded. She was. 'Now things are beginning to fall into place.' she said, having recovered from the initial surprise. 'Of course, I never had anything to do with the grants department. And I hadn't realised that Muckley was responsible for authorising payment of the grants. Come to think of it, he never ever spoke about that side of things. I wonder if he knew about the fiddle. I'd be surprised if he didn't. We shall have to see what the police come up with. By the way, how is your case coming along?

'Oh, it seems to be going very slowly at the moment. I'm seeing Jim in two weeks' time. I've just told him about these papers from Allan Goble. He thinks it could be a really big breakthrough.'

'I do hope so, Ron.' replied Anne anxiously. 'You can't really afford to lose. Anyway, I'm sure you'll keep me posted. Good luck. And we'll speak again soon.'

Allan Goble's word was good. His letter arrived the following day. It was hand written on his headed notepaper, Borough Construction, and it was dated 21 March 1985. He wrote:

> With reference to our recent discussion regarding the police enquiries into serious irregularities in the Southend Council Housing Department's

administration of home improvement grants, I would confirm that I first brought the matter to the attention of Councillor Copley early in October 1984. Councillor Copley called at my home, together with Nigel Smith, secretary of Southend Labour Party, and I gave him copies of papers similar to those which I enclose with this letter to you. The contents of these papers indicate very clearly a prima facie case of misconduct, because of the colossal difference between my estimated costs of carrying out the improvements, and the cost of improvement grant claimed, and approved, under the Improvement Grant scheme. Councillor Copley and Mr Smith expressed their concern at the situation and suggested the Town Clerk, Mr Laws, be informed. This Cllr Copley did within 24 hrs. It appears that Mr Laws failed to inform the police of the matter. Cllr Copley frequently contacted Mr Laws regarding the complaint and it was only when the new Town Clerk, Mr Roy Peacock, took over that the police were informed immediately. As you know, the Fraud Squad are now investigating and charges have already been brought against the Director of a local development company who was involved in the matter. In fact the actual building costs were £10,000, works being carried out by a Mr D. Carter. This has been confirmed to the police.

If I can be of any further assistance please contact me again.

Attached to Allan's letter was a letter from the housing

department to a Mr Hanlon of 30, Seaview Road, regarding 26, Park Road, informing him that his application dated 1December 1983 for an Improvement Grant had been authorised in the sum of £14,019.75 being 75% of the cost eligible for grant purposes.

To Ron's astonishment, and delight, the letter was actually signed by W M Muckley. It gets better and better, he thought. Attached to the letter was a copy of the Certificate of Approval which gave a detailed breakdown of the grant and costs. This was signed by T F Herman, the council's Home Improvement Grant officer. Allan had also enclosed a copy of his estimate for the work to 26, Park Road with full details of the improvements to be carried out.

This was the full picture: the specimen fraud documents that triggered the police investigation. Ron read them through again, this time with Patricia. Their conclusions were mutual. It was no surprise that the police had decided immediately to investigate. Any first year law student would have instantly reasoned that the situation was a prima facie case of serious fraud and that the police should have been informed without delay.

Ron and Patricia would have dearly liked to talk more about this incredible development but the children had to be prepared for school, and the shop had to be opened.

Ron wasted no time. During the lunch break he quickly typed a letter to Jim Nicol and sent copies of Allan Goble's papers to him. As he dropped the letter in the post box he felt good. The tide was turning in his favour and hope took a great leap forward. The truth is now out and he no longer feared his day in court.

Chapter 12

Thursday 21 March 1985:

The period of inactivity in the legal process had provided valuable time to enable Ron to work on his search to find a buyer for 55, West Road, which had now produced a firm offer. He had already chosen to use a solicitor in Colchester who would also deal with the purchase of their new home there. If the sale went through without a hitch it would take only three or four months to complete.

Ron and Patricia immediately set a date to visit Colchester, to call on estate agents and to scan local papers to find a property. They eagerly took down the wall calendar and opened their diaries. 'Oh, don't forget the shop appointment book, Ron,' urged Patricia.

Oh yes. Of course, I'll go and get it now. Thanks, Patricia.' He disappeared and quickly returned with the book He set it down beside the calendar and diaries and they both studied them. 'There we are... next Monday 25 March or Thursday 28' suggested Ron. Patricia looked at the dates and agreed. 'Perhaps Gill will spend the day here looking after the shop and Rachel, the older ones can look after themselves. Let's phone her now... see if she's free.'

Gill could manage either of the days and was thrilled that

their plans seemed to be going well. So, with great excitement the visit to Colchester to find a new home was to take place on the Thursday.

The journey to Colchester began under a grey sky. Patricia and Ron talked over their plans and hopes for the day. Their feelings were of optimism, tinged with a little excitement. They wanted to view as many houses as was practically possible and had decided that they were prepared, if necessary to choose one that could be a temporary home whilst they searched at leisure for the ideal home in the ideal location..

When they arrived they made their way to the St Mary's multi-story car park in the Town Centre. From there they walked across the narrow footbridge over Balkerne Hill and through the ancient archway in the Roman Wall, along the narrow streets past the Mercury Theatre and into Head Street: There they called in at a newsagent and bought a copy of the *Essex County Standard* and then found the nearest coffee shop to study the 'Properties for Sale' columns over a hot drink: None of them caught their attention.

They then turned to the pages of estate agents' advertisements and worked their way through them. Despite the large number of houses listed there were only five that appeared to be worth following up, fortunately, they were listed between just two of the many agents, which should help to save time arranging to view

William H Brown was the estate agent that held three of the five properties that Ron and Patricia had selected and they were soon entering their offices. Ron was first to speak after both being made comfortable at a desk of one of the sales assistants, Mr Boyland. After the formalities Ron produced the newspaper and indicated that they would like to see details of the three properties in their advertisement.

Ron and Patricia carefully read through the agent's broadsheet of each of the selected properties and decided that it would be worth viewing them. Mr Boyden telephoned the owners immediately and, surprisingly, was able to make appointments with all three owners for that day; one during the remainder of this morning, the other two after lunch. Mr Boyland produced a local street map and marked the exact location of each property.

Armed with the map, and with feelings of nervous apprehension, Ron and Patricia set off to the first viewing to find their new home. The first house was on a small, fairly new estate named 'The Painters', in an area about two miles south of the town centre called Prettygate. They pulled up outside the house and looked at it for a few seconds. They turned to each other and could tell that they both had the same feeling about it; doubts that it was the right one. But they decided to view it anyway.

When they returned to the car to discuss it they were pleased that their instincts had not let them down. There being very little left of the morning they decided to go back into town for some lunch.

Over lunch they took a closer look at the agent's broadsheet for their next viewing: It was a late 1930s built three bedroom semi-detached house, which was also in

Prettygate, with an eighty-foot rear garden, and a front drive that could easily accommodate three cars.

They arrived at the house, which was in All Saints Avenue. Even a quick glance told them that this was very different from the first one they had viewed. There was something about it that was warm and inviting: Perhaps it was its age, or even the location. And at a price of £34,000 seemed pretty good value. This time they approached the house with eager anticipation. As they were shown from room to room they gave no indication of how they felt about it, which was what they had previously agreed to. They thanked the owner for showing them around her lovely home and told her that they had one more property to view following this one.

On the way back to the car Ron slid his arm around Patricia's waist and briefly drew her close to his side. Patricia knew what he meant but, like him, was struggling to conceal her feelings about this house, and gave him a quick smile. Once inside the car they agreed that they should be careful not to make any hasty decisions, but both of them equally agreed that it was a really lovely house. There was one more to view; when they had seen it they both felt that it was quite nice, but that it was no real comparison to the All Saint's Avenue home.

It was now mid-afternoon and there was time for another visit to the coffee shop. They both felt elated, and they just knew they needed to talk about their viewings before going back to the estate agent. The first and third properties were soon dismissed as of no interest. As they sipped their coffee they took a closer look at the details described on the spreadsheet for the All Saints Avenue house, relating them to what they had seen at the viewing. There was no doubt in their minds that this would really suit their needs, and that they had both taken an immediate liking to the house and garden, and to the neighbourhood. They just could not believe that they had so quickly found a property that they both felt so excited about; that they would like to live in. There was just time to go back to Mr Boyland and discuss the way forward. Patricia told Ron that she would like him to conduct the main discussions, especially if those discussions led to making an offer, which she would be very happy to agree with.

Mr Boyland welcomed Ron and Patricia back into his office and they resumed the positions they held on their first visit. There were many questions to be answered, which Mr Boyland dealt with expertly and helpfully. Patricia reminded him that it was important to synchronise the purchase of the Colchester house with the sale of their property in Shoeburyness: they didn't want to find themselves in limbo, homeless, between the two transactions. Mr Boyland smiled and reassured her. William H Brown had been established in Colchester for more than 120 years and had a really good reputation, he assured her that the company would do everything possible to achieve a speedy completion, and told her the owner was anxious to find a buyer quickly because they, too, had found their ideal property and didn't want to lose it. Ron and Patricia glanced at each other and nodded: Ron turned to Mr Boyland and made an offer at the asking price.

The move to Colchester finally took place on 7 July 1985.

CHAPTER 13

Months dragged by. Ron had several further meetings with Jim Nicol, preparing all the papers for the trial. Every document had to be listed in meticulous order and numbered. This was the Discovery List that Jim had referred to in the early days of the action. A copy of the list must be sent to Fred Laws' solicitors who, in turn, would be required to send a copy of their Discovery List to Jim.

Both sides would then be allowed to request copies of these, and any other documents, for their own use at the trial. When both sides were satisfied that all relevant documents had been disclosed the two lists would be put together. Each page would then be numbered and the new list would be known as the Trial Bundle.

Copies of the Trial Bundle would be given to the Judge, to each member of the jury, and would be used by Fred Laws' counsel and by Ron during the conduct of the trial. It all seemed very fair and civilised. But this was a very serious contest which would be fought vigorously by both contestants.

With Jim's guidance Ron set about his task, meticulously making notes for his defence argument and cross-referencing them individually to each numbered document in the Trial Bundles.

It was a painstaking, time consuming task but a picture was emerging which he hoped would convince a jury in his favour. Normally this part of the preparation would be undertaken for Ron by a barrister, but it had already been established that the employment of such legal representation was far beyond his financial means: unlike Fred Laws who had unlimited public funds available to him to pay for a barrister of his choice.

For Ron to carry out this very important task was difficult on its own, to do so whilst travelling back and forth between Shoeburyness and Colchester trying to arrange the house move was extreme

Apart from Allan Goble's revelations, the silence that had descended on the town so many months earlier came to a dramatic end. On 10 October 1985 the *Evening Echo* published a story, again written by Del Flatley, the paper's political correspondent, under a bold heading that declared:

Police tell of huge investigation

Council grants:

Fraud squad probes 500 cases

Fraud squad officers at Essex Police HQ are investigating more than 500 cases of alleged building improvement grant irregularities at Southend Council.

This was revealed at a conference attended by Deputy Chief Constable Mr Roy Stone.

Tory council leader Norman Clarke, Labour leader Reg Copley and Tory councillors John Croft and Christopher Hudson were also there.

Deception

The meeting followed a call by Councillor Croft to Chief Constable Mr Robert Bunyard.

The alleged irregularities first came to light through a complaint made to Councillor Copley on October 16 last year.

Officers of Southend Council's internal audit investigated and the matter was then referred to the police.

Further enquiries followed and a council official was sacked in January.

Then police brought a charge of deception against a builder. This was later withdrawn.

The investigation then developed into a probe into the council's entire home improvement grant organisation.

Fraud squad officers then took over.

In a statement after the meeting, Southend Town Clerk Mr Roy Peacock said: "Since then a considerable amount of research has been undertaken by fraud squad detectives working in close liaison with the council's internal auditors and under the direction of the Director of Public Prosecutions."

The investigations have to be very thorough and a considerable number of files have been referred to the police, although it is unlikely that irregularities will be found in every case.

"The council has given the police unlimited access to all its files, ensuring their investigation can be completely independent of all enquiries being carried out by the council's own officers."

Mr Peacock feels the size and complexity of the investigation, mainly in fraudulent claims for grants, mean it will take a considerable amount time.

The final decision on any action will rest with the Director of Public Prosecutions.

Investigated

A full report is also being prepared for councillors by the internal auditors.

The Town Clerk added: "In the past few weeks, Councillor Hudson has given details of grants which he considers should be investigated. However, all these cases were already under investigation. No new cases have been brought to the council's attention since Councillor Copley raised the original query."

Councillor Clarke said everyone at the meeting expressed complete support and confidence in the conduct of the enquiry by the fraud squad.

The story was sensational. It raised Ron to even greater heights of exhilaration. His mind was in turmoil; question after unanswerable question racing through it. Fortunately he had read the story after the last customer had departed and the shop closed. Had he seen it before closing he could not possibly have concentrated on his work. And there were so many people he wanted to phone.

He took the paper through to the kitchen to show Patricia, but the children were milling around noisily. It wasn't the right time. At the moment the children needed her attention more than he did. He would phone Anne Archer instead. Returning to the shop the phone rang before he could reach it. It was Anne. 'Have you seen the today's *Echo*?' she asked, with astonishing calmness.

'Anne. Hi. I was just about to ring you. You beat me to it. I certainly have read it. It's mind-boggling ... unbelievable.'

There was a chuckle in Ann's voice. 'Yes, good isn't it.'

'Good? Good? Anne, that has to be the understatement of the year. And to think we all thought 26, Park Road was the only one: That on its own was serious... but five hundred? However long has it all been going on? And did Muckley sign them all? I wonder if he was one of those charged.' I tell you what really puzzles me in the report: It says Chris Hudson gave details of other grants which should be investigated, which the Town Clerk said were already under investigation; It then goes on to say that no new cases have been brought to the council's attention since Reg Copley raised the original query. Since Reg Copley raised only one query, ie 26, Park Road, all the other subsequent cases which the Town Clerk said were already under investigation must have been new cases. So the Town Clerk is surely contradicting himself.'

'Yes, Ron. I can see that. But how many others will? It just shows what a devious lot they are at the Civic Centre. I can think of quite a few questions I'd like answered, too. But I think we are going to have to wait until the police have finished their investigations.' She chuckled again mischievously. 'I can't wait.'

It was several more phone calls, and at least an hour later, before Ron took the paper through to Patricia to share the excitement with her of these latest revelations.

Again, months passed and nothing seemed to be happening. Ron plodded on with his task. He now had scores of pages filled with numbered notes and references to his trial documents. There were some gaps, but as Jim had said, these could be filled by documents from Fred Laws' solicitors. As he worked, he listed what other papers he needed from Fred Laws and the council.

Then on 30 May 1986 another sensational story appeared in the *Evening Echo*. It was a front page story this time under a headline that pulled no punches:

COUNCIL FIDDLE: POLICE QUIZ 12

TWELVE people were helping police with enquiries into the alleged housing improvement grant fiddle at Southend.

All, including one who was stopped waiting to board a plane at Gatwick, were being interviewed by CID.

Essex Deputy Chief Constable Mr Ronald Stone confirmed today that the investigations had reached its final stages.

He said: "We concentrated on inspecting properties concerned. We then waded through masses of paperwork.

"We have established that a number of offences have been committed."

A spokesman at county police headquarters said today some had gone voluntarily to police headquarters for questioning.

He added: "Others have been arrested. All those concerned have been released on bail to appear at Southend police HQ again in August.

"So far nobody has been charged."

Sacked

Essex Fraud Squad has been probing more than 500 cases of alleged grant irregularities.

Southend council officials have given large numbers of files over to the police.

The alleged irregularities came to light in October 1984 following a complaint by Labour leader Councillor Reg Copley.

Officers of Southend's internal audit investigated, and then police took over.

Further inquiries followed and a council official was sacked in January.

At one stage, documents and statements were presented to the Director of Public Prosecutions who ordered the Essex Fraud Squad to continue its investigation.

It has taken a long time to unravel everything.

Reports have been kept going to the DPP.

Ron wondered how much more of these shocks his

heart could take. He had to show the paper to Patricia immediately. He quickly went across to the newsagent and bought an extra copy. While she was reading it he phoned Anne Archer. As expected, Anne had already seen the story.

'What do you make of it, Anne?' asked Ron. 'All those people being questioned: twelve of them. I'd give a lot to know who they are.'

'So would I, Ron. So would I.' She replied with her usual calmness. 'But do you know what puzzled me about the story. The fact that the council's internal audit officials investigated before the police took over. That means Fred Laws and his officers would have questioned people in the grant section, and looked at the files before informing the police. If nothing else it would have alerted all those involved in the fiddle that their cosy little scam had been uncovered. That might explain why someone was picked up at Gatwick Airport. Makes you wonder if he would have ever been seen again if the police hadn't got there before the plane took off.'

'I hadn't thought of that, Anne. But you are absolutely right. That was a clever move. I wonder if the police were shown everything. But in any case, I've seen a copy of the grant for 26, Park Road. As you know Allan Goble gave me a copy. It was so obviously fraudulent. The difference between Allan's estimate and the grant claim was double the actual cost of the improvements. The police should have been informed immediately.

Anne chuckled cynically. 'I couldn't agree more. Of course, the likes of you and I would have reported such a matter immediately to the police. But that lot at the Civic Centre don't seem to behave in the same way as us lot.'

'Well, Allan said quite clearly in his letter that the police were not informed immediately, and that suits me fine because that's exactly what Jim Nicol asked me to find: to help my defence. He's already seen Allan's letter and the grant papers. But this story is a bonus. I can't wait to tell him about it. In fact, I'm going to do that next.'

'Brilliant! … brilliant.' said Jim Nicol, in a rare burst of excitement. 'Let me have a copy of that, Ron. I'll include it in the trial bundle. Well done. Keep digging and let me have every scrap of information you can get hold of on the matter. I think we're really getting somewhere now.'

Ron returned to his list of papers that he needed from Jackson for the Trial Bundle. Wasting no time he immediately wrote asking for copies of those papers.

CHAPTER 14

It was a bright, sunny May morning. The postman made his usual rattle of the letterbox, which was followed by the now-familiar thud of the mail hitting the hall carpet.

Ron casually made his way to the front door and gathered up the pile of envelopes, mostly large ones that he frequently received. He flicked through the bundle to see if there was anything particular that might catch his attention: and there was, a brown A4 envelope postmarked Aldwich London.

Ron took a sharp intake of breath. 'Could this be…?' he muttered to himself. Quickly tearing the envelope open he extracted the folded document. It looked official: and it was. As he unfolded it he immediately saw the heading and his pulse raced with excitement, it read; The Royal Courts of Justice.

'This is it… at last; A date for the hearing.' Ron hurried into the kitchen calling Patricia as he did so. Patricia turned towards him and took the document that he eagerly held out for her to read. 'Well, Ron, it's what you've been waiting for. August 12 1988, she read aloud: that's three months from now.'

Ron took the paper back and looked at it again. 'That's right. That will be… 4 years from the date of the writ being served, and… 3 years from our move here to Colchester. He paused again. But I wonder, why on earth has it taken so long? It doesn't make sense. Four years to come to trial? Surely this case should have been heard by now. I remember Jeffery Archer's libel action against the *Daily Star* newspaper was heard within 3 months. Perhaps Fred Laws was stalling; hoping that I might withdraw because of the potential costs of continuing to defend the case.'

Such a possibility had occurred to Ron many times throughout the long wait, and it *was* a very long wait. At one time the matter had reached a position where it seemed pointless to continue: where the objective seemed to have no real purpose.

Patricia took hold of Ron's hands and looked at him, almost pleadingly. 'Ron, darling. I know this means so much to you. You have fought so hard to right this wrong. And in so many ways you are right. But these are powerful people: and we are not. What happens if you lose the case? I am anxious. Could we lose our home?'

Ron drew her close to him and hugged her tenderly. Yes, I know you are, darling. And you know I don't want to do anything to hurt you. I know there is an element of risk in any legal action. But I have fairly strong evidence in my defence. Jim feels that I have a good chance of proving my case. After so much suffering and sacrifice I can't help feeling it would be tragic if I were to withdraw now. And no, we wouldn't lose our home if I were to lose the case: as you are joint owner of the house they couldn't force a sale because the debt would be mine and they could not force the sale of your interest in the property.

Patricia gripped his hands again, very tightly, and looked into his eyes for what seemed an eternity: silent. Ron could not know, exactly, what was going through her mind. He knew he should say nothing more. She slowly released her grip and wrapped her arms around him. He held her close. Ron... darling... I do love you. Ron was choked. He had tears. He could not speak. They kissed briefly, tenderly. He knew that Patricia needed to be alone. They slowly parted and

Ron went to his study.

He sat staring at his blank computer screen. He knew he should write something... about all that had brought him this... that had almost broken his precious relationship with Patricia. But it had all been so heavy. It had to be something light. He switched on the computer. While he waited for it to open up the answer came to him... he would commit the whole story to verse. Inspiration came to him and he started writing:

> This sad tale began,
> when Fred said to Anne
> "Twenty years to Southend you have given.
> With conduct obscure,
> from Bill Muckley, 'tis sure,
> from your post you have surely been driven."

> "Justice," Fred cried,
> "you'll not be denied,
> I'll examine this case: You'll be heard."
> Muckley's conduct absurd
> did continue uncurbed.
> Fred Laws had failed with his word.

> Thus Anne did depart,
> but she did not lose heart.
> Fred Laws to reveal she did vow.
> A new councillor friend,
> whom truth would not bend,
> and to pressure from high would not bow.

> So Councillor Ron,
> pressed relentlessly on
> with tales of the rules being bent.

"Tis not so," cried old Fred,
"too much has been said.
I'm not aware of such an event."

Ron gathered facts
of unscrupulous acts,
and insisted the Council should hear.
As pressure was spent
Fred had to relent.
An 'enquiry' date thus appeard.

But cunning old Fred
was not yet dead,
and a special report was contrived.
Poor Ron could not know
to the slaughter he'd go
when the 'enquiry' conclusion arrived.

Councillors Harris and Clarke
shook their heads and said "hark,
Ron's conduct we surely deplore.
In making such claims
he discredits our aims.
We must stop him before he says more."

Ron showed papers he'd taken.
The Council was shaken.
How did he get hold of those files?
Fred's vain appeal,
their source to reveal,
was unable to break Ron's denials.

To Muckley's relief
Ron's branded a thief.

Fred pondered what deed to release.
"I've got it" he shook,
"it's in the rule book.
I can call in the chief of police."

Fred surely did well,
Ron's locked in a cell
for hours, while police search his pad.
Though inquiries are large,
the police bring no charge.
Ron's freedom's at last to be had.

These stories we hear
have come to the ear
of Paul Foot,
The notorious scribe.
In his page he has said,
all these tales about Fred.
And did Muckley's conduct describe.

Paul's tales Fred denies,
"they're a pack of lies.
It's disgraceful the way Foot has hinted.
What he says is untrue,
but I don't think I'll sue.
Could be he can prove what he's printed."

Fred's taken aback
by Ron's counter-attack,
which says Fred's action was wrong.
To have Ron thrown in clink.
What else could he think
when Fred knew Ron was right all along.

Fred's anger emerged,
and from Ron he has urged
a retraction of words he did say.
"I'll defend my good name
from such damaging claim."
And issued a writ straight away.

Tis more than a year
since the writ did appear
and a hearing is nowhere in sight.
Why does Fred delay?
is he dreading the day
the court will consider his plight?

Thus will battle commence
and with Ron's strong defence
Fred's libel can hardly be won.
Though the cost will be high,
let no one deny,
it must be shown what the Council has done.

Now, apart from a few more papers he had requested from Jackson, Ron's preparations were complete. He had written pages of questions he wanted to put to Fred Laws and other witnesses in court. Each question was numbered and cross-referenced to a numbered document or file in the Trial Bundle. The list had taken more than a year to compile in the little spare time that he had. But it was worth it. Jim Nicol had agreed it was looking good. Jane Saxby had agreed to give evidence in Ron's defence. And with the help of the Office at The Royal Courts of Justice he had obtained subpoenas to call Muckley, Purrot, Daniels and others if needed.

The suspense was nerve-wracking. Ron was finding it more

and more difficult to continue living a normal life with this cloud of uncertainty hanging over him. The strain was beginning to take its toll. His temper was shorter. His mind frequently wandered, unable to concentrate for very long. And there was still the gap in his preparations which he had been unable to fill without those additional papers he had requested from Jackson. When the envelope eventually arrived Ron was astonished to find that the contents were incomplete. Jackson's explanation for the absence of some of the papers was staggering, beyond belief: he had written:

We are informed by the Town Clerk's department that the personal files that you requested of Mr Lythe and Mrs Archer, who were former officers of the Housing Department, are no longer available. They may have been amongst some housing administration files which were destroyed in a recent fire in the Council strong room. There are some remains of these files but they are too seriously damaged to enable a check to be made.

Ron's laughter brought Patricia hurrying into the room. 'Whatever's the matter, Ron? Whatever has brought on such mirth, and so early in the day?

'It's the post... this letter from Jackson... he says the papers I asked for were destroyed in a fire in a council strong room.'

Patricia took the letter from him. 'That's ridiculous, papers don't just burst into flames for no reason.'

'Apparently they do at the Civic Centre. But only documents that are helpful to my defence,' he said, cynically. 'They really are a cunning lot at the council. I don't know how they get away with it.'

Patricia handed the letter back to Ron. 'Are those papers very important?'

'Well, they're not vital. But they do form part of the whole picture. To me it just seems so dishonest. I've disclosed all my documents, but they won't disclose all of theirs. Perhaps I should have mislaid some of my papers that they wanted.'

'You're certainly learning the hard way, Ron. Why don't you leave it for a while, come and have some breakfast. It'll be good for your mind to switch off and return to the problem refreshed.'

As usual, Patricia was right. Ron had often wondered how he would manage without her common sense guidance and support.

This development meant that Ron would need to speak to Jim again. But it was becoming more and more difficult to contact of him. He was always up in Durham or somewhere up north seeing the 'Bridgewater Four' about their appeal.

Ron beavered on with his task, inserting the few papers that Jackson had sent, creating questions and comments and slotting them into his defence preparations. What he would really like to get hold of that would be extremely helpful, was some of the evidence held by the police in the council home improvement grant fraud investigation. But that was out of the question. The matter was sub-judice and as such would not be available to him until the fraud trial finishes. The thought reminded him that the police investigation had begun three and a half years ago. It must be a very big case. He had never known a criminal investigation to last such a long time. The outcome would surely prove to be very interesting.

He was adding the finishing touches to his defence notes when he received a telephone call from Jackson. Fred Laws' barrister, Patric Milmo, had decided to divide the Trial Bundle into two - the Plaintiff's Bundle and the Defendant's Bundle. Jackson had therefore been instructed to visit Ron to implement the split. Ron didn't really understand what it all meant. In any case, he pointed out, there were only ten days to go before the hearing.

Jackson offered a brief explanation: 'What should now happen is that we meet you at the earliest possible moment so that we can go through all the documents to go into the Jury Bundle and then each page can be numbered. There are certain documents that we do not think should go in the Jury Bundle, but we can discuss these with you when we meet. We are not saying they should not go before the court, naturally, you can produce documents that you may feel necessary and they may or may not be relevant. If, of course, Counsel for Mr Laws objected to any documents going before the jury then he would say so and then the Judge would then decide whether the documents should go before the Jury. Therefore, there may have to be a separate bundle into which would go documents that you would like to put before the Jury but that we could not agree to going into a Jury bundle. We can explain this in more detail to you when we meet.'

It didn't really make much sense to Ron, and he was beginning to mistrust Jackson. 'I'm sorry, Mr Jackson. It all sounds very complicated and confusing. I don't like this at all. I shall have to speak to my solicitor before I agree to a meeting. I shall have to ring you back.'

'That's quite understandable, Mr Levy. But as you say, there are only ten days to go. If you could do that urgently we would be grateful.'

Ron immediately phoned Jim's office. Linda was very apologetic. Jim was away again. In Durham working on the 'Bridgewater' case. He was expected to be away for several days. She would try to get in touch with him. But he wouldn't be able to help because of the distance and the time limits.

Feeling alone and abandoned, Ron desperately needed Jim's help but it seemed he would have to cope without it. Fighting back the onset of panic, Ron believed he was left with no alternative but to arrange the meeting with Jackson. But without legal support and guidance he knew he would be at Jackson's mercy. The meeting would have to be tomorrow.

Jackson's degree of preparation aroused Ron's suspicions further. The original bundle that had taken such an enormous long time to assemble had been divided into two and each page given a different number in its respective new bundle. On the surface it looked quite straight forward, but Ron immediately saw that these changes threw his prepared notes and questions into disarray. He would have to go through them meticulously all over again and relate them to the new page numbers. It would be a daunting task. But Jackson was firm, Patric Milmo had decided that that is what must be done, and Ron knew that it must be completed before the trial date or the presentation of his defence in court would be in chaos.

Reluctantly, Ron submitted to this dramatic change that had been imposed upon him, although he felt instinctively that he shouldn't have to: that his defence was being compromised, was being placed at a serious disadvantage. Now was the time that he needed Jim's advice, probably more than at any other time. But it was not to be. He was not available. Ron would have to do the best he could in the limited time left before the trial date.

'I've said it before, haven't I, Ron.' commented Anne Archer, in her usual cynical tone. 'They're a cunning load of foxes. Look, why don't you let me come with you to the court. You need someone beside you…to support you. I could be your note-taker. Jim obviously won't be there. Barristers have their assistants in court. I don't see why you shouldn't be allowed to have your own assistant. I can't guarantee to be there every day, but I'll do my best. And on the days I can't make it perhaps you could get someone else to be there. Perhaps Chris Hudson, or even your son.'

'That's a good idea, Anne. I would appreciate that. I must admit I don't cherish the thought of being there on my own. I still haven't been able to get hold of Jim. He really has let me down on this. That's why I had to phone you. I needed someone besides Patricia to talk with. And you've always been such a pillar. I don't think I could have got this far without your support and friendship. Shall I see you there...on the day?'

'I think that would be best, Ron, in case of any problems. I'm sure I'll make it, but you never know. Now you go and spend some time with Patricia and the children. Switch off for a while.'

'That sounds like a good idea, Anne. And thanks. Thanks a million. Speak to you soon. Bye.'

Chapter 15

Now, apart from a few more papers he had requested from Jackson, Ron's preparations were complete. He had written pages of questions he wanted to put to Fred Laws and other witnesses in court. Each question was numbered and cross-referenced to a numbered document or file in the trial bundle. The list had taken more than a year to compile in the little spare time that he had. But it was worth it. Jim Nicol had agreed it was looking good. Jane Saxby had agreed to give evidence in Ron's defence. And with the help of the Office at The Royal Courts of Justice he had obtained subpoenas to call Muckley, Purrot, Daniels and others if needed.

The suspense was nerve-wracking. Ron was finding it more and more difficult to continue living a normal life with this cloud of uncertainty hanging over him. The strain was beginning to take its toll. His temper was shorter. His mind frequently wandered, unable to concentrate for very long. And there was still the gap in his preparations which he had been unable to fill without those additional papers he had requested from Jackson. When the envelope eventually arrived Ron was astonished to find that the contents were incomplete. Jackson's explanation for the absence of some of the papers was staggering, beyond belief: he had written:

We are informed by the Town Clerk's department that the personal files that you requested of Mr Lythe and Mrs Archer, who were former officers of the Housing

Department, are no longer available. They may have been amongst some housing administration files which were destroyed in a recent fire in the Council strong room. There are some remains of these files but they are too seriously damaged to enable a check to be made.

Ron's laughter brought Patricia hurrying into the room. 'Whatever's the matter, Ron? Whatever has brought on such mirth, and so early in the day?

'It's the post... this letter from Jackson... he says the papers I asked for were destroyed in a fire in a council strong room.'

Patricia took the letter from him. 'That's ridiculous, papers don't just burst into flames for no reason.'

'Apparently they do at the Civic Centre. But only documents that are helpful to my defence,' he said, cynically. 'They really are a cunning lot at the Council. I don't know how they get away with it.'

Patricia handed the letter back to Ron. 'Are those papers very important?'

'Well, they're not vital. But they do form part of the whole picture. To me it just seems so dishonest. I've disclosed all my documents, but they won't disclose all of theirs. Perhaps I should have mislaid some of my papers that they wanted.'

'You're certainly learning the hard way, Ron. Why don't you leave it for a while, come and have some breakfast. It'll be good for your mind to switch off and return to the problem refreshed.'

As usual, Patricia was right. Ron had often wondered how he would manage without her common sense guidance and support.

This development meant that Ron would need to speak to Jim again. But it was becoming more and more difficult to contact of him. He was always up in Durham or somewhere up north seeing the *'Bridgewater Four'* about their appeal.

Ron beavered on with his task, inserting the few papers that Jackson had sent, creating questions and comments and slotting them into his defence preparations. What he would really like to get hold of that would be extremely helpful, was some of the evidence held by the police in the council home improvement grant fraud investigation. But that was out of the question. The matter was sub-judice and as such would not be available to him until the fraud trial has finished. The thought reminded him that the police investigation had begun almost 4 years ago. It must be a very big case. He had never known a criminal investigation to last such a long time. The outcome would surely prove to be very interesting.

He was adding the finishing touches to his defence notes when he received a telephone call from Jackson. Fred Laws' barrister, Patric Milmo, had decided to divide the Trial Bundle into two, the Plaintiff's Bundle and the Defendant's Bundle. Jackson had therefore been instructed to visit Ron to implement the split. Ron didn't really understand what it all meant. In any case, he pointed out, there were only twelve days to go before the hearing.

Jackson offered a brief explanation: 'What should now happen is that we meet you at the earliest possible moment so that we can go through all the documents to go into the Jury Bundle and then each page can be numbered. There are certain documents that we do not think should go in the Jury Bundle, but we can discuss these with you when we meet. We are not saying they should not go before the court, naturally, you can produce documents that you may feel necessary and they may or may not be relevant. If, of course, Counsel for Mr Laws objected to any documents going before the Jury then he would say so and then the Judge would then decide whether the documents should go before the Jury. Therefore, there may have to be a separate bundle into which would go documents that you would like to put before the Jury but that we could not agree to going into a Jury Bundle. We can explain this in more detail to you when we meet.'

It didn't really make much sense to Ron, and he was beginning to mistrust Jackson. 'I'm sorry, Mr Jackson. It all sounds very complicated and confusing. I don't like this at all. I shall have to speak to my solicitor before I agree to a meeting. I shall have to ring you back.'

'That's quite understandable, Mr Levy. But as you say, there are only twelve days to go. If you could do that urgently we would be grateful.'

Ron immediately phoned Jim's office. Linda was very apologetic. Jim was away again. In Durham working on the 'Bridgewater' case. He was expected to be away for several days. She would try to get in touch with him. But he wouldn't be able to help because of the distance and the time limits.

Feeling alone and abandoned, Ron desperately needed Jim's help but it seemed he would have to cope without it. Fighting back the onset of panic, Ron believed he was left with no alternative but to arrange the meeting with Jackson. But without legal support and guidance he knew he would be at Jackson's mercy. The meeting would have to be tomorrow.

Jackson's degree of preparation aroused Ron's suspicions further. The original bundle that had taken such an enormous long time to assemble had been divided into two and each page given a different number in its respective new bundle. On the surface it looked quite straightforward, but Ron immediately saw that these changes threw his prepared notes and questions into disarray. He would have to go through them meticulously all over again and relate them to the new page numbers. It would be a daunting task. But Jackson was firm, Patric Milmo had decided that that is what must be done, and Ron knew that it must be completed before the trial date or the presentation of his defence in court would be in chaos.

Reluctantly, Ron submitted to this dramatic change that had been imposed upon him, although he felt instinctively that he shouldn't have to: that his defence was being compromised, was being placed at a serious disadvantage. Now was the time that he needed Jim's advice, probably more than at any other time. But it was not to be. He was not available. Ron would have to do the best he could in the limited time left before the trial date.

'I've said it before, haven't I, Ron.' commented Anne Archer, in her usual cynical tone. 'They're a cunning load of foxes. Look, why don't you let me come with you to the court. You need someone beside you... to support you. I could be your note-taker. Jim obviously won't be there. Barristers have their assistants in court. I don't see why you shouldn't be allowed to have your own assistant. I can't guarantee to be there every day, but I'll do my best. And on the days I can't make it perhaps you could get someone else to be there. Perhaps Chris Hudson, or even your son.'

'That's a good idea, Anne. I would appreciate that. I must admit I don't cherish the thought of being there on my own. I still haven't been able to get hold of Jim. He really has let me down on this. Anne. I would appreciate that. I must admit I don't cherish the thought of being there on my own. I still haven't been able to get hold of Jim. He really has let me down on this. That's why I had to phone you. I needed someone beside Patricia to talk with. And you've always been such a pillar. I don't think I could have got this far without your support and friendship. Shall I see you there... on the day?'

'I think that would be best, Ron, in case of any problems. I'm sure I'll make it, but you never know. Now you go and spend some time with Patricia and the children. Switch off for a while.'

'That sounds like a good idea, Anne. And thanks. Thanks a million. Speak to you soon. Bye.'

CHAPTER 16

Fear, optimism, suspicion, faith, hope, dread, elation, anxiety, relief and doubt: like a tumble dryer turning over the family wash, all these emotions drifted through Ron's mind as he headed towards London's Liverpool Street Station on the 08.06 train from Colchester. However hard he tried he could not discharge his thoughts from the ordeal that lay ahead of him.

The number 26 bus dropped Ron off at The Strand, a few minutes from his destination: and this was it; The Royal Courts of Justice. He paused on the steps of this historic building, looking exactly as he had seen it so many times on the television news. He would have liked to stay longer, to take in the complexity and intricacies of this magnificent building. But there was too little time, and too much on his mind to do it justice: perhaps at a later date.

As he gazed up in awe at the enormous Gothic portals and archways, he felt small and inadequate. His inadequacy was brought home to him further as he stepped into the cavernous hall and saw, beyond the security desks, the bewigged barristers knowingly going about their business; black gowns flowing; legal briefs, tied together in traditional red ribbons, clutched unceremoniously in folded arms, and in the wake of these masters of litigation followed the suited entourage of supporting solicitors and legal executives carrying enormous bundles of files and law books. So many ordinary people, just like me, some in smart suits, some in casual, everyday wear, trying to look relaxed, as though they were doing this every day of their lives.

The large black brief case, which he had bought specially for this hearing, was heavily laden with his trial papers and files: It was now getting heavier by the minute and Ron decided he had paused long enough. He took one last look around, to see if Anne had arrived, before stepping through the opening and joining the flow of visitors that streamed towards the security desks. Apart from the uniforms the security officers looked strangely like checkout assistants at a supermarket. Cases and bags were opened and checked; checked for what? Bombs? Weapons? Placing his case on the desk was a welcome, albeit brief, respite from his heavy load. Ron must have appeared harmless to the security officer. His case was opened, given a cursory glance and unceremoniously shoved to the end of the desk to make way for the next visitor.

The information bureau in the cavernous hall provided details of the courtroom number in which the hearing was to take place. Ron felt unexpectedly calm as he made his way to courtroom 11. It was one of the old courts. He glanced at his watch. He was in good time.

With caution borne of uncertainty and anxiety, he stepped into the room. It was silent.. There was a distinctive smell of old wood and stone. The court was smaller than he had expected. Looking up towards the high, arched ceiling he noticed what looked like microphones suspended above the benches. Immediately below the Judge's dais sat a man in a black gown. He was studying some papers on the small table in front of him. Without raising his head he looked up over his half-spectacles. Ron cleared his throat. 'I think my hearing is in this court... today... Laws v Levy. I'm Levy.'

'Ah, yes, Mr Levy. 'I'm the Clerk of the Court. Are you familiar with court proceedings?'

Ron shook his head. 'No. I'm afraid I have no idea.'

'Let me show you where you will sit.' He indicated one of the benches in front of him: the second one from the front: Ron edged his way between the pews and deposited his case on the narrow bench-top in front of him. With a sigh that was half relief and half apprehension he gently lowered himself onto the hard wooden bench. Glancing forward directly above and behind the Clerk of the Court Ron realised he had placed himself immediately opposite the Judge's elevated green and gold leather throne. He tried to take in more of his awesome surroundings.

'Are you being represented?'

'No. I couldn't afford a barrister. I've had some guidance from my solicitor, and I've prepared my papers as best as I've been able to.'

The Clerk smiled reassuringly. 'The Court will help you. You'll find the Judge very helpful and patient. Mr Justice McKinnon is hearing the case, and he is addressed as "My Lord" or "Your Worship".'

'Thank you. I'm sure I'll remember that.' Ron opened his briefcase and started to lay his papers out in some order that would be easiest to cope with. He knew it was going to be difficult. He cursed Jackson and Milmo for dividing the bundle. He still wasn't confident with the two bundles with their new numbering.

The tranquillity of the room magnified the rustling of Ron's papers. The door creaked, announcing someone's entrance, he turned to see who. To his delight, and relief, it was Anne Archer. They exchanged smiles. Anne shuffled along the bench and sat beside him. 'Are you ready to do battle?' She asked. 'As ready as possible, Anne. But I'm glad to see you. I could have done with a bit more help from Jim, though, but I just haven't been able to get hold of him.'

'Yes, that was a bit naughty of him to disappear like that. He should have been around, especially at this stage. How

223

did you get on after all… with your re-numbering?'

Before he could answer, the door creaked again. Three men entered the court: one of them was Jackson: the one wearing a wig and black gown must have been Milmo. They made their way to the benches immediately behind and to the left of Ron. He half-turned to them. Milmo nodded a greeting, extended pleasantries and introduced himself. The third man was introduced as his Junior Counsel. It all seemed so civilised and yet it felt so artificial. After all, Milmo wasn't here to befriend Ron; he was here to demolish him: to destroy him.

'The Court rise' commanded the Clerk. Silence descended. Mr Justice Mckinnon entered from a door to the right of the dais. His bearing carried the authority and importance of his role. Resplendent in his scarlet robe and off-white wig, he made his way unhurriedly to his ample seat, placed his black folder on the desk-top in front of him and glanced around the court room at its occupants as he took his seat. Ron had imagined he would be taller, larger. He was certainly older than Ron had expected, looking past retirement age.

The Clerk lowered himself back into his seat, it was the signal for all others in the courtroom to do likewise.

The Judge addressed the Court first. He explained how the case would be conducted: How a Jury would be selected. His explanation was lengthy and frequently couched in legal terms that Ron found difficult to fully understand…

The Jury had been ushered in and had settled down. Mr Justice McKinnon addressed them, instructing them on their role and responsibilities during the hearing, and describing how it would be conducted. He then explained that the bundle of papers in front of each of them is the Jury's discovery bundle. He also explained that there was another bundle, the Defendant's bundle, which would be revealed to the Jury, document by document, during the hearing as the court deemed appropriate to so do.

There followed a lengthy exchange between the Judge and Mr Milmo covering various legal and procedural aspects of the hearing. This included an explanation by Mr Milmo of his reasons for deciding that the Defendant's discovery documents should be divided into two bundles; that some of Mr Levy's documents should not go before the Jury because they may not be pertinent to the defence, unless the Court ruled that they could be seen by the Jury.

The Judge then addressed Ron; 'Mr Levy, you are not represented in your defence. Is that correct?'

Ron glanced up from his two bundles of documents, still trying to make sense of the splitting, and stood up 'That is correct, My Lord.'

'Will you have any legal representation or support during this hearing?'

'No, My Lord, I am unable to fund appointment of Counsel, and my solicitor is away in another part of the country assisting with another of his clients.' Ron gently placed his hand on Anne's shoulder. 'But I do have the comfort and support of a friend, this lady on my right, Mrs Anne Archer, if that is in order, my Lord.'

The Judge nodded his approval as he put pen to paper. 'Is that Anne with an 'e', Mrs Archer?

'Yes, My Lord.' replied Anne.

The Judge carefully placed his pen in the spine of his note book and returned to Ron. 'Mr Levy, it is perfectly in order for your friend, Mrs Archer, to support you. You may confer together during the hearing but Mrs Archer may not address the Court or question any of the witnesses. In the circumstances the Court will assist you in any way that it can. Do you understand the direction and proceedings so far, and do you have any questions or concerns to put to me?'

'Yes, My Lord. I do understand so far, but I would like to explain that I have spent many months preparing my documents, numbering them, cross-referencing them according to my notes for my defence. Mr Milmo's insistence on the splitting of my bundle of documents, renumbering many of them, has caused me considerable difficulties...'

'Mr Levy, I do understand. And it is right that there may be some of your documents that need not, or even, perhaps, should not go before members of the Jury, but in the circumstances this Court will give you whatever assistance it is able to, and will take your situation into account during the proceedings.'

Ron was certainly not happy with that. In fact, he felt rather angry, but was surprised at how successfully he managed to conceal it.

The Judge looked up at the large clock at the back of the Court Room, closed his note book and announced that this would be an appropriate time to adjourn for lunch.

The Clerk quickly rose from his seat and ordered; 'The Court rise.'

Mr Justice Mckinnon declared that the hearing will resume in one hour, and left the Court.

The silence that had prevailed during the Judge's departure ended abruptly as most of the occupants hurriedly made to leave the court. Ron and Anne decided that a cup of tea and a snack would go down very well, with an opportunity to assess the hearing's progress.

'The Court rise,' commanded the Clerk, as the Judge entered the Court and took his seat for the afternoon session.

When the Court had returned to silence The Judge turned

his attention to Patric Milmo. 'Mr Milmo, I understand that you are representing the Plaintiff in this matter and you will be familiar with the direction and proceedings of this Court. You may address the Court now on the Plaintiff's behalf.

'Thank you, My Lord. I shall present the Plaintiff's prosecution case in defending my client from the libellous allegations made against him by the defendant.' It was a lengthy, robust presentation in which Mr Milmo paused from time to time, referring to many of the documents in the bundles which he went through with members of the jury, giving detailed explanations and implications of each document; he wanted to make sure that they fully understood their importance in the prosecution case. In doing so he sought to discredit Ron to the absolute maximum. He was very clever and manipulative, declaring to the Jury that he would show the Court how the Defendant could not possibly justify making such damaging claims against a man of such professional integrity and status as Mr Laws.

Ron turned to Anne, pointed at his watch, and shrugged. Anne understood his gesture: 'Yes, Mr Milmo was certainly making a meal of this, thought Ron. There was little doubt that he would be taking up most of the afternoon.

Throughout Mr Milmo's presentation the Judge asked questions, sought clarification, made copious notes, and addressed the Jury with explanations and guidance on points of law.

When Mr Milmo had completed his case the Judge announced that he would now adjourn the hearing until tomorrow. He then turned to Ron and asked; 'Mr Levy, how do you propose to begin your defence argument, will it be your intention to question the Plaintiff?'

Ron indicated that that was his intention.

'Then may I suggest that when you get home you burn

some midnight oil and put your papers in order in readiness for tomorrow.'

'The Court rise.' ordered the Clerk.

Mr Justice McKinnon gave a cursory bow to the Court, and departed.

'Well, Ron, I think you and I will have lots to talk about on the train journey home after that little performance.' Anne said

Chapter 17

Mr Justice McKinnon addressed the Jury, explaining how the reconvened hearing will be conducted and reminding them that the procedural rules and restrictions that they were informed of yesterday applied equally strictly today.

He then turned to Ron. 'Mr Levy, yesterday you indicated that in conducting your defence you wished to question the Plaintiff... is that still your intention?'

'Yes, My Lord. It is, indeed, but first of all I would like to present the outline of my defence to the Court, in much the same manner in which Mr Milmo presented the prosecution case for the Plaintiff: would your Lordship permit me to do that?

'Mr Levy, you may conduct your defence in whatever manner you think will benefit you, provided your presentation is kept within the proper procedures and dignity of this Court: please proceed.'

'Thank you, My Lord. As stated on page 11 of my defence statement, which is in my Defendant's Bundle, I was elected as a member of Southend Borough Council for the Shoeburyness Ward, and I was appointed to the Housing and Estates Committee.

'During my first two years as Councillor I became alarmed at the number of complaints I had received from my constituents about the unsatisfactory way in which their housing needs had been dealt with by the Council's Assistant Director of Housing Mr William Muckley. Mr Muckley denied all of the complaints. I prepared a report of those complaints and took them to the Director of Housing, Mr Cyril Purrott. Mr Purrot said he could do nothing about the complaints because Mr Muckley always denied them.

'My efforts to help my constituents appeared frequently in the local press and I started receiving through the post copies of documents from Housing Department files. Many of those documents gave considerable support to the substance of those complaints.

'And so I took the complaints to Mr Laws, the Plaintiff in this action, but I didn't tell him about the papers that had been sent to me. Mr Laws told me that he had heard about these complaints against Mr Muckley but investigations had failed to prove any of them. I told Mr Laws that I thought there should be an inquiry into the complaints and into the conduct of Mr Muckley. Mr Laws flatly refused to instigate any such inquiry.

'I then went to see the Leader of the Council, Councillor Norman Harris. Cllr Harris also refused to order an inquiry. I felt very frustrated at his reaction. I told him that there was clear evidence of misconduct by Mr Muckley. People were suffering because of that behaviour and I was determined that it should be looked into by the Council. Councillor Harris still refused my request.

'I would not be put off and I continued demanding an inquiry. Eventually, I told Councillor Harris that if he did not order an inquiry into my complaints against Mr Muckley, I would take the matter up with the appropriate Government department.

'With considerable reluctance Cllr Harris capitulated and, grudgingly, instructed Mr Laws to investigate my complaints and to produce a report of the results. A Committee of Enquiry was then set up headed by Cllr Harris and to include three other Senior Councillors and four or five council officers. Mr Muckley was also present, accompanied by his

Union representative.

'Mr Laws went through the list of my allegations and proceeded to demolish each of them with the explanations from his report: It was very clever; I thought it was a whitewash.'

The Judge interrupted Ron sharply: 'Mr Levy I must stop you there. Your last comments cannot be allowed. I do not know if you are aware of the seriousness of your suggestion. You cannot discredit the Plaintiff with an opinion that you might hold unless that opinion can be properly substantiated with evidence.

Having closely examined all of your documents I can recall no such evidence that even remotely suggests that the Plaintiff's report to which you refer was anything other than a properly compiled response to your allegations against a Mr Muckley. Now, if I thought that your statement was a deliberate attempt to mislead the Jury I would be now charging you with contempt of this Court. However, in view of the fact that you do not have the benefit of a legal representative to advise you on the proper conduct that is required of you in a Court of Law I am going to give you the benefit of the doubt. Do you have anything to say, Mr Levy?'

Ron tried to clear his throat, but it was too dry. His face felt flushed, he needed water. He sipped from the glass. 'My Lord, may I respectfully say you are right. It was certainly not my intention to mislead the Jury. I take your just rebuke very seriously. And I apologise profusely for my offending of this Court. And I promise to take greater care in how I present my defence.'

'Thank you,' snapped the Judge. He turned to address the Jury. 'Members of the Jury, you are to disregard the Defendant's last two comments.' He turned back to Ron. 'Mr Levy, do you wish to continue?'

'Yes, please, my Lord.'

The Judge nodded.

'Thank you, My Lord. Now, where was I? Oh, yes, Mr Laws' report... my complaints against Mr Muckley. Mr Laws was going through my list. His answers were very convincing. But when it came to my complaints about revealing exam questions to a housing trainee and housing certain people, I started to reveal the papers that had been sent to me, The Plaintiff became very angry. He demanded to know how I came by those papers. Cllr Harris also urged me to answer Mr Laws. I was quite shocked at the reaction and for a few moments I lost my composure. I could only say they were sent to me through the post. During the disturbance that followed, the meeting was hurriedly concluded, with my remaining few complaints undecided.

'The following day Mr Laws contacted the police and reported my possession of the papers which were missing from the Housing Department files. I then received a phone call from the police asking me if I would be willing to come in and help them with their enquiries. I agreed and went to the police station. I was subjected to detailed questioning after which the investigating officer told me that he did not believe me and that I would be held in custody whilst he investigated further. I was searched by the jailer, and locked in a cell for five hours. My home was also searched. After five hours I was released, without charge. The whole episode was very distressing. I felt that although I was trying to expose misconduct in the Housing Department I was the one who was treated like an offender, like a criminal. I truly believed that reporting me to the police was extreme and unnecessary. And I wrote the words complained of by the Plaintiff in his Statement of Claim, which resulted in him serving upon me a Writ for Libel.' Ron placed his papers on the desk in front of him and lowered his head.

'Mr Levy, do you wish to continue?' asked the Judge.

'Thank you, My Lord. I would like to continue by now questioning the Plaintiff. In particular I would like to question him regarding document number 254 of my bundle. It is a hand written letter from Mr Muckley's first wife. It is addressed to Southend Cllr Chris Hudson.

The Judge raised his hand and halted Ron there. 'Please wait Mr Levy. Mr Laws, would you please take to the witness stand.'

Fred Laws reluctantly made his way to the stand. The Clerk of the Court approached him and offered up a Bible and a small card. Fred Laws took the Bible in his right hand, and the card in his left hand. He read from the card: 'I do solemnly swear to tell the truth, the whole truth, and nothing but the truth, so help me God.' He seemed familiar with this part of court proceedings. But then, he is a lawyer.

The Judge quickly perused the letter from Ron's bundle copy in front of him. It read:

Dear Mr Hudson,

Just a short note wishing you good luck with your fight to be reinstated on the committees you were banned from.

How you could have been banned beats me. Why did Mr Peacock sack him (Mr Muckley) if all was well in the Housing Department. Mistresses were housed and wives had to get out of their homes.

I am going to court myself soon because my ex-husband is three months behind with my money, but when I ask for it I get a stream of abuse – how she is a headmistress I don't know. If you lead a good life you get nowhere – you were only doing your proper job in asking for an investigation, so all the best of luck.

Yours truly,

Joan Muckley (Mrs)

PS And get your apology

'It is difficult to see at the moment, Mr Levy, how this is at all relevant.'

Before Ron could reply, Milmo hastily thrust a question at the Judge: 'Would Your Lordship notice that it is dated 8 August 1985?

'And it is written by the former wife of Mr Muckley.' retorted the Judge. He resumed his dialogue with Ron. 'We are getting rather a long way from any issue in this action, are we not? If you want to call a Mrs Muckley to give some relevant evidence that is a different matter, but to start putting things she has written to some third party, another councillor, Mr Hudson, is not going to help the Jury very much, is it?

Ron did not agree with the supposition, but he feared that to say so would possibly alienate the Judge. 'Thank you, My Lord. I am going to call Councillor Hudson. Shall I leave it till then?

'I think so.'

Ron selected the next document from his bundle. 'I have nearly completed, my Lord. Can I go on to item 252A?'

The Judge selected his copy of document 252A and addressed the Jury. 'You have not got that, members of the jury. You were not given some documents. If you were given all the documents you would be given some that are relevant and some that were not, and it is obviously important that you should only see material that is relevant material. We are now going to look at another one, 252A. Shall we read that to ourselves? Who is this from?

'It is from a local developer My Lord?'

'... A local developer to you in March 1985?'

'Yes, my Lord.'

'Let me read it:

Dear Mr Levy,

With reference to our recent discussion regarding the

police enquiries into serious irregularities in the Southend council Housing Department's administration of home improvement grants, I would confirm that I first brought the matter to the attention of Councillor Copley early in October 1984. Councillor Copley called at my home, together with Nigel Smith, secretary of Southend Labour Party, and I gave him copies of papers similar to those which I enclose with this letter to you. The contents of these papers indicate very clearly a prima facie case of misconduct, because of the colossal difference between my estimated costs of carrying out the improvements, and the cost of improvement grant claimed, and approved, under the Improvement Grant scheme. Councillor Copley and Mr Smith expressed their concern at the situation and suggested the Town Clerk, Mr Laws, be informed. This Cllr Copley did within 24 hours. It appears that Mr Laws failed to inform the police of the matter. Cllr Copley frequently contacted Mr Laws regarding the complaint and it was only when the new Town Clerk, Mr Roy Peacock, took over that the police were informed immediately. As you know, the Fraud Squad are now investigating and charges have already been brought against the director of a local development company who was involved in the matter. In fact the actual building costs were £10,000, for the work that was carried out by a Mr D. Carter. This has been confirmed to the police.

If I can be of any further assistance please contact me again.

Yours faithfully,

A W Goble

'I do not see how you can put a letter to the Jury that was written by somebody in some building firm, in March 1985 to you. If you want to put a general question, putting the letter away, that is a matter for you.'

'Yes, My Lord. This is a very important point which I would

beg your permission to pursue, not necessarily the contents of the letter but the general issue.'

'If you have got some questions to ask – put the letter away – then I will have to consider whether it's a proper question after you have asked it.

'Oh for goodness sake,' thought Ron, irritated. 'Is this Judge going to let the jury see any of my documents?' He paused, trying to conceal his displeasure. 'The question I want to ask, my lord, is whether Mr Laws had received a complaint from a councillor and this builder regarding certain building developments in the town, and who...'

'Whether he received a complaint from whom?'

'From a Councillor Copley, my Lord.'

The judge continued making notes as Ron answered his questions. 'From Councillor Copley and ...'

'Mr Gobal.'

'Gobal, about...?

'About...Councillor Copley's concerns for some home improvement grant applications.'

There followed a brief silence whilst the Judge completed noting Ron's replies. He turned his attention to Fred Laws: 'Do you understand the question, Mr Laws?

'Yes, indeed.' He replied boldly.

'What is the answer?'

'Yes, My Lord, I did.'

'Did ...?'

'...Did receive a complaint from Councillor Copley about a home improvement grant case.'

Ron continued his questioning. He was approaching the vital part of his defence. His pulse quickened. 'Did the subject of that complaint, Mr Laws, form a prima facie case... was it a prima facie case of a breach of law?'

'It revealed that possible criminal offences had been committed, yes.'

The Judge interjected, seeking clarification. 'Sorry. It revealed…'

'That possible criminal offences had been committed. May I add that it was nothing whatsoever to do with Mr Muckley.' added Fred Laws, hastily.

'I accept that, My Lord.' Ron told the Judge, before returning to Mr Laws. 'Having established in your mind that that was so, did you… did you report that to the police?

'Yes, immediately.'

Ron jotted down the reply. 'You reported it to the police, on what date, can you remember?'

'I think it was the month I left the service of the local authority.'

'How long after?'

'October1984.' Replied Laws, now clearly irritated by Ron's probing.

Again, Ron noted the reply. 'How long a time lapse was there between receiving the complaint and reporting to the police?

Fred Laws took a deep breath and, almost through gritted teeth, said; 'I do not know. It would have had to have been a short time. I left the service of the local authority at the end of the month.

The Judge decided to intervene and to put Ron's obvious objective into clear terms; 'I do not know what the suggestion is, but can I put this to you, Mr Laws. Is there any truth in a suggestion, if it was made, that you delayed in reporting this possibly criminal matter?'

Fred Laws quickly regained his composure. 'No, my lord, I can add with confidence it was then a prolonged matter that went on for a period of years since I left the local authority.'

His Lordship now turned to Ron. 'Is there anything else you want to ask about that?'

Ron raised Allan Goble's letter and turned it towards the Judge. 'My Lord, this letter clearly shows the time scale between Mr Laws being informed of the fraud…'

The judge interrupted Ron and spoke to him in a firm tone. 'I am not going to let you refer to a letter written by some third party to you.'

Ron was determined not to give up. His whole defence depended on persuading Fred Laws to admit that he had failed to inform the police of the crime immediately. 'Can I ask Mr Laws a question?'

'You can certainly ask him a question.'

'Mr Laws, was this complaint made to you in March 1984… approximately? '

I do not remember, I remember distinctly Councillor Copley telling me of the circumstances and to the best of my recollection I immediately informed the police because there was a prima facie case of crime.'

Ron felt sure he detected a hint of irritation in Fred Laws' voice… or perhaps it was anxiety. 'Did you go to the police within 24 hours, or two weeks, three weeks?

'I cannot answer… Immediately is the only answer I can give.'

'*Oh yes you can*' thought Ron, '*because you know that you didn't report it to the police at all.*'

Ron turned his attention to the Judge: to appeal to him: to explain his objective in his line of questioning. 'I'm sorry to labour this, my lord, but it is important to…'

'Do not apologise to me, Mr Levy. If you have a further question, ask the witness.'

The Judge's sharp interruption again unsettled Ron, but he was determined to get Fred Laws to admit the truth. 'Mr Laws, it is important I have as near precise answer as possible… in that you would say that the complaint was lodged in, or about… March?'

Fred Laws turned his gaze to the ceiling. 'No, I did not say that.' He snapped

'Could you tell us when? Ron urged.

The judge intervened again. 'He said "I do not remember when".'

Ron was determined not to give up. 'You do not remember when it was lodged?'

'No.' Snapped Fred Laws. 'I believe it was immediately before I left the service of the local authority. Councillor Copley is still available. If he had a record of when he came to see me that would prove the point... I do not remember.'

The interaction between Ron and Fred Laws was gathering momentum. 'You do not remember how long it was between receiving the complaint and informing the police, Mr Laws, is that correct?'

'I have already answered that. I informed the police, in my words, immediately.'

'What is "immediately", Mr Laws, within an hour, a day, a month?'

'I am not going beyond "immediately" because I do not remember.'

'So, it could have been a month?'

'No, it could not.'

'It could have been a week?'

'I am not going beyond "immediately".'

'Am I not going to know how long it was, the time lapse between receiving...

The Judge had obviously heard enough and intervened: 'Mr Laws, can you remember how long it was?'

'No, My Lord.'

'So, Mr Levy, the answer to your question is you are not going to know from this witness because he cannot remember.'

'Could I ask one final question, My Lord?'

The Judge agreed with a single nod of his head,'

'Mr Laws, who actually reported the complaint to the police, was it you yourself or your successor, Mr Roy Peacock?

'I did.' Replied Fred Laws sharply.

'And what was Mr Peacock's involvement?'

'I have no idea. I left the service of the local authority and left my successor to it.

'I beg your indulgence, My Lord. I thought it was my last question but I would like to ask a couple more.'

The Judge raised his head from his note-taking and glanced at Ron. 'Right.'

'Having reported to the police, Mr Laws, did you have any further discussions with the police...after reporting it?'

'No, I remember one or two Criminal Investigation Department Officers came to see me. I told them what I knew about it and then I left the service of the local authority before anything else happened.'

'Can I go back on one final question? This is to do with the Council meeting, the Committee of Enquiry into my complaints against the Council's Housing Department. Do you remember how long the period was between you seeing the papers I showed to the Committee, and informing the police of my possession of them?

'I am sorry?'

'What was the lapse of time, Mr Laws, between your seeing the Council documents which I produced at that inquiry, and the time that you informed the police... what was the time lapse there?

'Fred Laws hesitated, as though either unable, or unwilling to give an answer. 'Err... two days.'

Ron gave a sigh of relief. He knew that it was not quite the correct answer; which was actually the very next morning.' But he realised there could be no gain in pursuing the matter further. With the two most important questions answered wrongly, Ron resigned himself to the fact that his defence had been severely compromised: barely able to conceal his despair at his inevitable defeat he closed his questioning as courteously as he could manage: 'Thank you, Mr Laws. I think, My Lord, I have gone as far as I can with this witness.'

Mr Justice McKinnon checked the time, finished his note-taking and addressed Ron. 'So, Mr Levy. You have completed your cross-examination of Mr Laws.

'Yes my Lord, for the time being I have.'

'Then this Court will now adjourn and will reconvene at 10.30 on Monday.' He eased himself out of his seat as the Clerk of the Court loudly ordered the Court to rise.

As soon as the Judge disappeared from view there was a scurry of activity as the Jury and participants prepared to leave.

Ron remained seated, staring straight ahead. Most of the people in the Court room had departed. The room was quiet. '

'Ron, are you alright? Asked Anne Archer. He appeared not to hear her. Concerned, Anne placed her hand lightly on his shoulder and gently shook him. 'Ron, are you alright?'

Ron slowly turned his head towards her. 'I can't believe it... just cannot believe it: Laws gave the wrong answer: he said he did report the Grant fraud to the police. We know he didn't. How could he do that? He swore under oath to tell the truth. How could he do that, how could he do it?'

Anne could see that he was upset. 'Ron, I am not the least surprised. As I've said before, nothing that that lot does will ever surprise me.' She started to gather up his papers to place in his case. 'Come along Ron, let's leave this place and get some cool, clean air.

Ron had no illusions about the seriousness of his situation; He knew that by insisting that he had reported the Home Improvement Grant fraud to the police Fred Laws had completely demolished his defence. There wasn't really any point continuing. His spirit plummeted as he realised the consequences of his impending defeat.

The next day at the resumed hearing Ron announced to the Court that, following his questioning of the Plaintiff the previous day, he did not intend calling any other witnesses and that he would be presenting no further evidence.

The Judge asked Ron if he was aware of the consequences of such decision and invited him to give his reasons which Ron declined, explaining that there would be little point continuing defending the case; that to do so would delay the inevitable and would incur unnecessary costs.

Mr Justice McKinnon turned to address Patric Milmo. Mr Milmo, you have heard the Defendant; that he has nothing further to add in his defence. I am sure that you will fully understand the effect that Mr Levy's decision may have in your prosecution of this action. Is there anything further that you wish to say, or are there any further matters of evidence that you wish to present on the Plaintiff's behalf?

Milmo quickly rose to his feet, in eager anticipation of the opportunity to exploit the options that this unexpected development presented. 'I am much obliged to you, My Lord. I would indeed like to make further representation. I think it is very important that the jury fully understands the seriousness of the Defendant's conduct in this matter. His decision to defend the action in the first place without having any real evidence to support his written defamatory statement was reckless and irresponsible...'

Ron winced. Milmo was going in for the kill. There was nothing Ron could do about it, except hope that the Jury would be sympathetic to his plight.

There were legal processes to be dealt with in winding down to conclusion of the hearing when the Judge had completed these he addressed the Jury with his summing up.

'Members of the Jury, you have heard and seen the evidence. You heard the Defendant tell this Court that he wrote the words complained of by the Plaintiff and that he published and distributed them to various other parties. You also heard the Defendant explain, in some considerable detail, why he felt justified in writing those words; he felt aggrieved and frustrated that his allegations of misconduct within the Housing Department at Southend Borough Council had not been given serious, or even proper, consideration by the Plaintiff, who had subsequently reported him to the police about missing Council files. And it is for you, members of the jury, to decide whether or not you accept the Defendant's reasons for writing the words complained of: You cannot open up a man's head, look inside and see if he believes or thinks what he says.

'Now of course, and even if it were possible to so do in the Defendant's case, his argument alone would not generally be a proper defence in law; The Defendant would have needed to show beyond reasonable doubt that he had been treated differently by the Plaintiff, without just cause than someone else who had been treated by the Plaintiff in very similar circumstances.

'You will recall, Members of the Jury, that when the Defendant questioned the Plaintiff about a criminal matter that had been brought to the attention of the Plaintiff the Defendant repeatedly asked the Plaintiff if, and when, he had reported the said criminal matter to the police. You will also recall I am sure that, whilst the Plaintiff insisted that he had reported the said criminal matter to the police, he was unable to recall exactly when he had reported it.

'Now, in applying the same principle to the Plaintiff's evidence as I did earlier with regard to the Defendant's evidence... "you cannot open up a man's head and look inside it to see if he really believes what he has said, or that he is telling the truth." However, in the absence in this Court of any evidence to the contrary you are bound to accept the evidence given under oath by the Plaintiff that he did report the aforementioned criminal matter to the police.

'Members of the Jury, you will now retire to the Jury room to consider your verdict. This Court will now adjourn until you have completed your deliberations and have reached a verdict.'

Barely four hours later the jury returned to the Court and filed into their seats.

The Clerk of the court turned to face the Jury and addressed them: 'Would the Foreman of the jury please stand.'

Ron leaned expectantly forward as the Foreman slowly eased himself onto his feet.

The Clerk continued, his tone and manner unchanging. 'Do you find for the Plaintiff or for the Defendant?'

Unaware of how tightly he was gripping the edge of the bench, Ron's knuckles had turned white.

The Foreman hesitated. He appeared to throw a quick glance towards Fred Laws.

Ron's whole body trembled as the Foreman, in a dull monotone, announced the jury's verdict...'we find for the Plaintiff.'

Even though he had known what the verdict would be those few words came as a hammer-blow to Ron. His heart skipped a beat. His head was swimming. But there was worse yet to come.

The Clerk continued; 'And what is your verdict on the Plaintiff's claim for costs and damages?'

With his eyes now focussed on the Judge the Foreman replied, his voice still devoid of emotion; 'We agree the claim for costs and award damages in the sum of £10,000.'

Ron's spirits were already as low as he thought they could get, but this announcement from the Foreman threw him into utter despair. '£10,000' he thought. 'How could they?'

Mr Justice McKinnon thanked the Jury for carrying out their duties. With their responsibilities now completed they were dismissed and allowed to leave the Court.

The Judge waited until the last Juror had departed. He then turned to address Ron. 'Mr Levy, you have heard the Jury's verdict, this means that you will be liable to meet the Plaintiff's legal and other related costs and expenditure: These will be taxed, which means that they will be checked and approved, or otherwise, by the Court office to ensure that all claims are appropriate and permitted. It is, of course, your responsibility to discharge those costs as best you are able:

'In consequence I hereby direct that judgement be entered for the Plaintiff for the sum of £10,000 with costs.

'I further direct and order that the Defendant be restrained from in any manner publishing the words set out in paragraph 2 of the statement of claim herein as follows:

> "as you know Mr Laws' action following the "enquiry" resulted in my five hour incarceration in a police cell and my family's equally distressing search of my home by the police whilst I was in custody. Since this action could not possibly contribute anything productive to the "enquiry" Mr Laws' action can only be interpreted as malicious and vindictive. This together with Mr Laws' unprofessional conduct in the matter hardly gives

credence or dignity to the high office that he holds."
Or any other words conveying similar defamatory
allegations against the Plaintiff in perpetuity.'

'Mr Levy, do you understand this judgment?' asked the Judge.

Ron's mind was in turmoil. 'err... err sorry my Lord... err...yes My Lord, I think I do... do understand.'

'Very well, you will receive a copy of this judgment in due course. This hearing is now concluded.'

'The Court rise.' ordered the Clerk.

As the Judge disappeared from view Ron slowly slipped back into his seat. He gazed trance-like straight ahead. He could think of nothing else. He was oblivious to the chatter of the remaining litigants and the rustling of papers as they were hurriedly stuffed into briefcases.

Ron had lost all sense of time. Suddenly he became aware that his arm was being gently shaken: 'Dad, Dad, are you ok? Ron looked to his side. It was Peter. He had come forward from the public gallery. Ron had forgotten that Peter came to this final day of the hearing in case he needed any help. It was obvious to Peter that his father was in shock. Dad you're in no state to travel home on your own I'm coming with you... taking you right home. Come on, I'll help you pack your papers in your case.

Ron didn't argue. he wasn't able to. He just allowed Peter to lead him out of the Court and onto the bus which took them to Liverpool Street station. Ron did not speak throughout the journey home but Peter didn't press him; he knew his father needed time to cope with his distress.

Peter knew what he needed to do; to see his Father safely home and to let his mother know the disastrous outcome of the trial. He also knew that his mother would be very upset by it all and that she too would need supporting. The only consoling factor was that this long drawn-out saga was now over, bar compliance with the judgment.

Chapter 18

On the 2 April 1990 a report of the Southend Council Home Improvement Grant fraud trial and sentencing, which ended two days earlier, appeared on the front page of the Southend *Evening Echo* under the heading:

'OPERATION HERMIT'.

The trial, at Chelmsford Crown Court, finally closed a year and a day after opening: 16 Defendants were prosecuted

Several weeks into the trial Terrence Herman pleaded guilty to corruption and was sentenced to 27 months imprisonment and ordered to pay £40,000 costs.

Of the other 15 Defendants four pleaded guilty, seven denied but were convicted, three were acquitted, one changed his plea to guilty and no evidence was offered against one because of his age.

Together with this verdict came full details of when and how the criminal investigation began into the Home Improvement Grant fraud: At a meeting on 23 October 1984 at Southend on Sea Borough Council offices, Mr Roy Peacock, Borough Treasurer and Mr Phillip Stepney, the Council's Senior Auditor reported on one property, 26 Park Road, to two Detective Officers. Essex Police took the view at this time that the allegation of bad workmanship and work not being done was due to negligence rather than criminal intent, but undertook to investigate the matter if other evidence came to light.

As a result of further enquiries carried out by the Internal Audit Department, a written complaint referring to 26 Park Road, from Mr Roy Peacock, now the Town Clerk, dated 11 December 1984, was received by the Chief Superintendent, Southend Division. This resulted in a police investigation being started.

'No mention so far of Fred Laws,' thought Ron. 'In any case, if the first police visit was made on 23 October, a week before Fred Law's retirement, and Roy Peacock's Internal Audit, which resulted in the criminal complaint to the police during the second week of December, which was after Fred Law's retirement from the Council, then it was very difficult to see how Fred Laws could possibly have reported the complaint to the police: either 'immediately' or at any time.'

Ron continued reading the report:

At the beginning of January 1985 two senior Detectives from Essex Police Fraud Squad commenced the investigations into Southend Council's Home improvement Grant Department: These investigations established beyond any doubt that the Home Improvement Grant in respect of 26 Park Road was fraudulent.

The two Detectives then decided to take a look at all of the Home Improvement Grant applications for 1984: Their hunch was to be proved well justified; several other cases of fraud identical to that of 26 Park Road were uncovered.

The Detectives then decided to examine the Home Improvement Grants for the whole of 1983 and they found more fraudulent Grants. They then decided to see just how far back the fraudulent Grants went.

Four years after starting their investigations the Detectives called a halt at a staggering five hundred cases of fraud.

Ron read the report with growing astonishment, his hands were trembling. If the report was accurate, and there is every reason to believe that it was because it was based on police evidence at the trial, then it confirmed that it was Roy Peacock who reported the fraud to the police and not Fred Laws.

How different the outcome might have been if this evidence had been available during Ron's libel hearing. A really good barrister could have calculated that there was likely to be such evidence, which may have presented him with a strong argument to have the libel action deferred until after the conclusion of the fraud trial

In the face of such dramatic evidence Ron wondered if there might be some merit in considering an appeal against the libel verdict. But he knew that if he were to go down that road he would have to be more careful about the source and credibility of his evidence than he had been before.

It would be unwise to rely on press reports alone and other third party evidence or information; it would need to come from an official source... perhaps the police.

But in any case, an appeal was bound to be costly. And Ron and Patricia had settled into their new home in Colchester. They had recovered from the trauma of the trial and things were going well for them. Did he really want to rake up all the past and go through another stressful legal process? It seemed a shame not to take advantage of the possibility of redressing the balance of injustice of the trial. However, so much time had passed since the judgement an appeal was bound to be out of time... and yet, a strong instinct chipped away at his doubts. His mind returned to his brief discussion with Patrick Milmo outside the Court Room at the end of the trial: 'One day I shall write a book about all this'.

.

Ron decided to start writing his book straight away, and at the same time he could explore the possibility of laying the foundations of an Appeal against the judgement.

Eventually, his curiosity got the better of him. Following a little research he phoned the Civil Appeals Office at the Royal Courts of Justice. They told him that he was most definitely out of time to appeal, but to overcome that obstacle he would need to ask the Plaintiff's Solicitors for their agreement to extension of the time to appeal. He would also need to obtain from them a copy of the Sealed Order, which should be in their possession because it would have been their responsibility to have the Order Sealed thereby starting the clock for the Appeal time limit to run.

On 5 March 1991 Ron phoned the legal Services Ombudsman to seek advice on how to go about appealing against the Judgement. They advised him to contact the Royal Courts of Justice and enquire as to the procedure for making application for leave to appeal against the judgement.

Ron decided that it would be better to pay a visit to the Royal Courts of Justice, discuss it face to face with someone, rather than spend perhaps hours on the phone to them. A few days later Ron boarded the 09.38 train at Colchester North station heading for London. It was the start of his journey to the Royal Courts of Justice, and the beginning of his endeavour to appeal against Judgement. His visit proved to be well worth while. He received some very helpful guidance on the procedure to follow together with two important documents: 'Summary of Action and Grounds for Appeal', and Legal Aid Application Guidance papers.

During the train journey home Ron had lots to think about: He had by now dismissed thoughts of claiming damages; Patricia was right... he should receive no financial gain from a successful appeal, it would be enough to restore his good name; such a win would provide an excellent conclusion to his book.

When Ron arrived home he was still excited about the prospect of an appeal. Patricia listened intently to the details of his visit. But he could see that she was anxious. He wanted to reassure her and promised that he would be very cautious. It was early days yet and he assured her that he would only go ahead with the appeal if the evidence was irrefutable. It was also encouraging to know that if circumstances changed, it would be possible to withdraw the Appeal before it was set down. When he had calmed down they both set about completing the forms that Ron had brought home.

Three days later Ron was ready to lodge the completed forms. He knew he would have to wait whilst his request for consent to appeal was considered. If it was approved he would be sent the Appeal Application Forms plus a request for a fee of £100 towards the cost of appeal. The guidance notes advised that if the application was not approved he would be given an opportunity to discuss the reasons.

Within a week Ron received a response from the Civil Appeals Office saying:

I am enclosing forms to make an application for extending time against the Order dated 20 October 1988.

However, the Order which you lodged is in fact the Associate's Certificate. This is normally sent to the solicitors in order for them to draw up the Order and send it to the Court to be sealed.

Until we receive a copy of the Sealed Order and Court fee of £50 we will not be able to set down your application.

Ron hadn't realised how complicated the process would be. It made him aware how cautious he needed to be without legal representation, but he was determined to get it right.

Ron then responded as competently as he could to the Civil Appeals Office:

Thank you for your letter of 13 March and enclosures.

I am in the process of writing to the Plaintiff's solicitors requesting a letter of consent extending my time against the Order: They have replied and they inform me they are now awaiting their client's instructions. When my correspondence with them is concluded I shall write to you again with a view to proceed further in the matter.

On 18 March Ron completed his letter to Drysdales & Janes informing them that evidence had come into his possession which conflicted with evidence that Fred Laws gave at the libel action trial. His letter sought their consent to an extension of the time for setting down the appeal, together with a request for a copy of the Sealed Order:

Their prompt reply was a terse refusal of their consent to appeal out of time. It was signed by Philip Jackson.

Noting that Jackson was still acting for Fred Laws, Ron replied equally promptly reminding them that they had not responded to his request for a copy of the Sealed Order - and repeated his request. At the same time he informed them that he had submitted an application for extending time for appeal against the Order.

Jackson replied on 3 April saying:

We have written to Mr Laws for his instructions and as soon as they are to hand we will communicate further with you.

Until we receive those instructions we will refrain from making any comments on what you have to say.

A further five weeks passed before Jackson wrote again. This time it was to tell Ron that;

'We are unable to supply you with a copy of the Order because we cannot find the relevant file.'

Astounded by Jackson's reply, Ron's immediate response pulled no punches:

'You say that you are unable to supply me with a copy of the Order because you cannot find the relevant file. It seems almost beyond belief that you have 'mislaid' such an important file, especially so in such a short space of time. I would like to think that this is a genuine instance of ineptitude and not a deliberate act of obstruction: Although on reflection this whole business has been plagued with missing files, and documents that mysteriously burst into flames. I shall, as you suggest, apply to the Southend District Registry for a copy of the Order. It is to be hoped that they have taken greater care of their files than your firm appears to have done with its files.

Ron could not help but feel that Jackson's reply showed that he was clutching at straws:

We have obtained our Client's further instruction.

Our Client says that his memory of precise details of what occurred after the complaint by Councillor Copley, are now rather dim. He says that he is absolutely certain of one thing and it is that he initiated the enquiry. Our Client confirms that it was towards the end of October 1984 that he left the Council's service and he commenced his duties as a Commissioner on the 1st of November 1994 and it therefore follows that his successor, Mr Roy Peacock, who was previously the Borough Treasurer, held the prime responsibility for assisting the Police enquiries

In the circumstances, we cannot see that you have any grounds for appeal.

In his immediate reply Ron said:

I am in receipt of your letter of 31 May which is no less unsatisfactory than your previous replies to my correspondence in that it does not provide the information that I requested.

Your letter is also misleading in that you say that Mr Laws "... is absolutely certain...that he initiated the enquiry." This does not actually say whether he first reported the matter to the police: also, you say that Mr Laws confirms that "... Mr Roy Peacock... held the prime responsibility for assisting the police enquiries." Again, this does not actually say whether Mr Peacock first reported the matter to the police.

In view of your apparent difficulty in providing the information that I have requested perhaps it would be helpful if I put my questions in more precise terms:

1. Does Mr Laws deny that he lied to the Court?

2. Does Mr Laws insist that he first informed the police of Councillor Copley's complaint?

3. Does Mr Laws claim that evidence exists, or did exist, that he personally informed the police of Councillor Copley's complaint?

4. Does Mr Laws deny that Mr Peacock first reported Councillor Copley's complaint to the police?

5, Does Mr Laws claim that Mr Stepney's statement to the police is incorrect?

6. Is Mr Laws able to explain why his evidence to the Court conflicts with Mr Stepney's statement regarding the date that Councillor Copley's complaint was first reported to the police?

I have taken great care to ensure that the answers to these questions are within Mr Laws' capability either from the documents which I have already provided you with or from information which I am certain is known to him. Would *you now please let me have those answers as soon as possible.*

Any first-year law student will know that a judgment that is been obtained with false evidence is wrong and represents the strongest grounds for a successful appeal. In these circumstances I find your inability to see that I have any grounds for appeal quite astonishing.

In fairness to all concerned you will no doubt agree that this is a matter for the Court to decide.

Ron decided to let the matter rest at that for the time being, but he decided to write to Southend District Registry of the High Court of Justice, to ask if they are able to provide a copy of the Sealed Order:

'In respect of the above action (Sealed Order) new evidence has emerged which provides grounds for an appeal against the Order made on the twentieth day of October 1988.

I have initially lodged papers with the Civil Appeals Office but they inform me that the Order which I lodged is in fact an Associates Certificate and not the Sealed Order. I have approached the Plaintiff's solicitors to obtain a copy of the Sealed Order but they say that they are unable to find their file.

In their letter to me, a copy of which is enclosed for your guidance, the Civil Appeals Office advise that until they receive a copy of the Sealed Order they will not be able to set down my application.

I shall be most grateful if you will kindly assist me with a copy of the Sealed Order at your earliest convenience'.

The reply from Southend District Registry arrived on the 19 June:

'Following your letter of 5 June 1991 our file has been checked for an Order dated 20 October 1988. The District Registry has never been supplied with a Sealed copy for our file hence I cannot help you with your query.'

As disappointing as their reply was Ron knew he had to continue the search. And so he wrote again to Jackson to ask him which Court Sealed the Order and the date on which it was sealed

Jackson's reply brought no further enlightenment:

'We thank you for your letter of 21 instant.

As you know, we have informed you that our file has gone missing and, included in that file, was any Court Order. Our recollection is that the Order was sealed in London. If you contact the District Registry at Southend, quoting the case number, they should be able to tell you where the Order was sealed and the date, because they should have in their possession a copy on the Court File.'

Ron saw no point in telling Jackson the result of his enquiry to Southend District Registry. He decided to leave Jackson in the dark for a while longer. Instead he chose to try the Associates Department at the Royal Courts of Justice and on 2 July he wrote:

Re; Sealed Order

In respect of this action new evidence has emerged which provides grounds for appeal against the Order made on 20th day of October 1998.

I have initially lodged papers with the Civil Appeals office but they informed me that the Order which I lodged is in fact an Associates Certificate and not the Sealed Order. I have approached the Plaintiff's Solicitors to obtain a copy of the

Sealed Order but they say they are unable to find their file. I have written to Southend District Registry but they say they have no record of the Sealed Order on their file, or any other department of the Courts. I would be most grateful if you could assist me by sending me a copy so that I can set down my application.

Thank you for your assistance.

At the same time he wrote to the Civil Appeals Office to bring them up to date on his enquiries:

I write further to my letter of 5 April 1991.

My correspondence with the Plaintiff's Solicitors now appears to have gone as far as is possible. I feel that they have not been as helpful as they could have been; First, they have refused to consent to the extension of time which refusal would seem unreasonable in view of the new evidence which I copied to them: They have failed to provide me with a copy of the Sealed Order – they say that they have lost their file: Their response to my request for information relating to the new evidence has been misleading and evasive, although the Plaintiff does admit that he does not have any documentary evidence to support the statement that he made to the Court which conflicts with the new evidence.

In consequence, I wrote to Southend District Registry requesting a copy of the Sealed Order from their file. They replied stating that they have no record of the Sealed Order. I am now writing to the Associates Department of the Royal Courts of Justice requesting a copy of the Sealed Order from their file.

In view of the above information and admission by the

Plaintiff I am also submitting a further appeal to the Legal Aid Board requesting that they reconsider their dismissal of my earlier appeal.

It is disconcerting that there should be such a delay in lodging my Appeal but I am doing my best to achieve a solution and I look forward to early progress in the matter.

Many thanks for your consideration and assistance.

A week later Ron wrote to the Area Manager of the Legal Aid Office giving details to date of his preparations to appeal against the Order together the supporting evidence for the appeal.

With all this flurry of letter-writing Ron remembered that he hadn't replied to the District Registry of the Southend County Court. He thought it would be prudent to do so now and wrote:

Thank you for your letter of 18 June 1991.

I have written to the Plaintiff's Solicitors who say that to their recollection the Order was sealed in London. They again say that if I contact the District Registry of Southend you should be able to tell me where the Order was sealed and the date because you should have in your possession a copy on the Court file.

'I have also written to the Associates Department at the Royal Courts of Justice who advise me that the number quoted is not a London number in which case the Judgement would have to be entered in the District Registry and not in London and they would have no record of it.

'The Chief Associate also advises me that it would appear that the Plaintiff's solicitors may not have entered the Judgement. If that were the case then, unusual as such

situation would be I could possibly be entitled to draw the Judgement myself, in my own time, and enter it at Southend District Registry. This would then set the clock ticking for the time limit to lodge my Appeal. This I now wish to do and I would be grateful if you would advise me as to the required procedure: Whether it can be done by post and what the cost is likely to be.

'I would much prefer to have this matter dealt with by a solicitor but my financial situation prohibits this.
Thank you for your assistance and consideration.

Given the prevailing circumstances it seemed reasonable to assume that Jackson would be unaware of this bizarre situation, and Ron relished the prospect of being able to run rings round Jackson by not telling him. Ron was going to get a lot of mileage out of this. He would continue with the appeal process and see how long it would take Jackson to realise what an enormous legal blunder he had made.

The next most important task for Ron was to write to Southend police. He needed to ask them if they would be willing to let him have details of the evidence regarding the reporting of the Home Improvement Grant fraud to them that was used during the trial at Chelmsford Crown Court: this Ron did on 17 July 1991

The reply Ron received came from the Deputy Chief Constable, Mr P J Simpson, at Police Headquarters, Chelmsford, who confirmed that the press report was generally correct. However, DCC Simpson also explained that such requests for copies of evidence would need to be made through a solicitor.

In his reply Ron explained that his financial circumstances

were such that he could not afford to be legally represented in his request for the information that he needed in order to prepare his own case.

In the meantime, on 22 August, Ron visited the Civil Appeals Office with a list of questions about making application to appeal. He wanted to know exactly what he needed to do to prepare for his appeal; he wanted to hear the full details of the process, from making the application to preparing his evidence. Ron already knew that the most important requirement of all was a transcript of his questioning of Fred Laws during the trial when he insisted that he did report the fraud complaint to the police. Ron was told that he would need to make arrangements with the Mechanical Recordings Department to listen to the relative section on the tape and note the start and finish times which showed on a small screen as it was played. He then would need to contact a firm from a list of authorised transcribers to produce the typed transcript.

Ron knew that it was all going to take a great deal of time and dedication, but he was determined to see it through.

A few days later he received a reply from DCC Simpson saying:

'Thank you for advising me that you are unable to employ a solicitor for the purpose of interviewing the officer who investigated the Southend Borough Council home improvement grant inquiry.

Your request for information has been further considered and opinion taken about the facts which you ask to be confirmed. In view of the circumstances which require you to conduct your own case I am prepared, on this occasion, to release the information without the need for a solicitor's interview.

Accordingly, I give an abstract of the investigating officer's report:

"At a meeting on 23 October 1984 at Southend on sea Borough Council offices, Mr ROY PEACOCK, Town Clerk and Mr PHILIP STEPNEY, the Council's Senior Auditor reported on one property, 26, Park Road, to two Detective Officers. Essex Police took the view at this time that the allegation of bad workmanship and work not being done was due to negligence rather than criminal intent, but undertook to investigate the matter if other evidence came to light".

As a result of further enquiries carried out by the Internal Audit Department, a written complaint referring to 26 Park Road, from Mr Roy PEACOCK, dated 11 December 1984, was received by the Chief Superintendent, Southend Division. This resulted in a police investigation being started.

Ron read the final paragraph through again. He knew that if this statement was correct the implications were quite astonishing. Fred Laws retired at the end of October 1984: Roy Peacock would have automatically succeeded him as Chief Executive Officer on 1 November. Therefore, if the police investigation started following a written complaint dated 11 December, as DCC Simpson said, then It could not have been Fred Laws who reported the Home Improvement Grant fraud to the police because he had already retired from the post.

To Ron this was fantastic news. And yet, faint warning bells were ringing. The letter doesn't actually say that Fred Laws didn't report the fraud complaint. If it did that would really be an enormous help to Ron's appeal.

And so he decided to put some more questions to DCC Simpson, after all, the tone of his letter seemed to suggest that he was willing to help, and so Ron put together six of the most important questions for DCC Simpson and posted them to him on 12 September. He wrote:

The information which you have conveyed to me is most helpful. However, it would appear to expand the area of evidence that I now require in order to prepare the best possible case for my appeal. For example:

1. I shall need to know what prompted the visit to Southend Borough Council on 23 October by the two Detective Officers.

2. I shall need to know whether the allegation of bad workmanship and work not being done (to 26 Park Road) was the only allegation made either before, or at the, meeting on 23 October 1984.

3. I shall need to know how the written complaint from Mr Roy Peacock of 11 December differed from the allegations made at the meeting of 23 October.

4. I shall need to know what other 'evidence came to light' Which caused the two Detective Officers to keep their undertaking to investigate the matter.

5. I shall need to know if the investigating officer is aware of what 'further enquiries were carried out by the Internal Audit Department' that formed the basis of the written Complaint of 11 December.

6. Finally, I shall need to know the extent of Mr Laws' involvement in respect of the complaints to the police regarding 26 Park Road.

'I fully appreciate the demand on your valuable time that my request makes but I am equally certain that you will appreciate the importance of fully preparing and researching my case for appeal before going into Court.

Three anxious weeks later DCC Simpson's reply arrived. What he said gave a detailed explanation of how the complaint was dealt with, but it still missed the most important information that Ron desperately sought. DCC Simpson wrote:

The answers you requested are set out below:

1. The initial call to Southend Borough Council offices was as a result of a telephone call to Southend C.I.D as a result of a complaint by Councillor COPLEY, to the Chief Executive of Southend Borough Council.

2. The allegation being made by Councillor COPLEY only concerned 26 Park Road.

3. The written letter of complaint from Mr Roy PEACOCK dated 11 December 1984 reiterated the earlier verbal complaint to officers from the C.I.D. office at Southend after further enquiries had been made.

4. The officers who had received the earlier verbal complaint had asked for specific examples of bad workmanship and work not being done. Two qualified surveyors from the Southend Borough Council surveyors' department carried out a full survey of the property and found substantial evidence of work not being done, poor workmanship and work of poor value for money.

5. As a result of the initial complaint from Councillor Copley, the Chief Internal Auditor commenced an audit of the Grants Office. This initial enquiry revealed the group of names who were involved in the 26 Park Road property, also appeared in a large number of other applications. Further enquiries revealed other name groups who appeared time and again. During the interview of the people involved in the 26 Park Road property, including Mr HERMAN, the manager of the Grants Office, admissions were made by HERMAN and Graham BECK that corrupt payments had been received and made. These admissions together with the evidence coming to light as a result the audit investigation caused the start of 'Operation Hermit'.

5. The involvement of Mr Laws in this enquiry was only that of being the Chief Executive of the Southend Borough Council, a person to whom Mr HERMAN was responsible for a short period of time.

I hope this information will be of assistance to you.

Although DCC Simpson's reply gave more information than Ron had expected, it still did not contain the most vital information he needed to give strength to his appeal. Ron knew that to persist with further clarification might be pushing his luck, but he just had to take that chance – he wrote:

Thank you for your letter of 4 October the contents of which certainly are of assistance.

However, the answers are not quite as comprehensive as I had hoped. In consequence, it would be greatly appreciated if you would kindly agree my request for clarification in the following:

1. Who actually made the telephone call to Southend C.I.D and what was the date and nature of that call, as referred to in your reply to question 1?

2. Was the allegation of bad workmanship and work not having been done (to 26 Park Road) the only allegation made in respect of 26 Park Road either before, or at, the meeting on 23 October?

3. Did the written complaint from Mr Roy Peacock of 11 December contain complaints additional to those which reiterated the earlier complaints to officers from the C.I.D office at Southend?

4. What was the precise nature of the complaint from Councillor Copley and were the officers given any documents that Councillor Copley may have submitted to the Town Clerk together with that complaint? Furthermore, if Southend C.I.D. had interviewed Mr Herman immediately following the first telephone call to Southend C.I.D. (your reply question 1) would 'Operation Herman' have started there and then in October 1984 rather than in December... assuming that Mr Herman would make the same admissions to the police that he made to the Council's Chief Internal Auditor?

5, Do I take your reply to mean that Mr Laws took no part in the reporting of Councillor Copley's complaint to Southend C.I.D. and that he took no part in any of the subsequent police investigations of Councillor Copley's complaint?

I do not understand the legitimacy of the claim regarding Terry Herman's alleged autonomous administration of the Home Improvement Grants because all Grant applications required the approval of the Housing and Estates Committee (of which I was a member), and subsequent payments of the Grants required the approval and signature of the Director of Housing and Estates or the Assistant Director of Housing and Estates.

Thank you, again, for your most valuable assistance.

Again, no clear confirmation as to whether Fred Laws actually reported the complaint to the police. Ron was fearful that to persist with this request could alienate DCC Simpson and risk losing his willingness to help further... but it had to be done, and so Ron asked again:

On 12 November Ron received what was to be his final letter on the subject:

I refer to your letter dated 15 October 1991, and set out below is the only additional information that has been obtained from what you will appreciate is a very large police file and it has taken one of my officers a considerable amount of time to extract these details as the officer in charge of the case has now left the Force. I hope this information is of assistance to you:

1. The person who made the actual telephone call to Southend police was Mr Peacock, Chief Executive and Town Clerk to Chief Superintendent F SHEPHERD.

The actual detail of the call is unknown and is not recorded on the file.

3. There are no details of the meeting on the 23 October.

4. The only complaint was in relation to 26 Park Road.

5. As far as can be ascertained Mr LAWS took no part in the reporting of the complaint.

Yours faithfully,

James A Conlan

Assistant Chief Constable Administration.

'Wow' thought Ron. 'That's it. I've got it. He really didn't report the fraud to the police. This is dynamite. Roy Peacock made the call to the police in October, which was after Fred Laws retired, and, according to the police records, Fred Laws took no part in reporting the matter to them: well you can't make it clearer than that. So I can get cracking on my

Appeal straight away.

CHAPTER 19

During the following four months Ron made several visits to the Civil Appeals Office. The Legal Department Officers were very helpful in providing guidance on the actions that he needed to take, the documents that he should assemble in putting his appeal together and the necessary forms that had to be completed and submitted to the Appeals Office. By this time it had been established beyond doubt that Fred Laws' Solicitors had failed to have the Order sealed after the Libel hearing, which would have started the clock for the time limit of four weeks in which to appeal against the Judgement. It was beyond Ron's understanding, and belief, that they could have made such an enormous blunder. He was also advised that in the circumstances it was within his legal right to have the Order sealed himself, in his own time, thereby triggering the time limit for Appeal, without the consent of Fred Laws' Solicitors: Ron could not believe his luck that he should be able to do this eight years after the Judgement.

On 23 January 1992 Ron telephoned John Larkin, Verbatim Reporters at Chancery Lane, London from the list of Transcribers, and spoke to Mr James Chapman. Mr Chapman explained to Ron that he would need to call the

Royal Courts of Justice and speak to the Mechanical Recording Department, give them the case number and arrange an appointment to listen to the tape. He would then need to locate the part of the recording that contained the section of the hearing that he wanted transcribed. When he had completed this task Ron was to give the details to Mr Chapman who would obtain a copy of the recorded section and produce the required transcript.

Two weeks later Ron arrived at the Royal Courts of Justice and was directed to the Mechanical recordings Department. He was then escorted to a room which contained a number of upright tape machines with very large tape reels. He was offered a seat at one of the machines and shown how to run the tape backwards and forwards. A set of headphones was given to him together with instructions to listen to the recording and to note the number that appeared on the indicator at the start of the section that he wanted, and then to run the tape further forward until he reached the end of the required section. Ron's escort then told him that when he had completed his task he was to press the buzzer by the door and the escort would return to check that he was happy with what he had heard and noted.

Ron was beginning to feel quite excited. He hadn't realised it would be so simple – and such a charming, helpful escort. He placed the head phones comfortably over his ears – and pressed the start button.

The section that Ron heard surprised and amazed him, time had somewhat dulled his memory of exactly how much of what Fred Laws had said in evidence that was untrue: It was good to hear, and it raised Ron's hopes for his appeal.

Whilst in the building Ron's next call was to the Civil Appeals Office to seek clarification of the correct procedure for lodging his Appeal. The Official who dealt with his enquiry gave a very helpful explanation of the process. Ron now fully understood what he needed to do. But first, and most important, was to obtain the transcript.

It was more than a year later, during which time Ron managed to complete all of the essential preparations, that he received the official document from the Court of Appeal which was headed 'NOTICE of APPEAL'. Ron Read it through several times, his heart racing. He could barely believe he had managed it; and without a solicitor. He decided it was now time to write again to Jackson, and he eagerly set out on what he hoped would be the final part of his ambition to clear his name.

It was now mid June 1992. Ron set about writing his letter to Jackson:

I refer to correspondence in this matter last year.

I am now able to proceed with my application for appeal to the Court of Appeal and I would ask you please to provide me with the following:

1. Any list of exhibits made under Order 35, rule 11, or the schedule of evidence, as the case may be as were evidence in the Court below.

2. The 'note of judgement' of Counsel who appeared for your client in the Court below in accordance with Order 59 rule 9/6.

In view of the time limits which must be complied with and which will be strictly enforced I would ask you, please, to deal with this request without delay. Ron enclosed a copy of the NOTICE OF APPEAL.

Surprisingly, Jackson must have been composing a letter to Ron at the very same time, which must have crossed in the post with Ron's letter. Jackson wrote:

Dear Sir,

As you are aware, we have heard nothing further from you in this matter. When going through our files, we in fact noticed that you sent to us in March1991 a copy of a letter that you had received from the Civil Appeals Office in London. The first sentence in that letter reads, and we quote, "I am sending you forms to make an application for extending time against the Order dated 20th October 1988".

You seem to have completely ignored what that letter says, and as you know, we have already pointed out to you in correspondence that if you are intending to proceed with any Appeal, then it is necessary for you to make an application to the Court for an extension of time. We have also made it clear to you that if you apply for an extension, then this would be strenuously opposed.

Ron saw no point replying to this letter, Jackson would eventually realise that his comments are now irrelevant and that he would need to reply to Ron's latest letter. Jackson's reply came very promptly:

We thank you for your letter of the 18th instant, enclosing Notice of Appeal. We do not think that you have studied the Rules relating to an Appeal because under Order 59 Rule 4, you have to appeal not later four weeks after the Judgement or Order. You have never obtained any extension to appeal out of time, and therefore we cannot possibly see how you can proceed with your case. If you wish to proceed with an appeal, then in our view you would need to apply to the

Court for an extension of time for appealing, and of course this would be strenuously opposed in view of the enormous delay that there has been, and of course delay is one of the most serious matters that would need to be considered by the Court.

With regard to Order 59 Rule 9/6, we think you have misread what that has to say, You are the proposed Appellant, and of course it is up to you to make all the running in this case, and you have to prepare any documents and then they must be submitted to us for possible agreement or alteration. We cannot see the relevance of Order 35 Rule 11, but again it is up to you to prepare documents for the use of the Court of Appeal. And of course to supply us with details of what document you think should be before the Court.

We note that in the last paragraph of your letter, you refer to time limits. We do not know to what time limits you are referring, but as we see the situation, time limits are your problem, and not ours.

We would suggest with respect that you obtain legal advice if you are intending to proceed with an Appeal.

A few days later Ron received a letter from the Court of Appeal informing him that the Notice of Appeal which they sent earlier in the month was not published on the official Court of Appeal Form and was therefore not valid, and enclosing the properly published Notice of Appeal. Ron immediately wrote to inform Jackson of the Court's error, and enclosed the new Notice of Appeal.

In his reply to Ron, Jackson could barely conceal his irritation, and his confusion:

We thank you for your letter of the 3ʳᵈ ᴶᵘˡʸ instant enclosing a new Notice of Appeal. We repeat what we said in our letter, to you, of the 22 ultimo. We cannot see how you can proceed with any Appeal without obtaining leave and we will refer you to Order 59/4/4. Question of documents, in our view, does not arise at this stage. You seem to have completely ignored the time limits imposed for appeal, which is four weeks after the date on which the Judgement or Order was sealed, or was otherwise perfected. This is dealt with in Order 59 Rule 4. This is not a case where you are a few days, perhaps a week or two, out of time. In October, it will be four years since the case was dealt with. Again, we would suggest that you obtain legal advice if you intend doing anything about an Appeal.

In the meantime Ron had received a further notification from the High Court telling him that a date had been set for the hearing of his Appeal and that he must inform the Plaintiff's Solicitors immediately. 'With pleasure' thought Ron, and set about the task as instructed, making sure he dated his letter, it was the 10 July 1992:

'I have to give you notice (Rule 59/5/10) that the Appeal in the above action has been set down on the 9 day of July in the Queen's Bench Division Final List.

I am advised that the Appeal will be allocated a number in the next seven to ten days. When that number is made known to me I shall convey it to you immediately.

In reply to your recent letters rejecting my right to Appeal I enclose herewith a copy of the Sealed Order which should explain the authority for the Appeal.

How Ron wished he could be a fly on the wall when

Jackson reads his letter.

The High Court was as good as its word, on the 18 of July Ron received a letter from them informing him of the latest development in his Appeal, which he must convey to Drysdales & Janes. Ron eagerly wrote that letter without delay:

Further to my letter of 10 July I now have to notify you that my Appeal has been entered in the records of the Court of Appeal and has been allocated the reference Q BENF 92/0889/C. This case will enter the List of Forthcoming Appeals on 9th September 1992.

I refer to your recent letters. I have not ignored the time limits for Appeal. Indeed, The Civil Appeals Office would not have issued the necessary documents to enable me to do so in accordance with the Rules laid down in the Supreme Court Practice: This, of course, should have been known to you.
The Sealed Order that I sent to you was drawn up in accordance with Order 59/56/6 (paragraph 3).

With regard to your letter of 22 June the reason that you heard nothing further from me is that I was awaiting notification of my Appeal reference allocation. It should be clear to you now that I am able to make Appeal without application for an extension of time.

It is not for me to advise you, indeed it would be impudent of me to do so, but I would respectfully draw your attention to r. 6(4); para.59/6/7.

I have also to complete the Time Estimate Form (copy enclosed) although this does not have to be returned to the Civil Appeals Office until not later than 23 September. It is my opinion that the hearing of the case is likely to occupy the time of the Court for one day. I would be helpful if you would give this estimate your consideration as preparations proceed and let me know if you agree before I return the form.

Despite the urgency of the matter Jackson still took three weeks to reply:

We thank you for your letter of the 23 ultimo. We apologise for not replying to this sooner, but the person dealing with the matter was away from the office.

We have written to the Court about this matter because, we cannot see how your Appeal has been allowed to be entered. As soon as we receive a reply from the Court, we will be in touch with you,

By the 21 August Ron had completed the preparation of his documents bundle and the necessary papers to send to Drysdales & Janes. He was getting very tired of all the letter writing and legal processes but he was determined to see it through, and pressed on with the next letter to Jackson:

I would advise you that the bundles are ready for lodging with the Civil Appeals Office and I must immediately serve on you:-

1. A legible photocopy of the index to the Applicant's bundles. (Enclosed herewith)

2. A list specifying precisely what transcripts the Applicant has bespoken for the use of the Court of Appeal: These are;

3. (a) The Judge's Judgement.

(b) Extract from Proceedings from tape No. 755 16.12 hrs. to 16.24hrs:

Mr Laws' cross examination by Mr Levy.

I am also required to send you a copy of the Time Estimate form (annex D) with my estimate of the time that the Court is likely to occupy with this application. This is also enclosed herewith.

PS. Your letter of 20th August arrived after this letter was typed. I shall reply as soon as possible. In the meantime I would like you to let me have a copy of the Note of Judgment that you refer to so that I may consider my position: I never received such Note of Judgement.

'Also enclosed: Representation Sheet. Please advise if it is incorrect.

Two weeks later Ron received a notice from Drysdales & Janes stating that it was their intention to seek a Security of Costs Order and asked him to let them have full details of his financial situation as soon as possible.

This demand from Jackson didn't fool Ron. He knew it was an obstruction, a delaying tactic. Possibly even an attempt to prevent his Appeal by claiming that he would not be able to pay the costs if he loses it. In a way it showed that Jackson was afraid that Ron's evidence could mean a successful Appeal. If that was so Jackson would be desperate to prevent Ron's Appeal going ahead. The thought gave Ron fresh courage and he immediately set about putting together an appropriate reply:

I acknowledge receipt of your letter of 4 September which is receiving my attention.

Obviously my preparation of the Appeal Bundle to be lodged within the strict time scale takes priority and I shall reply in detail to your letter at the earliest moment thereafter.

Jackson's reply was equally prompt, and he was clearly

rattled by Ron's failure to treat the matter as urgent:

We thank you for your letter of the 7th instant.

So far as we can see it would take you less than 15 minutes to write to us and set down your financial situation and, therefore, will you please let us hear from you by return. In our view, the matter of security for costs takes precedent over any other issue because, in our view, if you are not able to cover the costs position, then the Court would not allow you to proceed any further with your Appeal. In the circumstances, unless we do hear from you, by return, we shall issue a summons for Security of Costs and, at the same time, we would ask that the appeal be stayed pending the hearing of the Summons'.

So, I was right', thought Ron'. 'They really are intent on stopping my Appeal. Things are really hotting up. They must think I have a strong case for them to get so anxious.' But Ron didn't really want to prolong the process by defending a summons and so he set about putting his financial status together. The task certainly took considerably more time than Jackson had estimated, but Ron was able to send the details off to him on 21st of September:

Ron's opening remarks dealt mainly with, though reluctantly, providing details of his income and capital position, he continued and wrote:

'Notwithstanding the foregoing it is my view that there is no necessity for you to make application for a Security of Costs Order and that if you still insist on so doing, that you do so for reasons that I have previously suggested. However, I accept that it is your right to make such application. It is also my right to oppose it, and I shall do so strenuously by

persuading the Registrar that the estimated costs are well within my ability to pay. If that fails I shall submit the view that the merit of my Appeal is such as to make a Security of Costs Order unnecessary.

I would advise you that I have now lodged the requisite bundle of Appeal documents and I am required to serve on you a copy of the index to my bundle, this index is enclosed herewith. As you will know the Appellant is not obliged to provide Appeal bundles and transcripts for the Respondent's side albeit that all the documents will be in your possession already. I am also required to let you know what transcripts I have bespoken which are:

Extract from Proceedings 14 October 1998.

The Judge's summing up and verdict 19/20 October 1988.

In your letter of 4 September you refer to my letter of the second instant. This was an error on my part. My letter should have been dated 26 August. I have adjusted my records accordingly and I would be grateful if you will do likewise with yours. In your letter you say that there is no question of you withholding any document from me or of trying to hide any fact that might have a bearing on this case. With that assurance in mind I would ask you, please, to check your file and let me know the date that you visited my home to carry out the exercise of splitting the Discovery documents into Plaintiff's Documents and Defendant's documents.

To Ron's surprise Jackson's reply arrived within two days:

We thank you for your letter of the 21st instant, with enclosures.

On the figures that you have disclosed, we do not think

that you would be in a position to meet any substantial Order for costs that may be made against you. We hardly think this is a satisfactory situation so far as security of cost is concerned.

With regard to documents, you have now supplied us with your List and you say that you have lodged bundles at the Court. We have written to the Registrar of Civil Appeals to say that we have now received your List and we are giving the matter our consideration, particularly, with regard to documents that we feel should be before the Court and, therefore, in our view, the Appeal should not be entered for hearing until we have had an opportunity of considering your List and dealing with the documentary position. We have also pointed out to the Registrar of Civil Appeals that we think this is a case where an Application for Security of costs will need to be made and we told the Registrar that we are now sending all the papers to Counsel for his advice on the situation.

We are, also, not in a position, at the moment, to say how long we think a hearing would last because this is a matter for Counsel to decide and he can only do this once he has looked at all the papers.

Ron shook his head in disbelief. They are going to try using the same strategy that they used at the Trial, he said to himself. They are going to split the bundles again. Well, I'm forewarned this time and I'm not going to let them get away with it quite that easily. He carefully read the letter again to make sure of how to reply:

I thank you for your letter of 23 September 1992.

I note what you say regarding costs and I disagree with

your view that I would be unable to meet such costs. I also note that you use the word "substantial". I do not regard the estimate of costs, which is your own estimate, as substantial. Your application is exactly as I anticipated and it will be for the Registrar to decide.

You seem to have disregarded my request for information regarding your visit to my home prior to the trial. As you know, I have co-operated fully with you in all your requests for documents and information. Please will you reciprocate and let me have the details that I have requested by return.

Ron waited until the 12th 0f October and decided that Jackson should have replied by now, and so he wrote to him again:

It is now more than three weeks since I last wrote to you (25 September) with a request for information regarding your visit to my home prior to the trial. To date I have not received either reply or acknowledgement.

I would remind you again of your previous assurance that you would not try to hide from me any fact that may have a bearing on this case. So, for the third time of asking, on what date in 1988 did you call at my home to split and re-number the Discovery Documents?

With regard to a Security of Costs Order (rule 59/10/26) I have not yet received a Summons: If you have made the Application please would you advise me the date of such Application.

The following day Ron received a letter from Jackson, dated 12 October, stating that they were unable to find any reference in their files relating to the exact day that he called on Ron do discuss the splitting and re-numbering of the bundles. It occurred to Ron that the two letters crossed in the post.

Thank you for your letter of 12 October.

I note the information regarding the date that Mr Jackson attended my home. However, I recall my telephone discussion with Mr Jackson to make arrangements for that visit when he advised me of Counsel's decision to split and re-number the bundle of Discovery Documents. Please would you search your file again and let me know the date on which you were advised of his decision to split them. I shall be grateful if you would provide this information without the need to make repeated requests.

With regard to the matter of Security of Costs I note what you say regarding a Summons and I await receipt of same. I am aware that on 15 October your Application was entered in the records of the Court of Appeal and given the reference number REG 926284. If your Application is to proceed then in this respect I suggest that you let me have a complete list of the documents that you intend to put before the Court.

A further ten days passed before Jackson replied to Ron's request. The letter contained vague excuses about searching their files, but contained no information of any real value to Ron: He would have to write again:

I thank you for your letter of 30 October.

You say that you have had to do a considerable search of your files to try and answer the questions posed in my letter of 20 October: What you have come up with is not a reply to that question but a reply to a question that I asked in my letter of 12 October which you have already answered. The question, in simple terms is: on what date did Mr Milmo advise you of his decision to split and renumber the Discovery Documents to go before the Court?

With regard to the Affidavit which I am putting before the Court in support of my Application for leave to adduce further evidence, I would advise you that the attestation clause is attached to the original Affidavit which has been lodged with the Civil Appeals Office. I have, in fact, been sworn to the Affidavit on 16 July 1992 in the Oaths and Swearing Room at the Civil Appeals Office before a properly authorised officer of the Civil Appeals Office.

With regard to the exhibit referred to as 'RAL2' I have not served you with a copy of that document' because you did not ask for a copy and because, as the rules say, The Appellant's side are not obliged to provide Appeal bundles and transcripts for the use of the respondent's side. However, since it is the practice for the appellants to often make arrangements with respondents to provide them with a copy of the transcript on the respondent's side agreeing to pay the additional cost of providing that transcript I am sending you a copy and I would invite you to make some contribution towards the cost of so doing.

If your application for a Security of Costs Order is to proceed then I would suggest that you let me have a complete list of the documents that you intend to put before the Court in support of your application.

The reply this time came from Drysdales & Janes and was dated12 November 1992. Ron wondered if the matter was now being dealt with by another partner in the firm:

We thank you for your letter of the fifth instant.

We had a number of discussions with Counsel, both before

and after Mr Jackson's visit to your premises. Our recollection of the situation is that we spoke to you on the telephone on more than one occasion concerning the bundles being split and this was both before and after the 6 October. We cannot be precise as to an exact date when we first spoke to you about splitting the bundles.

We note what you say with regard to the attestation clause of your Affidavit. What should have happened is that when you served us with a copy of your Affidavit, it should have had details of the Jurat contained therein but the Affidavit was blank.

We are obliged to you for sending us a copy of Exhibit RAL2. We think that you have misunderstood the rules so far as supplying documents are concerned. Where you serve an Affidavit, and there are documents referred to in that Affidavit, then it is incumbent upon you to supply those exhibits or copies thereof when you serve the Affidavit. It has nothing to do with bundles being prepared for the trial. However, be that as it may, we appreciate that you have incurred some expense in obtaining copies and, accordingly, we enclose cheque for £10.00 as a contribution towards expenses.

With regard to the Summons that we have issued, relating to Security for Costs, we have been in touch with the Court and we have spoken to the Clerk dealing with the matter, who informs us that the Summons has been passed to a Registrar for directions and that, as soon as those directions are issued, then the Court will be in touch with us with a hearing date. At that stage, we will send you a copy of the Affidavit, together with a copy of any exhibits.

Ron was now beginning to wonder if he would ever get a straight answer to his question, and so he set about replying, this time in stronger terms:

Thank you for your letter of 12 November.

I am now very concerned at your failure to provide the information that I have requested. It seems most unlikely to me that you did not understand my request and so I must assume that you are trying to hide facts which have a bearing on this case.

I have no doubt that you had discussions with Counsel before Mr Jackson's visit to my home: I also have no doubt that you made attendance notes of those discussions. Likewise, I have no doubt that the information that I seek is in those attendance notes. Therefore, again, and for the third time of asking, please will you search those notes and answer the actual question that I am putting to you:

Q. On which specific date in his discussion with you did Counsel tell you that he had decided to split the bundle into Plaintiff's Documents and Defendant's Documents?

'do not need to know when you advised me of Counsel's decision to split the bundle, you have told me that three times already. I do need to know when Counsel told you.

With regard to cheque for £10.00 as a contribution towards the cost of providing you with a photocopy of the Extract from Proceedings, the sum is smaller than I expected but I thank you nonetheless for that contribution.

I note your comments regarding the Summons and I await the Registrar's directions in the matter.

Again, the reply appeared to not come directly from Jackson:

We thank you for your letter of 17 instant.

We think that we have taken this matter as far as it can go, so far as answering your questions. There is absolutely nothing to hide in this matter and we cannot understand what it is you are pursuing, Reading your Notice of Appeal, It would seem you are trying to say that you were taken by surprise with regard to the bundles being split and that, in some way, this affected your conduct of the case.

As you know, at the beginning of the trial, the Judge was informed of the position with regard to the bundles and he made it absolutely clear to you that, if there was any document that you wanted to go before the Jury that was not in any bundle already before the Jury, then you would have plenty of opportunity to put the document to the Judge so that he could consider whether it was relevant and then, if it was relevant, it could go before the Jury. Perhaps it is some other point that you are trying to make with regard to the documents and, if so, please let us know.

Ron was beginning to despair about all this correspondence. He was so sure that Drysdales & Janes had the information that he wanted, but he began to doubt that they would ever surrender it to him. But he knew that with so much at stake he had to keep trying:

Thank you for your letter of 23 November.

I do not accept that you have taken this matter as far as it can go, so far as answering my question: In the matter of the Appeal you are obliged to disclose all information and facts which have a bearing on the case. I think you know exactly what it is I am pursuing and I think that you are aware of the implications that the correct answer would reveal. Yes, I was taken by surprise at the bundle being split and the documents re-numbered although it was the closeness to the trial that this was sprung upon me that affected the conduct of the case.

I do not think it is appropriate at this stage to put to you the whole of this part of the Appeal argument but I will reply to the points made in the third paragraph of your letter. I do know what the Judge said at the beginning of the trial regarding the bundles. However, it was Mr Milmo who decided on the strategy of splitting the bundle. There was no beneficial reason for splitting and re-numbering the bundle other than to disadvantage the conduct of my defence: All of my documents were relevant and they should have remained in the single trial bundle that had been prepared during the four-year period preceeding the trial. Mr Milmo would have had plenty of opportunity during the trial to challenge any of my documents and to seek the Judge's ruling as to their relevance.

The point that I am making, which I suspect is known to you, with regard to the splitting and re-numbering of the documents is quite simple; I had spent a year or so preparing my defence: I had made hundreds of notes and arguments all meticulously numbered and cross-referenced to the numbered document/s to which they related in the single bundle: Splitting the documents into two separate bundles and re-numbering them had the effect of throwing my defence preparations into disarray: Since you imposed the splitting of the bundle on me only five clear days before the trial there was insufficient time to effectively rearrange my preparations. As you know, during the trial I frequently struggled to find the relative notes for the documents that were at issue. My fumbling caused delay and confusion. The Judge's patience was clearly tested. I am sure you recall his advice to me: Mr Levy, I suggest you go home and burn some midnight oil and put your papers in order. What the Judge did not know is that I had already burned many pints of midnight oil trying to arrange my papers to the changes that you had dictated: Mr Milmo's strategy proved very successful.

Important though this ground of the Appeal is, it is, as you know, secondary to the principal ground of the Appeal; which relates to the false evidence that Mr Laws gave in relation to the Home Improvement Grant fraud.

You should now fully understand my reasons for requiring the information that I have asked for. I can understand your reluctance to make such disclosure but I must insist that these facts be made known to me. Would you please, therefore, let me know when Counsel informed you that he had decided to split and re-number the Discovery Documents.

Ron waited three weeks… but no reply from Jackson. And so he wrote a short letter reminding them that he had received nothing from them.

Christmas came and went, still no response from Jackson. Ron waited a further three weeks, and then on 15th January 1993, which was seven weeks after Ron's final request, he received a letter from Jackson dated 14 January:

We have now heard from the Court that our application for Security of Costs will be heard on 28th January 1993 by the Registrar of Civil Appeals in Chambers at the Royal Courts of

Justice, Strand, London WC2. We now enclose a copy of the Summons, together with the Affidavit in Support and Exhibits and we should be pleased if you will acknowledge receipt.

The Court tells us that they cannot give us a time for the hearing of the application until after 2 p.m. on the afternoon of the 27th January. In the circumstances, you should telephone the Court on the afternoon of the 27th, in order to find out the Court number and the time. The telephone number that the Court have given to us is 071 936 6917/6891 and the reference is REG 92/6284.

With regard to the correspondence that we have had with you concerning the Appeal Bundles, relating to the hearing in 1988, we have nothing further to add.

Ron gave a wry smile he saw the humour in that statement. 'I bet they have nothing further to add, they know I am right. That is why they are so anxious to stop my Appeal. Well, it won't work. I'll pay the Costs Order and Fred Laws will have to answer my claim about the evidence he gave under oath'.

On 28 January 1993 Ron attended the Appeal Court for the hearing on the application for the Security of Costs which, as he expected, was granted. Immediately following that hearing the Judge dealt with Jackson's application to have the Appeal struck: To Ron's enormous relief the application was rejected.

The following day Ron had a telephone conversation about the previous day's hearings. Ron wasn't quite sure what Jackson wanted but from what he said Ron suspected that Jackson was now going to try and stop him adducing new evidence for his Appeal.

Ron was uneasy with what Jackson had said. He dwelt upon the matter for a few days and decided to write to the Civil Appeals Office to seek their guidance:

In your letter to me dated 4th August1992, you advised me that my application to adduce new evidence (FC3 92/6056/C) will be listed for hearing with appeal hearing QBENF 92/0889/C).

Immediately following the Security of Costs hearing last week (Reg 92/6284), I had discussions with the Plaintiff's solicitors. Following that discussion it occurred to me that, should my Application to Adduce New Evidence (FC3 92/6056/C) be refused, there would cease to be any grounds for the Appeal to proceed. I am concerned that the Court's time would be wasted in such an event, and at the subsequent cumulative costs of an abortive Appeal hearing.

'Whilst I would not presume to question the decision to list this application immediately before the appeal hearing, I would be most obliged for any direction that you may feel is appropriate in the above circumstances.

Three weeks later Ron received a short note from Jackson:

You have no doubt received direct from the Court of Appeal a copy of the Order that the Court have now drawn pursuant to the Judgement of Mr Registrar Adams. However, in case this has not been sent to you, we enclose a copy of the Order.

Ron replied immediately:

Thank you for your letter of 17 February. I am grateful to you for sending me a copy of the Order because I had not, as you suggest, received a copy direct from the Court despite two telephone calls in the matter.

In accordance with the Rules of the Supreme Court, Order 22, rule 8(1) I hereby give notice that the security in the above Order has been given by way of a Bankers Draft, in the sum of £5,000, to the Accountant General to receive into Court for Lodgment to the above account.

That's foiled Jackson's main plan to stop my appeal, thought Ron. He really believed I wouldn't be able to raise the money. How little he knows me, or how determined I am to see Fred Laws in court to answer to his perjury.

For the next five months there followed the occasional exchange of brief letters requesting various documents for the Hearing. By the beginning of August Ron began to wonder why nothing seemed to be happening, and so he telephoned the Civil Appeals Office for an update on the situation, which they provided in good detail together with further instructions on what he needed to do. This included information which he needed to convey to Drysdales & Janes, which he did without delay:

I have today spoken to the Civil Appeals Office who confirmed that one full set of the trial Documents has to be lodged with the Civil Appeals Office in case, unexpectedly, reference has to be made to some document which is not in the core bundle.

it may be that you intend lodging a full set of the Trial Documents for your own purposes and if that is the case then I shall not need to do so and I shall be pleased if you will let me know.

In any event I am advised that the Skeleton Argument that I have already lodged with the requisite bundle is incomplete as each point needs to be cross referenced to the appropriate document in the Trial Bundles. Of course, this has been made more difficult by the splitting of the documents into two bundles and renumbering. However, it would help to avoid confusion at the Appeal Hearing if you could let me have copies of the indexes to the Plaintiff's and the Defendant's Bundles. I would, of course, expect to pay the cost of providing such documents which are also needed to complete the amended Skeleton Argument, a copy of which I shall send to you immediately the task is completed.

Three weeks passed with no reply from Drysdales & Janes. Ron was getting anxious about the time and sent them a reminder:

I wrote to you on the 5th of August and at the time of writing I have not received a reply. As you will appreciate time is now beginning to run out to the date of the Appeal Hearing on 7 October and I would ask you, please, to now give this matter your most urgent attention.

I am sure I do not need to remind you that according to the rules you will not be able to introduce any documents or evidence that was not used in the original Trial without an application to the Registrar. Please let me know if it is your intention to introduce such new evidence and, if so, let me have copies of such evidence.

Ron wanted to think that it was his reminder that brought a prompt reply, but it was more than like a coincidence bearing in mind their poor record of communicating:

We thank you for your letter of 24th instant. The reason why we have not replied sooner to your letter is that in the first place, Mr Jackson was on holiday and secondly, our *papers have been with Counsel. Counsel has advised that Mr Laws should swear an Affidavit in connection with certain matters. We are in the process of preparing that affidavit and as soon as Mr Laws has been sworn to it, we will, of course, send you a copy. Counsel has also advised that we should issue a Summons which will say that your appeal should be struck out on the ground that you Appeal is scandalous, frivolous and or vexatious or an abuse of the process of the Court by virtue of the agreement that we reached with you when you paid the sum of £5,000 in full and final settlement of Mr Laws' claim and costs. The Summons will be issued within the next few days, supported by an affidavit and as soon as this has occurred, we will, of course, serve you with the Summons and the accompanying Affidavit correspondence that took place between ourselves and the solicitors that you had acting for you in 1989 and 1990.*

We would also be asking the Registrar to give certain directions with regard to the putting in of transcripts which we have requested from the Court and also with regard to documents to go before the Court of Appeal.

So, Fred Laws' legal team is getting really rattled now', thought Ron. 'They are going to do whatever is within their means to stop my Appeal. Well, I am going to do what I can to prevent them doing that'.

The summons was duly served and Ron responded robustly, insisting that his Appeal was: neither scandalous, frivolous and, or vexatious or an abuse of the process of the Court. It was based on credible evidence from the police and should be allowed to proceed.

Jackson's attempt to obtain a Security of Costs order, his efforts to have the Appeal struck out and his request to the Registrar to give directions with regard to the documents that Ron intended to put before the Court meant that the original date set for the hearing could not now be met and a new hearing was to be arranged. This was later set down for 21 of July 1994.

On the 30 June1994 Jackson wrote to Ron telling him that Southend Borough Council had searched their archives and had found an attendance note dated 23 October 1984 which showed that Mr Laws was present when the police came to investigate the complaint about the Home Improvement Grant fraud.

Ron was deeply shocked. He read the letter several times. He couldn't believe it. Despite the Housing Department's history of disappearing files and documents that mysteriously burst into flames in the strong room this vital document, that could save Fred Laws from ruin in the Appeal Court, miraculously appears at the very last minute, unscathed, after lying hidden in the Council's archives for ten years.

Jackson gave no explanation as to what prompted the search for this document, but Ron could hazard a guess. Ron also realised that the note, if genuine, would have a devastating impact on his Appeal Argument.

With only two week to go before the deadline for submitting documents Ron knew he could proceed no further without advice from the Appeals Office. Since he had received no reply from them to his letter of 4th of February he decided to phone them immediately.

Mr Graham at the Appeals office listened patiently to Ron's dilemma. He suggested that, ideally, he should withdraw the Application for Appeal but that according to the Rules it was now too late to do that. Ron pointed out that had Fred Laws' Solicitors produced the Council's Note during the early stages of his Appeal Application and not within a few days of the fourteen-day deadline for the submission of all documents Ron would very likely have not submitted the Application, which would have saved a great deal of time and money.

There followed a few seconds silence before Mr Graham replied. 'From what you say, Mr Levy, and I can understand your dilemma, there may be a possible way round your difficulty. I vaguely recall a situation similar to your one where a litigant changed the Appeal against Judgement to an Appeal against the Costs of the aborted Appeal. Leave it with me for an hour or two and I'll come back to you'.

Mr Graham was as good as his word: 'Yes, Mr Levy, there was such a case and so I have looked up the procedure for making the change. I've also obtained the necessary forms together with printed direction for completing them. I will put them in the post for you today'.

Ron thanked Mr Graham profusely: He couldn't help feeling that the man had gone beyond his dutiful requirement in guiding him as he did. It was not an ideal development but perhaps something worthwhile could be rescued from the whole sorry mess. 'After all... ' thought Ron. '...why should Fred Laws have all the running, ducking and diving, always able to fend off, without lasting injury, whatever legal blows that are thrust at him? And yet... the answer might possibly be found in the most prominent difference between himself and Fred Laws – money.

And so Ron completed the forms that Mr Graham had sent to him in order to prepare the ground for what should be the final contest set to take place at the Royal Courts of Justice in just five week from now.

CHAPTER 20

Thursday 21 July 1994.

Ron alighted from a red no. 26 bus as it laboriously pulled in to The Strand on this bright, cloudless morning that heralded yet another scorching day.

Already, at this early hour, combustion fumes lay heavily suspended by fierce sunlight, but through it all delightful aromas drifted across from a sandwich bar on the corner of Essex Street, attracting cockney-wise pigeons gliding effortlessly among tall buildings, gradually descending to the pavement, crash-landing and jerkily pecking at dropped morsels as they skillfully avoided scurrying feet of Londoners on the move.

He walked back a few yards to where Fleet Street divides, separating Aldwych from The Strand. Facing him as they had done so many times during this long-drawn-out legal contest were the Law Courts, The Royal Courts of Justice. Checking his watch, he was glad he had almost an hour in which to absorb his surroundings and to prepare himself for what would surely be the final episode in this perplexing legal wrangle.

Deep in thought, he stepped off the kerb - and was immediately blasted by a taxi-horn. Acknowledging the driver's warning with a wave of his hand, he was met by a long-suffering glare: This *is* a wide crossing!

Chastened, he carefully made his way to the broad pavement fronting the Courts, and found himself among a placard-waving group of demonstrators aligned against the railings and chatting noisily with an outside broadcast team. Something to do with *Eastenders,* or was it *Coronation Street*? Whatever it was, it made little impression on passers-by. They had seen it all before.

Ron marveled once more at the impressive façade of the Law Courts. His earlier visits had inspired him to research well the environs and proceedings, and here he was again, one more participant in a never-ending procession of those who had prosecuted or defended actions on this ground: the very ground which had replaced courtrooms that Dickens had portrayed as being 'inconveniently located, unsatisfactory in design, and simply too small for the ever-increasing demands of the nineteenth century'. An observation echoed in the *Law Times* which stated: 'Surely justice is entitled to be lodged in a palace, if Government and Legislation and Art are to be so domiciled.'

Then, eventually bowing to the demands from Benthamite reformers, Parliament had agreed an Act in 1866 whereby designs were invited for construction of the new Law Courts, resulting in George Edmund Street beating five other contestants to erect this awe-inspiring complex that had stood the test of time.

Now, despite oppressive heat, Ron shivered. Cold comfort as he looked about him, in the laughing faces of the demonstrators. Fleetingly it crossed his mind that demonstrations and railings were inseparable: perhaps

Emily Pankhurst had started it all... the traditional pairing for all those with an axe to grind.

He looked down at the great marble steps hollowed by countless feet and glinting brazenly in the morning sunlight. Taking a deep breath he walked up them and through the massive portals that could easily have graced a cathedral; an illusion that was soon dispelled as he was confronted by a modern screen monitor and security officers.

Now familiar with the procedure, he placed metal objects from his pockets on a counter, laid his briefcase on a conveyor-belt and watched as it passed through an x-ray tunnel, the screen image indicating that the contents were harmless.

Retrieving his belongings, he approached the information desk, which was prominently located just inside the cavernous Central Hall.

A young dark-haired woman wearing a lapel badge giving her name as Janet smiled and said. 'Good morning, sir. May I help you?'

'Good morning, miss,' he answered. 'Could you tell me, please, in which court Laws v Levy is listed to be heard?'

Without preamble a beautifully manicured finger traced along the index.

'Ah, here it is. That will be in Court number 66, sir. It's one of the new courtrooms. Do you know its location?'

'66! I had no idea there were so many courtrooms in this building. I would be grateful for directions. I only know the old courtrooms.'

As instructed, he headed for the wide exit at the furthest end of the hall. On reaching there he paused to admire again the two larger-than-life statues, one either side of a short marble stairway. One was of Queen Victoria and the other of The Right Honourable Charles Baron Russell, Lord Chief Justice of England 1894 to 1900; both positioned to gaze imperiously towards the great hall entrance.

Looking back, he marvel ed at the hall's interior, as he had done on previous visits. Massive paintings of past luminaries, tall multiple columns and English Decorated Gothic framed dark recesses, leading to the old courtrooms. Through these recesses figures constantly emerged and disappeared, some robed, some in smart suits.

Glancing at his watch, his own predicament precluded him from further exploration. Time was running out and he quickly mounted the steps that led to a corridor where directional arrows pointed the way to Courtroom Sixty-Six. There a notice stated that there were to be two actions before his, one at 10.15, another at 10.30; His was at 10.45.

The presiding judge for his case was given as Lord Justice Butler-Sloss.

The name rang a bell. Ron remembered reading about a Child Abuse Inquiry, some 5 or 6 years ago, of which she had been chairman.

He pushed the swing doors and on entering the courtroom caught his breath in the cool atmosphere. Air conditioning! and such bright lights. How different from the old courtrooms! The judge's dais was lower, and mellow maple furnishings complimented the modern, spacious decor, in complete contrast to the stuffiness encountered at the previous hearings.

A lady attendant, wearing a black cape, which singled her

out as an usher stood before the dais. Ron approached her.

'Excuse me, madam. My name is Levy. I'm listed this morning.'

She consulted her papers. 'Yes sir. There are two other cases before yours, but they are both very brief hearings. You can sit at the back of the court. In fact, it will be best if you do that so that you are here when you are called.'

'Thank you,' replied Ron. 'Oh, by the way, how do I address Lady Butler-Sloss?'

She smiled. She must have been asked that question many times. 'When you speak to her, personally, it is "my lady". When you speak to the Judges collectively, you address them as "my lords".'

'Oh, and one other thing, would it be possible to have a glass of water available... where I'm going to sit, I mean?'

'Of course Mr Levy, that'll be arranged.'

He thanked her and made his way to the public gallery at the back of the court.

He sat quietly, taking in the scene. Patric Milmo, resplendent in wig and gown, was seated in the second row, whispering to his two assistants seated behind him. Ron smiled to himself... strangely, this time he did not feel intimidated by Milmo's presence. There were only three other occupants and somehow this, and the refreshing coolness, gave him comfort.

Quietly he opened his briefcase, and started to go over his notes... to marshal his thoughts for the coming hearing. As he was doing so, a door adjacent to the dais suddenly opened. The usher immediately stood up and in a firm voice commanded: 'The Court rise.'

Ron quickly replaced his notes as three robed figures emerged: Lord Justice Rose, followed by Lord Justice Butler-Sloss and Sir Tasker Watkins. They bowed to the court and all present responded likewise.

The two cases preceding Ron's were soon dealt with, but this gave him some idea of what was expected in appeal court proceedings

The Clerk of the Court focused attention on Ron, the last to be heard, and beckoned him to come forward to the front bench. Quickly, as one does when called to a dentist's chair, Ron strode purposefully to the well of the court, slid into a narrow seat, opened his briefcase and placed it on the bench-top. He had practised this movement many times and soon had his papers set out. Because he had complete conviction that his cause was just he had been confident that all would be well; but here it was different. Here he must persuade the Court that his argument was right. His confidence was gradually eroding, the enormity of his task descending like a cloak that threatened to muffle him. He suddenly thought of his wife, his children, and knew that he was going to see this through come what may. The loneliness that he had known since starting out from home receded and now he felt ready. Reaching for the water flask that the Clerk had provided, he poured some into a glass and as he did so glanced at her in gratitude. She rewarded him with a faint smile of recognition. The cold, crystal clear water was wonderfully refreshing. He was thankful that the flask had been filled to the brim... he was going to need it.

Once again he rifled through his papers, anxious that they were in order of precedence. He didn't want to relive the experience of the first hearing, the trial, that had embarrassed him when his notes were in disarray - caused mainly by the judge's insistence on a course that was to prove disastrous to him, the main parts ignored, the very areas of his evidence that were crucial to his case. This time he was prepared, and determined that there wouldn't be a repetition of that disaster.

'Mr Levy. Would you like some time to get your papers in order?' the judge gently enquired. Ron straightened up and looked at Lady Butler-Sloss, her tone immediately putting him at ease.

'Thank you, My Lady. I'm most grateful to you. It shouldn't take too long. I'm sorry to hold up the proceedings.'

She, sensing his anxiety, said gently: 'Please don't worry. Just let me know when you are ready, Mr Levy.'

She had charmed him, and despite the amplified rustling of papers in this almost-empty courtroom, where all eyes were focused on him, his confidence returned.

'My Lady, thank you for your patience. I am ready now.'

She leaned forward, resting on her arms in a confidential manner as if what they had to say to one another was for them only.

Quietly she said 'Why are you here with this application if you wish to have your appeal dismissed. You do want the appeal dismissed, don't you?

This didn't sound right.

'I'm not sure of the correct terminology, My Lady. I discontinued the Appeal because the Plaintiff produced a document at the last minute, and I felt it would be irresponsible to continue, but in the circumstances I felt

304

that I should not have to bear the costs that had accrued, since the appeal was lodged more than a year ago.'

Her Ladyship flipped the pages of the file in front of her. 'Mr Levy, you do understand that in a legal action such as this it is usual for the losing party to pay the costs in the action, so how have you come to take this course... to bring the matter before this Court?'

This unsettled him. He thought he had made it clear in his skeleton argument why he felt it wrong to make him bear the full burden of the costs. 'My Lady, when I first received the document about the alleged meeting with the police - and I knew I couldn't continue with the appeal. I telephoned the Civil Appeals Office and told them how I felt and they told me that I could ask for a Hearing on the Costs and to see if the Court would agree with me.' He picked up his bundle of notes, holding them aloft, 'And so I prepared my argument on that principle in the hope that I might be able to obtain a fair judgment in the matter.'

'Right then, Mr Levy. You had better continue.' She eased back in her chair, one hand resting lightly against her chin as she and the other judges calmly awaited his reply.

'Thank you, My Lady. I am mindful that this is not a re-run of the trial in the Lower Court - the libel action. Neither is it a hearing of the appeal that I reluctantly had to abandon.' He was anxious to assure their Lordships that his motives for this hearing were valid. 'I am also aware that it is not a hearing of my application to adduce new evidence. However, there is one issue that is central to those three actions that is equally central to this hearing.' He glanced at his notes, anxious to get the wording exactly right. 'That

305

issue, My Lords, is the criminal matter that was reported to Mr Laws by Councillor Copley on 16 October 1984, which is revealed in the documents that I have numbered A5 to A9. You will see that they are the home improvement grant details that accompanied Mr Goble's letter to me about Mr Laws... about his failure to report the complaint to the police. I shall make reference to the detail of those documents later when I make my points.'

'As my chronology reveals and puts very simply, Mr Laws issued libel proceedings following an internal inquiry by the Council into my complaints against the conduct of the Assistant Director of Housing, Mr Muckley. At that inquiry I produced copies of documents from housing files in support of my allegations. Mr Laws claimed that the documents were from a missing file.   he reported my

possession of the documents to the police, asking them to investigate me. That is shown in his letter to the police dated 20 April 1982. That is numbered L1 in the bundle, My Lady. I would add that according to Lord Widdecombe's report into the conduct of local government I had a right, as a councillor, a right of access to those documents anyway.

'I accused Mr Laws of acting maliciously and vindictively in reporting me to the police. I tell you the truth, My Lords, I believed that then and I still believe that now.

'In defending the action I included the housing grant papers into the Jury bundle. These papers were not an issue in the Pleadings (although I do not know why my solicitor failed to make them so). But Mr Milmo is not a fool, he would have immediately identified the strong suggestion that Mr Laws had failed to report the criminal matter to the police and he would have undoubtedly discussed the matter with him in pre-trial briefings.'

Ron's throat was tightening. His mouth felt dry. He sensed a movement behind him. Mr Milmo was shifting in his seat, perhaps uncomfortably, at what he had just said about him. Another sip from the glass restored Ron's clarity and enabled him to continue.

'So, here was a situation where Mr Laws had reported me to the police within 24 hours of my producing those documents at the inquiry, documents which he claimed had been improperly taken from the housing files. a relatively minor matter, I thought, compared to the very serious matter of the home improvement grant fraud which he did not report to the police at all. It was this failure to report such evidence that confirmed my belief that Mr Laws had singled me out, by reporting me to the police, as revenge for all the difficulties that I had caused him over the preceding three years with my persistent complaints against the Housing Department.

'There was no reason to doubt the validity of Mr Goble's evidence of the fraud. It had been widely reported in the press that police investigations into the complaint had commenced in December 1984. Armed with this evidence my solicitor was satisfied that defence of the libel action had a reasonable chance of succeeding. I think it is true to say that had this evidence not come to light it is extremely unlikely that I would have continued with the defence of the action'

Her Ladyship raised her hand, interrupting his flow. 'I'm reluctant to stop you at this point, Mr Levy, but I don't quite see where this is leading to... its relevance to this hearing.'

'I am very close to that point, My Lady. I'm sure it will become clear when I get there. It is important to my argument.' She signalled him to continue.

'Mr Milmo argues that the incident concerning the fraud complaint was irrelevant because it took place some two months after the alleged libel was published. Well, the purpose of using this evidence was to show the Jury that Mr Laws was capable of acting partially in two similar situations involving prima facie evidence of a crime, he reported me to the police, but not his own housing official.

'Whilst it was disappointing that Mr Justice McKinnon refused to let the Jury see Mr Goble's letter and the specimen fraud, it was of no real consequence because when I questioned Mr Laws he told the Court that he did report Councillor Copley's complaint to the police. You will have seen where he did that, My Lords, on pages 3 and 4 of the transcript of the trial before you.'

He paused whilst their Lordships searched the papers and read the relevant passages. They looked up and Ron continued.

'It was not the reply that I expected. I was shaken, to say the least. I knew that I was no longer able to put to the Jury that he had singled me out. Without Mr Laws' admission that he did not report the matter to the police my defence had no hope of succeeding; It would fail. I began to panic. There didn't seem much point continuing with the trial. I don't think at that point that I even wanted to go on with it. But I didn't know how to end it. I even began to wonder if I had been wrong about Mr Laws. It seemed to me that all I could do was to let the trial take its course to the end.'

He was becoming unsettled. He took another drink and regained his composure. 'My Lords, I accepted the Judgment and resolved to deal with the consequences as best I could. A settlement was negotiated in the maximum terms that were within my financial capability and the Judgement was satisfied on agreed terms in March 1990.'

Lord Justice Rose leaned forward expectantly. 'The Judgment was for costs and damages, that was £27,000 and £10,000 respectively wasn't it? And what was the sum agreed in settlement?'

'£5,000, my Lord.'

'And you paid that, did you?'

'Yes, My Lord. In March 1990.'

His Lordship raised his eyebrows in passive acceptance.

'My Lords, I was relieved that it was all over and I resolved to put the whole business behind me and to put that episode of my life down to experience. That is until a year later, March 1991.

'It was then that a copy of an extract from a statement by Mr Stepney, Southend Council's Assistant Director of Finance, came into my possession. You have a copy of that in your file, numbered 7, 8 and 9. This is a statement that Mr Stepney made in September 1987 to Fraud Squad officers investigating the 26 Park Road matter. On page 21 of that statement, which I have highlighted, Mr Stepney states:

"I was aware that on the 11th December, 1984, the matters were reported to the police at Southend Division via the Chief Executive Officer and Town Clerk."

'Since Mr Laws had resigned as Town Clerk on 31 October, 1984, it was reasonable to conclude that he could not possibly have reported the matter to the police. It follows from there that Mr Laws' successor, Roy Peacock, the new Town Clerk, was the person who reported the matter to the police on 11th December, 1984, as Mr Stepney had indeed sworn.'

Her Ladyship understood exactly what he was leading up to. 'So what you are saying, Mr Levy, is that when Mr Laws told the Court that he had reported this criminal matter to the police he was not telling the truth.'

'My Lady, you are ahead of me. That is exactly what I am saying.'

'But how does that affect the question of costs... why you think that you should not have to pay them?'

'I hope to make that clear later, My Lady. I do think these points have an important bearing on my argument and I would be most grateful if I could be permitted to continue with this line of reasoning.'

'If you think it will help your case, please continue.'

He felt relieved. 'Thank you, My Lady. This development seemed to me cause for concern: if Mr Stepney's statement was correct, then it would appear that Mr Laws had indeed made a false statement to the Court. Thoughts of an appeal against the Judgment then entered my mind, I immediately made enquiries at the Civil Appeals Office and took the preliminary steps to proceed with an appeal.

'At the same time, that was April 1991, I wrote to Mr Laws' solicitors informing them of the new evidence which I copied to them, I asked them to provide me with any evidence that Mr Laws might have which would show that he did report the matter to the police so that I could reconsider my decision to appeal.' Ron lifted his bundle of papers, indicating his letter. 'You will see from their reply that they completely ignored my request.'

'Before lodging the Appeal Application, and with the benefit of legal advice, I entered into correspondence with the Chief Constable of Essex Police who confirmed in a letter dated 12 November 1991 that Mr Laws took no part in reporting Councillor Copley's complaint to the police: That's document number 13 in the bundle.'

He paused while they sifted through their papers and found the relevant document.

Her Ladyship looked up from the paper. 'I see that, Mr Levy. Please continue.'

'Thank you. The Chief Constable had already confirmed in a previous letter that a written complaint, dated 11 December, 1984, referring to 26 Park Road, came from Mr Roy Peacock. It was his letter that resulted in the police investigation commencing. That letter is number 12A, My Lords.'

'And you saw this as a further indication, confirmation by the police that Mr Laws had lied to the Court?'

'Yes, My Lady. I most certainly did. It seemed to me that this new evidence, which was extracted from police records following a highly successful prosecution - that this fresh evidence was credible and that it should be possible to satisfy the Court that it could be admitted as new evidence for the purpose of an appeal. My Lords, Notice of Appeal was served on 7 July, 1992.

Ron returned to his notes. He felt better now that he was fleshing out the bones of his argument, and the Court seemed to be impressed by the manner in which he, as a layman, was conducting himself.

'In his Skeleton Argument, Mr Milmo claims that the new evidence satisfies none of the conditions in *Ladd v Marshall*. For example: on Condition 1 he says that I could have easily obtained the information from the police or Mr Peacock before the trial; on Condition 2 he says the evidence would have a negligible influence on the result of the case. It would probably not have been admissible in the first place... no reasonable Jury would have given it serious consideration; on Condition 3 the information from the police records can be shown to be inaccurate. No reliance could be placed upon it. He goes on to give a complex list of reasons why he thinks the Court will not admit the new evidence! My Lords, he could hardly say otherwise... especially with so much at stake!'

Behind him, he was aware of Patric Milmo's consternation, of his silent anger as he shuffled through his portfolio.

Ron had the situation in control. With renewed vigour but conscious that he mustn't appear facetious, he continued: 'I could not possibly be expected to match the legal dexterity of Mr Milmo, My Lords, but I hope my deficiency in that area is more than compensated for by the application of common sense. In response to Mr Milmo's submission, I would argue: on Condition 1, the police evidence could not have been obtained before the trial because it was still the subject of an investigation and was sub-judice; on Condition two, principally, Ladd v Marshall conditions state...'

In a kindly tone her Ladyship interrupted. 'Mr Levy, I think you can take it that we are well aware of *Ladd v Marshall*.'

He could not conceal his embarrassment. 'Of course, My Lady, I should have known.' He continued: 'I take the view that Condition Two, that the evidence would probably have an important influence on the result of the case, need not be decisive. I take the view that that condition was satisfied. However, in the absence of a Judicial Review of the application to adduce the new evidence Mr Milmo's argument stands untested.

'On Condition 3, the only inaccuracy, if it can be called that, is the reference to Mr Roy Peacock, Town Clerk... he was in fact Town Clerk Designate. In his affidavit Mr Laws states "It would seem that police records confirm that Councillor Copley's complaint to me was passed on to them in October 1984". My Lady - it does nothing of the sort! What the police records *do* show is that the complaint passed to them on 23 October, 1984 consisted of allegations of bad workmanship and work not having been done - which constituted negligence rather than criminal intent. My Lords, Mr Copley did not complain of bad workmanship or work not being done... he complained of fraud and he produced evidence of that fraud.

'In the police records that Mr Laws refers to there is no mention of the complaint of fraud. There is no mention of the Grant Documents that Councillor Copley handed over to him. In fact there is no mention of either Mr Copley or of Mr Goble. And yet by Mr Laws' own admission to the Court, those documents showed prima facie evidence of a criminal offence.'

He paused. The Court seemed to hold its breath, the scratching of their Lordship's pens faintly audible in the silence. He waited until they had finished:

'My Lords, it would seem from this that the police records suggest that Councillor Copley's complaint of fraud, together with the supporting evidence, was not passed on to the police in October 1984.

'To return to the Appeal Application...14 months had passed since the appeal was entered, during that time various communications passed between Mr Laws' solicitors and myself in the conduct of the appeal preparations... this included an Application for Security of Costs which was heard, and granted in the sum of five thousand pounds, in January 1993.

'Shortly before the deadline for lodging Appeal Bundles Mr Jackson phoned me and read out to me the letter and documents he had received from Southend Town Clerk, Mr Preddy: that's the letter and copy of notes of a meeting between Mr Laws, a Mr Lawrence (who was Mr Stepney's Deputy at the time) and two police officers. My Lords, I was devastated at what I had just heard. I knew immediately this meant that I could not possibly continue with the appeal. Indeed, it would have been foolish, even reckless, to do so having had sight of the documents which had just been faxed to me.'

Reliving the experience distressed him, he was unaware that he had stopped speaking; that the Court was waiting for him to continue.

'Mr Levy, are you all right'? Her Ladyship's gentle voice eased him back to the present. He was grateful for her concern.

'Thank you, My Lady. I'm sorry. I'm fine, thank you.' He recovered his composure and returned to his notes.

'On the face of it, My Lords, it did seem, after all, that Mr Laws had discussed the Grant matter with the police. I immediately contacted the Civil Appeals Office and advised them of this new development. I sought their advice on how to extricate myself from the appeal. I also expressed my concern that the Plaintiff's solicitors had failed to obtain this new evidence when first served with the Notice of Appeal and supporting evidence.

'The Court Office advised me of my right to make application for dismissal of the appeal without costs, which, of course, I did, and which is why I am here today. But I am even more disturbed by the contents of these notes which purport to show that the Plaintiff did report the criminal matter of Councillor Copley's complaint to the police.

'A closer scrutiny of the notes suggests to me that that might not be the case; as with the police records to which I referred a short time ago. For example, there is no mention of Councillor Copley's complaint. There is no mention of Mr Goble's quotation for the works to 26 Park Road. The author of the note writes: "We outlined what had occurred". My Lords, I can't help wondering what that "outline" consisted of for the police to see it more as slackness by Council officers than wrongdoing and for them to ask: "how the grant came to be paid when the work had not been done."

'My Lords, I ask where in these notes of his meeting with the police... is the prima facie evidence of a criminal offence which the Plaintiff told the Court was immediately apparent to him on sight of those documents?

This again suggests that Mr Laws did not, after all, inform the police of Councillor Copley's complaint. I accepted this document at its face value and I discontinued the appeal. With hindsight I feel that I need not have been so hasty... that I could have continued the appeal. But I accept that that opportunity is now lost.

'In making application to this Court on the costs, I seek to salvage what I can from this extraordinary situation. It is a fact that had the Plaintiff's solicitors obtained this attendance note shortly after July 1992 the appeal would have been discontinued then, so avoiding the bulk of the costs.'

Lady Butler-Sloss removed her spectacles and leaned forward. 'Mr Levy. What you are saying is that Mr Laws' legal advisers could have produced these documents many months ago but because of their incompetence, their inefficiency or laziness, they failed to do so and that in consequence you have been burdened with these enormous costs. Is that so?'

Ron could not believe what he was hearing. His burden was lifted. It was what he had wanted to say for so long but thought that to do so might make matters worse. He replied with renewed confidence: 'My Lady, that is exactly what I am saying.' He sensed waves of anger directed at him from Patric Milmo, the recipient of such severe admonishment from the Judge.

He continued: 'Counsel for the Plaintiff contends that he is under no duty to search and find immediately or at all any existing evidence to controvert my fresh evidence.'

Her Ladyship intervened impatiently: 'I can see your point, Mr Levy, and I agree with what you are saying; but where is it getting us?'

'I'm leading up to that, My Lady. What Mr Milmo says - about being under no such duty - may or may not be so, but in view of the seriousness of the allegation that Mr Laws lied to the Court, it surely begs the question: Why wasn't he under such obligation?

'I think I know the answer to that: Mr Milmo employed a strategy at the trial which he has repeated at this appeal. A week before the trial was due to begin, Mr Laws' solicitor came to my home and went through the Jury Bundle rearranging the documents according to advice given by Mr Milmo and altering the numbers on most of the documents. On the first day of the trial the Court was presented with two separate bundles: the Plaintiff's Bundle and the Defendant's Bundle. This was the first sight I had had of the two bundles in their separated form. Mr Milmo told the Court that the first Jury Bundle had to be changed because he considered that "it contains a lot of material that was not relevant and which would confuse the Jury". He went on to say: "Thus Mr Levy is in the unfortunate position of having notes which refer to documents which are not the right numbers in the right bundles". How right he was! that is precisely the effect he intended with his strategy. He had been in possession of all the discovery documents for two or three years, yet he delayed until a week before the trial the extraction and renumbering of my documents that he did not want the Jury to see. This was a ploy that was intended to disrupt and confuse all my preparations; it was a deliberate manoeuvre to disadvantage my defence - and it worked!

'In much the same way, My Lords, he has delayed, until the last moment, producing this alleged attendance note... which threw my appeal preparations into confusion and difficulty. It was produced, conveniently for him and Mr Laws, too late to trace the author of the note and obtain an affidavit as to its authenticity and too late to make an accurate analysis of its contents. And, again, the strategy worked! After all, the date that was fixed for the Appeal Hearing was notified to him nine months earlier in February 1993. Are we expected to accept that Mr Milmo had still not given advice on the case to Mr Laws? That no action whatsoever had been taken to prepare a reply or defence to the allegation of perjury?'

Ron smiled to himself as he sensed Patric Milmo's anger. But what he had said was true; Milmo had been rumbled... and he didn't like it! Turning to the next document, he continued.

'In his Outline Argument, Mr Milmo claims that it was neither necessary nor appropriate to incur costs searching the Borough Council files dating back some eight years for a document which Mr Laws and his advisers had no knowledge existed. That argument is unconvincing to say the least! Mr Laws' solicitors wrote to the Borough Council on 26 August, 1993 and the Council replied within seven working days announcing that they had traced a copy of the attendance note, dated 23 October 1984, which was made when Mr Stepney was the Council's Chief Internal Auditor. That does not suggest either a lengthy or a costly search.

'Mr Milmo says "the document came to light as a result of the Council using their initiative carrying out a search at the beginning of September 1993".' Ron paused briefly, lowered his notes and looked up at the Judges. They peered at him attentively. 'My Lords, that is also nonsense! The sworn Affidavit of Mr Jackson says very differently why the Note appeared.'

Selecting the affidavit from his carefully numbered bundle, Ron read out the conflicting section: '"The reason why a Note has appeared from the files of the Southend Borough Council is because I received from Mr Milmo QC advice on Mr Levy's Appeal. I sent a copy of that Advice to the Borough Solicitor, Mr D G Preddy, under cover of a letter dated 26 August 1993 pointing out to him what the latest situation was in the matter. I have spoken to Mr Preddy on the telephone and he has stated to me that when he received my letter of the 26 August 1993 and Counsel's Opinion, he instigated enquiries through the Assistant Borough Treasurer, Mr P Stepney, because he was vitally involved in the investigation by the police and the Housing Department. I understand from Mr Preddy that when Mr Stepney searched through Council records he found a Note dated 23 October 1984 and for subsequent days relating to the police enquiry and it is quite clear from the Note that Mr Laws was present at an interview with the police and a Mr Lawrence who was the Deputy to Mr Stepney in 1984.".'

'My Lords, it follows clearly from that Statement that the Council's search of their files was not carried out on their own initiative. It is also very difficult to believe that Mr Laws did not know that the Attendance Note had been made;

apart from the author of the Note he was the only other Council official present at the meeting... it was standard practice to make such notes of important meetings and Mr Laws would have witnessed the notes being written. It seems to me that these circumstances would certainly be consistent with Mr Jackson approaching the Borough Council asking for such evidence.'

With controlled anger he slammed the document down on the bench. 'How different it all was when I corresponded with Mr Jackson regarding my request for discovery of documents to assist with my defence preparations! In his reply, dated 30 September 1988, Mr Jackson says: "We are informed by the Town Clerk's Department that the personal files of Mr Lithe and Mrs Archer who were former officers of the Housing Department are no longer available. They may have been amongst some housing administration files which were destroyed in a recent fire in the Council strong room." In a later paragraph he says: "With regard to your request for a copy of a short-term agreement between Mrs Holliday and the Southend Borough Council, we are informed that the Housing Department says that there should have been a document relating to Mrs Holliday's residence at 33, Exeter Close, which we are informed was from October 1979 to June 1980, but no trace can be found of a file relating to this matter.'

Ron's mind flashed back to the time when, preparing his defence notes, he first learned of the destroyed files. The anger he had felt then rose again now. 'My Lords, it really is quite astonishing that the Town Clerk can produce, almost instantly, a document (which had allegedly lain undisturbed for 9 years, and which had miraculously escaped the ravages of spontaneous combustion), a document that greatly assists Mr Laws, which gets him off the hook, but a similar request from myself proved most unproductive, as I described earlier.

'My Lords, this Attendance Note could have been produced in July 1992 if Mr Laws and his legal advisers had taken the action then which they took in 1993. I do not accept that he was under no duty to search and find immediately, or at any other time, any existing evidence to controvert my new evidence; if not to himself, there surely must have been a responsibility to this Court. After all, had he produced those documents a year earlier there would have been no waste of the many hours spent on the matter by the Civil Appeals Office. And it would certainly have avoided wasting the time and cost to the taxpayer of this hearing today.'

Ron paused, he was nearly finished. He presented his closing plea.

'My Lords, if you accept my argument that the appeal should now be dismissed without an order as to costs for the Plaintiff I would ask you most earnestly to give consideration to my request for an order for costs under the Litigants In Person (Costs And Expenses) Act 1995.

He put down his papers and leaned wearily on the bench, head bowed. The Court was silent for a few seconds. Ron raised his head slowly, looking at each of the three Judges in turn, searching for some indication of their feelings. He saw nothing. Nervously he cleared his throat. 'I thank you most humbly, My Lords, for your patience and tolerance.' He sat down.

'That's it,' thought Ron. 'Now it's Mr Milmo's turn. I wonder what he will have to say about that lot!'

The Judges conferred softly, their words unheard despite a hushed Court.

When they had finished, Her Ladyship turned to Mr Milmo. With a faint smile she said: 'Mr Milmo, we shall not be asking you to give evidence.' His gasp was audible as he abandoned his intention to stand up.

Their Lordships rose. 'The Court rise,' intoned the Usher.

They were absent for no more than five or six minutes. During that time the Court was strangely silent. Patric Milmo was still simmering at being deprived the opportunity to reply to the stinging remarks that Ron had made about him in his argument.

Their Lordships returned.

'The Court rise.'

Her Ladyship spoke. 'We have completed our deliberations and I will ask Lord Justice Rose to give the first judgement.'

His Lordship picked up his papers. In his preamble, he gave a condensed description of the trial, and its outcome, in the High Court: The reason why Ron was able to lodge an appeal outside the usual time limit, the Security of Costs Order and the circumstances surrounding the discontinuance of the appeal, and the late appearance of the Council Attendance Note.

Then came the Judgment.

'Accordingly, for my part, although one sympathises with the defendant in relation to the background in this matter, it being apparent that it was as a consequence of his activities that serious and significant fraud was uncovered, that is not a matter which it seems to me avails him in relation to the first point which this Court has to consider, namely whether the normal order for costs to follow the event should remain.'

Lord Justice Rose paused and glanced at Ron. 'For my part I am wholly unpersuaded, despite Mr Levy's courteous and careful submissions, that that order should not be made and therefore, for my part, I would dismiss the application.' He placed his papers in front of him in a gesture of resignation and settled back in his seat.

Sir Tasker Watkins' contribution was brief and directly to the point: 'I agree, though I, too, have very considerable sympathy with him.'

In the natural order of such proceedings it was for the Presiding Judge to give the final judgment and Her Ladyship said, 'I also agree. I am also grateful for the restrained and courteous way in which Mr Levy presented his arguments and, like my brethren, I have considerable sympathy for the position in which he has found himself; but the appeal is to be dismissed, and I also have found no reason to say that it should not be dismissed with the usual order following of costs.'

With a sardonic smile, she turned her attention to Patric Milmo: 'Tell me, Mr Milmo. Why the big guns for such an uncomplicated hearing? Surely Junior Counsel would have been more appropriate?'

Patric Milmo was momentarily stunned. This admonishment from one of his own profession had caught him off-balance, and for once he struggled to find the right words. 'I... err... well, My Lady. You are quite right. Err... Junior Counsel was indeed intended to represent the Plaintiff in this matter, but he was called away at the last moment and was unable to attend.' He sat down, discomfited.

Ron was jubilant, overjoyed that he had been instrumental in deflating this eminent QC, but grudgingly he admired him and had a strong feeling that if he had him in his corner he could have won the day.

Her Ladyship had not yet finished with him. 'Then you won't mind if I order costs to be set at Junior Counsel rates will you, Mr Milmo?'

Although Ron had been unsuccessful at this hearing, her summing-up consoled him, so much so that he could have hugged her. It was almost worth the five thousand pounds to hear Milmo put down so exquisitely.

Summoning all the self control he could muster, Milmo replied: 'As My Lady pleases.'

'Then that concludes this hearing.'

Their Lordships gathered up their papers and went into huddled conference.

Milmo and his two clerks did likewise, then left the Court.

It was over. Ron gathered his papers together, inserted them in his briefcase and had a last look round before going through the swing door into the corridor where, somewhat to his embarrassment, Patric Milmo was engrossed in debriefing his clerks. As he approached, the venerable barrister smiled benignly and said: 'Well, Mr Levy, you certainly got a very sympathetic hearing.'

'Yes, Mr Milmo. I believe I did.'

'Of course, it's going to cost you a lot of money, isn't it?'

'Well, I had written off those costs a long time ago. I felt that I had to see it through to the end. But I'm glad it is all over.'

'Many people before you have fought campaigns on issues they believe in. I'm pleased you think it was worth the cost.'

Ron hadn't expected such a philosophical response from him. Perhaps he, too, was sympathetic. 'I tell you this, Mr Milmo: the story will make a very interesting book, which I have already started.'

Milmo looked genuinely surprised. 'And how do I come out in your book, Mr Levy? Not too well, I suspect.'

'Actually, you come out quite well. In fact I make the point that had you been acting for me there was a good chance that the outcome may have been very different.'

With this parting volley he nodded goodbye as he departed through the labyrinth of corridors, out into the bright sunshine, and headed for the nearest coffee-bar.

Epilogue

Ordinary beings can encounter extraordinary experiences. I was certainly an ordinary being, but I must have encountered far, far more extraordinary experiences than most others. However, I strongly believe that whatever the experiences it should be possible to learn valuable lessons from them.

Throughout this story the two most extraordinary experiences that I encountered were those that involved me as a litigant in the High Court: The first as the Defendant in a libel action; the second as an appellant in the Court of Appeal. In both cases the plaintiff had access to unlimited funds to appoint one of the very best QCs; Patric Milmo. I had no such funding and I was compelled to represent myself or withdraw from the action, which would have meant that my long battle for justice would have counted for nothing.

I have no doubts that, had Patric Milmo been representing me, the outcome of the trial could have been very different.

This leads me to believe that in this country litigants get the kind of justice that they can afford: that's not justice, that's just us.

Ron Levy 2018

AUTHOR'S NOTE

The names quoted in this story are true, with the exception of Mary Bates and her three children whose names have been changed for legal reasons.

Printed in Great Britain
by Amazon